Organizational Development and Change Theory

This book offers a fresh perspective on organizational development and change theory and practice. Building on their recent work in quantum storytelling theory and complexity theory, Henderson and Boje consider the implications of fractal patterns in human behavior with a view toward ethics in organizational development for the modern world.

Building on Gilles Deleuze and Felix Guattari's (1987) ontology of multiple moving and intersecting fractal processes, the authors offer readers an understanding of how managing and organizing can be adapted to cope with the turbulence and complexity of different organizational situations and environments. They advocate a sustainable, co-creative brand of agency and introduce appropriate, simple tools to support organizational development practitioners. This book offers theory and research methods to management and organization scholars, along with praxis advice to practicing managers.

Tonya L. Henderson is a Consultant, Author, and Speaker for Gly Solutions, LLC, USA.

David M. Boje is Professor of Management and the Arthur Owens Chair in Business Administration at New Mexico State University, USA, and has an Aalborg University Honorary Doctorate, affiliated with the Material Storytelling Lab, Denmark.

Routledge Studies in Organizational Change & Development

1 **Organizational Change for Corporate Sustainability 3rd Edition**
By Suzanne Benn, Dexter Dunphy, Andrew Griffiths

2 **Organizational Change, Leadership and Ethics**
Leading Organizations Toward Sustainability
Edited by Rune Todnem By, Bernard Burnes

3 **Managing Organizational Change in Public Services**
International Issues, Challenges and Cases
Edited by Rune Todnem By, Calum Macleod

4 **Organizational Change for Corporate Sustainability**
A Guide for Leaders and Change Agents of the Future, 2nd Edition
By Suzanne Benn, Dexter Dunphy, Andrew Griffiths

5 **The Sustainability and Spread of Organizational Change**
Modernizing Healthcare
Edited by David A. Buchanan, Louise Fitzgerald, Diane Ketley

6 **Agency and Change**
Rethinking Change Agency in Organizations
By Raymond Caldwell

7 **Reshaping Change**
A Processual Perspective
By Patrick Dawson

8 **Organizational Change for Corporate Sustainability**
A Guide for Leaders and Change Agents of the Future
By Suzanne Benn, Dexter Dunphy, Andrew Griffiths, Suzanne Benn, Dexter Dunphy, Andrew Griffiths

9 **Change Competence**
Implementing Effective Change
By Steven ten Have, Wouter ten Have, Anne-Bregje Huijsmans & Niels van der Eng

10 **Organizational Change and Global Standardization**
Solutions to Standards and Norms Overwhelming Organizations
By David M. Boje

11 **Organizational Development and Change Theory**
Managing Fractal Organizing Processes
By Tonya L. Henderson and David M. Boje

Organizational Development and Change Theory

Managing Fractal Organizing Processes

**Tonya L. Henderson
and David M. Boje**

LONDON AND NEW YORK

First published 2016 by Routledge

2 Park Square, Milton Park, Abingdon, Oxfordshire OX14 4RN
52 Vanderbilt Avenue, New York, NY 10017

Routledge is an imprint of the Taylor & Francis Group, an informa business

First issued in paperback 2018

Library of Congress Cataloging-in-Publication Data

Henderson, Tonya L.
Organizational development and change theory : managing fractal organizing processes / by Tonya L. Henderson and David M. Boje.
pages cm. — (Routledge studies in organizational change & development ; 11)
Includes bibliographical references and index.
1. Organizational change. 2. Organizational behavior.
3. Organizational sociology. I. Boje, David M. II. Title.
HD58.8.H459 2015
658.4'06—dc23
2015009777

ISBN: 978-1-138-80120-2 (hbk)
ISBN: 978-1-138-62407-8 (pbk)

Typeset in Sabon
by Apex CoVantage, LLC

This work is dedicated to the friends and family members who have supported us on the journey.

For Tonya, Robert Wakefield has been a wonderful and supportive son, whose kindness, consistency, and patience are without measure. Jack Wakefield, has been a source of inspiration with his love of all things mathematical and contagious enthusiasm in that regard. Finally, Patrick Merrigan has been supportive, kind, and a blessing since the day we met. His encouragement during the final months of this project has meant the world to me.

For Grace Ann who taught David that horses are people too. To Henri Savall, Veronique Zardet, and Marc Bonnet for their groundbreaking socioeconomic approach which we see as taking a step toward understanding fractality and change management.

Contents

List of Figures and Tables ix
Acknowledgments xi
Introduction xiii

PART I
Fractal Change Management Theory: A Bold New Tool for a Brave New World

1 What Is Fractal Change Management? 5

2 What Are Fractals in Management Science? 45

3 Fractal Organizing Processes: Knowing One When You See It! 65

4 Fractal Storytelling 79

PART II
Exploring Fractal Organizing Processes in Situ

5 From the Ashes: What We Can Learn From Nonprofit Leaders during a Crisis 107

6 How Fractal Organizing Processes Unfold in Day-To-Day Business and Being 120

PART III
The Fractal Manager's Toolkit

7 The Fractal Action Research Method (FARM) 151

8 A Fractal-Based Strategic Change Model 159

9 Ontological Systems Mapping: A Tool for Ethical Engagement 174

Commencement 183
Glossary 187
References 189
About the Authors 201
Index 203

Figures and Tables

Figures

i.1	Influences Affecting the post-Newtonian View of the World	xvii
i.2	Mandelbrot Set Fractal	xxii
1.1	Separation Model of S (social) and M (materiality)	7
1.2	Social Domination Model of Socio (S) Materiality (M)	8
1.3	Materialism Dominance Model	9
1.4	Balance Model of Sociomaterialism	9
1.5	Intra-Activity Model of Sociomateriality	10
1.6	Re-Con-Figuring Model	11
1.7	Contrast a 3D Nonaka Knowledge Management (slinky-like) Spiral Model with a 3D Fibonacci-Fractal-Spiral Model	15
1.8	Tonya Working on Formidable Face Pose	29
2.1	Branching Fractal	46
2.2	Branching in Non-Duality Branching Fractal with Unequal Nodes	47
2.3	Branching Fractal in Three Dimensions: Time, Power, and Efficacy	48
2.4	Example of a Branching Fractal	49
2.5	Fibonacci Spiral	51
2.6	Broccoli Romanesco Approximates Fractal Structures and Fractal-Spiral Cones	53
2.7	Koch Snowflake	54
2.8	Cantor Fractal Measurement Example	56
2.9	Generating a Sierpinski Gasket	60
2.10	Sierpinski Pyramid	60
2.11	Multiple Unfolding Fractal Processes with Different Effects	61
4.1	Four *B*s of Antenarrative	81
4.2	Polyphony of Systemicity Contexts and Their Interplay	82
4.3	Critical Ontologic-Selfhood in Contexts of Multiplicity	83

4.4 Four Types of Antenarrative 83
4.5 Fractal Stories Worksheet 94
4.6 Cyclic-Antenarrative, Common in Management Practice 98
5.1 Relational Introspection 108
6.1 Wikia Fractal Story 129
6.2 Zooming In on the Fractal-Story Pattern 130
6.3 Fibonacci Fractal-Spiral 131
6.4 Fractal Nautilus 131
6.5 Daniel Q Boje US Pat NO. 3,384,007 issued May 21, 1968 Patented April 9, 1974 (approved) 133
6.6 Cumulative Number of Patents Referencing Daniel Boje's Patent in Their Own 134
6.7 Fractal Change Management Model 141
6.8 Moving from Two-Dimensional to Three-Dimensional Branching Fractal Depictions of FCM 141
6.9 SPUDS and Shifting Veterans' Fractal Patterns in Generative Ways 145
7.1 FARM Process Ontological Inquiry Steps 152
7.2 Simple Model of Choice 156
8.1 Five *As* of Fractal Change Management: The Pinwheel Approach to Organizational Change 161
8.2 Moods of Systemicity Attunement 163
8.3 Changing the Trajectory of an Organization 167
9.1 Ontological Systems Mapping Process 177
9.2 Ontological Systems Model of a City's Nonprofit Community 181
9.3 Ontological Systems Map of a Community of Western Yoga Practitioners 181
c.1 Wings of Tetranormalizing 185

Tables

3.1 A Worksheet for Identifying Fractal Organizing Processes 71
6.1 An Exercise in Branching Fractals 132
6.2 Contrasts of Old and New Agribusiness Fish Farm Models 140

Acknowledgments

We wish to thank David Varley and Bernard Burnes for believing in this project from the start.

We also wish to thank Mike Bonifer, Glenda Eoyang, Ken Baskin, Renée Walker, Kristine Quade, and Srikanth Velamakanni for granting us interviews in support of this work. Their stories were both inspiring and enlightening as we worked to bring fractal organizing processes to life. They are featured in Chapter 6 as a way for readers to engage with real-world examples. We are also especially grateful to Daphne Deporres for her role in further developing the ontological systems mapping methodology.

Introduction

To quote Mandelbrot (1983, p. 1), "Clouds are not spheres, mountains are not cones, coastlines are not circles, and bark is not smooth, nor does lightning travel in a straight line."

The word fractal in Latin is *fractus* and means to be broken, jagged, and uneven, with repeating shapes of self-sameness or irregular curves across different scales. Latin verb *frangere* means to break or create irregular fragments. We will relate fractal (*fractus* and *frangere*) to attunement. People in organizations are somehow attuned to fractality. First, starting definitions: "A fractal is most generally defined as a structure which displays increasingly more detail as one zooms into it" (Vrobel 2011, 18). Benoit Mandelbrot (1975) coined the term fractals. Mandelbrot's definition of fractals: "irregular and/or fragmented at all scales" (Nottalle 2011, 44). Fractal Change Management (FCM) is defined here as an attunement to repeating and nonrepeating sameness and irregularity in managing and organizing the sociomateriality of organizations. Sociomateriality is how the social and the material are interactive (or intra-active), and interpenetrating.

Human systems self-organize, often fractally. The exact outcomes are tough to predict, but the kinds of patterns we see in aggregate human behavior and fractal storytelling seem to provide a system-specific signature for the groups of people using fractal concepts to change organizations today. We human beings seem to like to coalesce around a common goal or belief, grow in harmony, eventually create in and out groups, then cling to an illusion of control when the fighting gets bad enough to threaten those who have managed to place themselves atop the hierarchy. We build cohesion, strengthen it, and rebuild it anew when the outside world's complexity proves too much for it. All too frequently, we grow accustomed to the team structure we've labored to be a part of, and then collectively cling to it stubbornly long after its purpose is served. We even cling to structures that we know to be unhealthy or ill-suited to the environment or the task at hand, grasping for familiarity like a drowning man reaches for a life raft. Change then comes from the bottom up, sometimes violently, and the cycle begins again.

This is a book about organizations, change, and the ways that change unfolds in sociomaterial ways. Here we develop Fractal Change Management (FCM) and Fractal Action Research Methods (FARM) for intervening in the unfolding of organizations. We include interviews from people doing change management in ways that are keenly attuned to fractal organizing processes. Their clients include major corporations and government entities. The work is intended to provide practical tools for managing fractal organizing processes in a world where change is the only constant. Our other works in this area are largely theoretical, exploring some of the implications of quantum thought and complexity (Boje 2011a, 2011d, 2011f; Boje and Henderson 2014; Henderson 2014a; Henderson and Deporres 2014; Wakefield 2012). Yet as Kurt Lewin famously said, "there is nothing so practical as a good theory" (Lewin 1951). To that end, we wish to explore the practical side of fractal change management theory in the modern world, bridging the gap between nascent theory and "boots on the ground" utility, building on more recent work with practitioners and engagement outside of academia (Henderson 2014c). In this book we develop FCM and FARM for intervening in the unfolding of organizations.

In this work, we explore organizations as unfolding, emergent, and dissipative sociomaterial fractal processes, building on prior works addressing systemicity (Boje 2008, Boje 2014b, Boje and Wakefield 2011, Wakefield 2012). With a view toward practical utility and methods, we tie these ideas into an overarching model that is at once theoretical and intuitively applicable in today's fractal organizations (Eoyang 2009, Hoverstadt 2008, Quade 2011, Quade and Holladay 2010, Wakefield 2012b). We draw from the experiences of many skilled scholars and practitioners to develop cases, exercises and practical examples are offered to assist in visualizing and understanding fractals where appropriate. In order to pursue such an approach, it may be useful to take a walk through history to examine its origins.

THE MARCH TOWARD A FRACTAL VIEW OF ORGANIZATIONS

The age of enlightenment ushered in the mechanistic view of the universe, the notion that all interactions could be predicted through the use of science and mathematics. The positivist view suggested that all could be known and predicted with the right set of equations. This belief led to the dissection of anything people wanted to understand. To get at the heart of anything, one had only to break it down and learn the details of its parts, which could then be reassembled into a working machine. In human organizations this led to Taylor's scientific method and Weber's bureaucracy, as part of a push toward efficiency. The idea that men could be assigned specific functions and perform rote tasks characterized the industrial revolution and brought tremendous economic growth, but it did so at the expense of the human spirit (Wiener 1954).

So within the context of top-down control and carefully designed processes of production, something unexpected happened. Workers began to self-organize, unionizing and fighting for recognition of their own interests within the industrial production apparatus. The cogs in the machine combined forces and changed the face of industry. In some cases this was destructive, as with the US automobile industry's inability to support the cost of negotiated benefits over the long haul, once it became necessary to compete with Japanese companies and produce smaller, more fuel efficient vehicles that Detroit was late to recognize as the emergent demand of the US consumer. In other ways the long-term, systemic effects were positive, as managers were forced to recognize that a worker is more than the number of correctly assembled parts on a given day.

Workers had in many cases been trained to pursue the one best way to do their tasks, based solely on technical efficiency. If a worker was inclined to do anything but follow directions, he was easily replaced. As long as there were enough hungry people willing to do menial, rote tasks there was no need to change.

The idea that workers were disposable people, somehow less human than their more educated bosses, became frighteningly common, leading to such abuses as the widespread use of asbestos for decades after its link to lung cancer was discovered. Workers were exposed routinely, without warning or proper safety equipment as millionaire CEOs cashed in on the fact that the cancer grows slowly enough that the link was easily concealed. Tonya's father's life was cut short this way. Oddly enough, as he moved up through the ranks and became a manager himself, he always proudly carried his union card and agonized over layoffs and tough decisions. The sinister implications of the schism between leaders and workers that is inherent in the machine metaphor are endless.

Faced with dehumanizing conditions, oppressed human beings invariably organize themselves, collaborating to enforce change from the bottom up. Despite the role that intellect and free will play in human affairs, our aggregate behaviors tend to be scalable, repeated, self-similar patterns. We create hierarchies and dissolve them over time. Witness the rise and fall of empires throughout history as our aggregate behaviors in multiple contexts suggest the species' vacillation between a compulsion to create order and the need to destroy it and make room for something new and, presumably, better to emerge (Baskin 2007b, Lewin 1999). These self-similar patterns of emergence and dissipation have always been a component of not only the human condition, but the signature of the very universe's breathing in and out. This understanding, temporarily lost to the Westernized, mechanistic mind, was known in ancient Hindu philosophy and is also evident in the Chinese view of history as the rise and fall of empires in a cyclical fashion. Man and his environment cocreate variations on ancient attractor states, as mountains rise and fall, empires grow and crumble, companies spring up and shut their doors, couples fall into and out of love. This transience of any given state is part and parcel to the universe's dance around a nonstatic equilibrium.

"To be effective, today's leaders must recognize that the environment is constantly changing, and strategies that worked in other situations don't work in the current context" (Quade and Holladay 2010, p. 49). The way people think and relate to one another is changing amid the socioeconomic turbulence of the modern age. Evolutionary biology, quantum physics, globalism, and the Internet have converged to create a new worldview. Organizations need new ways to assess the environment and their own structures as predictability falters and fluidity increases. These changes necessitate an approach to management that is more principle-based than controlling, emphasizing recurring, scalable patterns in lieu of, or at least in addition to, linear projections.

Today organizations are moving increasingly toward process ontology as they become less rigid and strive for adaptability in a turbulent socioeconomic environment. Everyone wants to know exactly how to manage chaos, but the reality is that traditional organizational structures are ill suited to develop the kind of flexibility needed to navigate the future marketplace. Here we take a cue from the ad-hocracies that spring up around particular interests or short-term projects. We expand on prior definitions of third order cybernetic systems and systemicity, bringing them to life for the skeptical reader. Third-order cybernetic systems include social networks, ad hoc project teams, and communities assembled through the mutual interests or voluntary association of their members. They are characterized by dynamic self-organization and boundaries that shift rapidly, often exhibiting varying levels of rigidity at the same time, depending on what aspects one chooses to focus on. Boje (2008) terms this mode of existence "systemicity," using the suffix "-icity" to indicate something that is not quite a pure form of that which precedes it.

We have just described changes in human thought arising from the widespread acceptance of evolutionary biology, quantum physics, and the Internet. Many scholars see the convergence of these matters as revolutionary for the way they affect our processing of information as human beings, how we relate to one another, and their accompanying socio-economic turbulence. Among the changes to be described are the shift from the view of man as a detached external observer to that of a cocreative agent; the changing analytical focus from an atomistic, individualistic one toward greater consideration of aggregate effects; a move to accept multiple, nonlinear time constructs; and Boje's antenarrative typology. We address these ideas by first exploring the post-Newtonian worldview itself, considering complexity theory as an evolutionary step toward understanding human systems, tie in the concept of antenarrative, then bring in the lessons of quantum storytelling theory and sociomateriality.

Man exists as part of a larger system, within, not at the mercy of, nature. Western thought would have us harness nature, fight the wild beast, tame it, and turn its power to our service as superior beings. For those who cannot stomach constant change, awareness is wrought with fear. The simplicity and solid nature of the machine metaphor and Tayoristic modes of thought ring of nostalgic stability as leaders cling to "the good old days," which may or may not have served the greater good insomuch as their own self-interests. Figure i.1 shows the convergence of multiple influences to shape a new era of human thought.

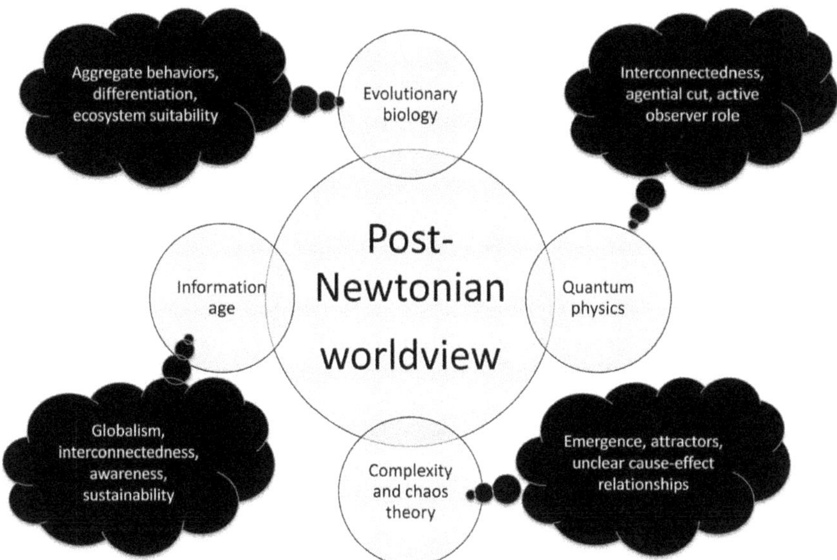

Figure i.1 Influences Affecting the post-Newtonian View of the World
Source: By Tonya L. Henderson. Used by permission.

COMPLEXITY IN HUMAN SYSTEMS

A priori to any movement toward a fractal understanding of organizations is the acceptance of the complexity metaphor applied in the human frame. One must understand that human systems are necessarily complex adaptive systems and apply that in business settings. A complex adaptive system is necessarily a system with permeable boundaries, if it has definable boundaries at all. Such systems are subject to an influx of information and/or energy from the outside world, spawning self-organizing behaviors internally, as agents react to iterative feedback from the environment. Ashby's (1958) law of requisite variety suggests that for a system to be viable, its internal complexity must match that of the outside environment. Thus, as information and/or resources flow into and out of a human organization, one can expect a certain amount of individual reactions to these stimuli to combine cocreatively, forming aggregate behaviors that are at once familiar and difficult to predict. Thus, order emerges from the ground up, not inconsistent with the notion that power vacuums tend to be filled even in organizations that are egalitarian by design.

Bruno Latour (1999) describes Pasteur's work with cultures as largely setting the stage for an emergent phenomenon. Just as Pasteur assembled the right mixture of material elements in space and time to create an opportunity for an emergent phenomenon, it is our intention to bring together a generative mixture of ideas, examples, and exercises to facilitate the emergence of a generative approach to management in today's organizations. Our contributions build on this notion to explore the fractal unfolding and dissipation of sociomaterial processes with a view toward practical use in organizational development. In doing so, we build on our prior works in complexity, storytelling, and materiality to support another perspective about fractal organizing processes (Boje 2008, 2011d, 2011e, 2011f, 2010a, 2012; Boje and Henderson 2014; Wakefield 2012).

Today there is ample evidence to support a complexity-inspired view in myriad settings. For example, Antonicopoulu and Chia (2007) describe learning organizations as CAS and identify two approaches to understanding organizational complexity: one which considers organizational learning to be about "the process of transforming, creating, refining, or validating schemas" and the participation metaphor, wherein social interactions bring about learning (p. 280). Comunian (2011) applies these ideas to the cultural development of cities. The "creative city" is tied to innovation in solving problems. "Soft/ideological infrastructure and spatial/physical structures" are cited as the means of self-organizing. Hazy (2006) describes organizations is "as (a) complex adaptive socio-technical system(s) composed of agents, resources (including knowledge), tasks, and their interrelationships" (p. 58). Sandkuhl and Kirikova (2011) found self-similarity to be relevant for the process and product perspectives but noted that "it is important to see and respect limitations of self-similarity, because some levels of the product structure have similarities, but these similarities disappear with increasing specialization" (p. 204). Many other works have brought complexity into the realm of management science and leadership, gaining widespread acceptance of the complexity-derived view of the organization (Boje 2008, Eoyang 2009, Jantsch 1973, Letiche and Boje 2001, Quade and Holladay 2010).

When examining self-organization, predictability via coarse-grained linear analysis of individual trajectories is abandoned in favor of aggregate possibilities (Sheldrake 1988, Talbot 1993, Tsoukas and Dooley 2011, Prigogine 1996, Waddington 1961). Heisenberg and Bohr collectively force acceptance that not every attribute of an entity can be predicted or even measured at a given time and place, albeit for different reasons (Barad 2007, Hawking and Mlodinow 2005, Talbot 1993, Wheatley 2006). Probability and statistics rise from the status of an accommodation of ignorance about actual values to that of "best descriptions" for aggregate interaction-derived possibilities (Antonacopoulou and Chia 2007, Prigogine 1996, Sheldrake 1988). Taleb (2007) takes it further, accommodating unlikely, high amplitude events and rejecting overuse of the normal distribution in statistical analysis and risk modeling.

These lessons drive one to consider more holistic approaches, in the interest of taking a systems level view. Holistic thinking abandons reductionist and functional analyses, viewing the parts of a system as integrated, sometimes self-similar, parts of a whole that must be examined in its entirety. Gershenson and Heylighen (2003) suggest systems that appear self-organizing at one level of granularity may not be if considered from a different perspective (Gershenson and Heylighen 2003). Talbot (1993) considers the universe "a hologram, a dynamic web of interrelated events in which each part of the web determines the structure of the whole" (p. 41). Haley and Boje (2015) liken interference patterns from multiple beams of light constructing holograms to the interaction among micro-stories and dominant narratives (Haley and Boje 2015). Such approaches expand on traditional systems thinking and pave the way for exploration of more complex, emergent systems.

Yet such an approach is not without its critics. To use a scientifically derived term like fractal in a social context can cause much debate over whether there is a different term that might be more appropriate, whether the term is misappropriated, etc. For example, Ken Baskin cautions us that the vocabulary of complexity, while descriptive, can sometimes detract from common understanding because of its cumbersome nature and very specific meanings in scientific contexts.

Times have changed. Today, science is no longer limited to the understanding of a small, elite group of highly educated individuals. It has become the domain of the common man insofar as it permeates our society, through lived experiences of modern medicine, computing, global telecommunications, etc. We now live in a society whose culture lives in cocreative symbiosis with scientific thought. This realization, coupled with the understanding that man is, despite all efforts to remain an objective outside observer, a part of nature and therefore, whether consciously or unconsciously, subject to its patterns, leads us to conclude that it is not inappropriate to consider scalable self-similar patterns in aggregate human behavior to be fractal-like. Furthermore, other management scholars have successfully used the term, making it confusing to add a synonym for something that is clearly established as a phenomenon of human systems (Eoyang 2009, Hoverstadt 2008, Quade and Holladay 2010, Stacey 1996, Svyantek and Deshon 1993, Tsoukas and Dooley 2011, Williams 2000, Zimmerman and Hurst 1993). To that end, we use the term fractal in the descriptive sense, begging the pardon of mathematical purists.

After all, it was in his quest to understand nature itself that Mandelbrot famously coined the term. As if to avoid the limitations of scientific snobbery, he stated,

> Most emphatically, I do not consider the fractal point of view as a panacea, and each case analysis should be assessed by the criteria holding in its field, that is, mostly upon the basis of its powers of explanation, and prediction, not as [an] example of a mathematical structure.
>
> (Mandelbrot 1983, p. 3)

It is in this spirit that we apply the term to social systems, following the lead of other scholars, drawing on its powers of explanation and demonstrated utility in understanding organizations.

In our context, we are interested in helping managers to spot scalable self-similarity in ways that are immediately and practically useful, which may not allow sufficient time for rigorous testing of each case to ensure that we can identify fracticality, which we define as the exhibition of fractal-like structures in the sociomaterial emergence and dissipation of organizations. There is a lot of great quantitative work being done to measure the fracticality of social systems from a scientific perspective.[1]

Mandelbrot termed his book The Fractal Geometry of Nature an essay despite its length, stating, "I describe it as a scientific Essay because it is written from a personal point of view and without attempting completeness. Also, like many essays, it tends to digressions and interruptions" (Mandelbrot 1983, p. 2). We ask that this work be accepted in a similar fashion, as the exposition of ideas with practical use for those who would venture into these pages with an open mind. As we as authors grow and learn, expanding through cocreative lived experience with others, so do our concepts of FCM and FARM.

What this suggests is that whereas fractal math, fractal graphics, and fractal simulations are suggestive, we must be careful in assuming that every thing is a fractal scalability. Perhaps the fractal story patterns David observed in Daniel Q. Boje's trash compactor patents being embodied (as they call it in the patent field) in 52 subsequent patents in spin off industries, is not an exact Fibonacci spiral fractal. Rather, there are deviations, approximations, and the spiral could collapse into a rhizome, or disappear, altogether in the reappropriation process of entrepreneurial creative destruction. We discuss this case later in the book. We invite you to take what you can use and, in the famous words of George Eliot, "with the breath of kindness, blow the rest away."

SOCIAL RULES AS FRACTAL GENERATORS

By way of introduction to the practicality of these ideas, we offer the reader an example of simple rules governing individual behavior that may drive fractal patterns of sociomaterial unfolding in organizations, families, and society as a whole. There are rules of behavior adopted by many combat veterans that must be changed in order for the same individuals to be successful in the civilian sector.

We veterans run our life by the fractal rules we learn in the military. A fractal rule is way your storytelling patterns your life in material ways. David is the godfather to the 'Material Storytelling' Lab founded by Anete

Strand in Denmark (Strand, 2011). We use sand trays and let people pick material objects (action 2s, toy animals, military ware, vehicles, etc.) to non-verbally tell stories.

We also use a big sandtray, an arena with live humans and horse, interacting with each other and with material objects such as rails, cones, hula hoops, barrels, and so on. At some point we ask veterans and their family members to set up the objects to depict their life story before and after deployment, and then the challenging part, walk the horses through it.

The 'We' is Kenneth Hacker and Jeanne Flora (Arts & Science College, Communication Studies Department, New Mexico State University); Elizabeth England-Kennedy and Wanda Whittlesey-Jerome (Health & Social Services College, Social Work Department); Kourtney Vaillancourt and Merranda Marin (College of Agriculture Consumer & Environmental Sciences, Family and Consumer Sciences Department; and Grace Ann Rosile, Meghan Downes, and David Boje (College of Business, Management Department). Fractal material storytelling is an assemblage of rules that create behavioral interaction cycles (or loops). Here are examples of military fractal rules that generate recurring patterns in a veteran's life story.

1. *Be strong, always!*
2. *Never show weakness!*
3. *Man Up! Suck it up! Get back to work!*
4. *Never ever tell the 'man' you have PTSD!*
5. *Telling a PTSD story in the military means you return from deployment to PTSD confinement!*
6. *Telling a PTSD story means you will never get promoted!*
7. *Telling a PTSD story means you will be discharged!*
8. *Telling a PTSD story leads to Social Stereotyping!*
9. *Telling a PTSD story leads to permanent Pathologizing!*
10. *Here's a fractal rule: Just take your meds and keep quiet!*

These simple rules create fractal patterns in veterans' life and work stories. We elaborate on this particular case in Chapter 6, this volume, but it is provided here for illustrative purposes. The pattern below is a Mandelbrot set. When we zoom in to explore the patterns at different levels of granularity, we see the same kinds of patterns on multiple scales, generated through the recursive application of a mathematical rule. These kinds of patterns continue to develop at infinitem, as the same rule is applied. In nature we see the same kind of self-similar, scalable repetition but with variation where an organism intra-acts with its environment and other organisms—not so very different from our veterans' stories!

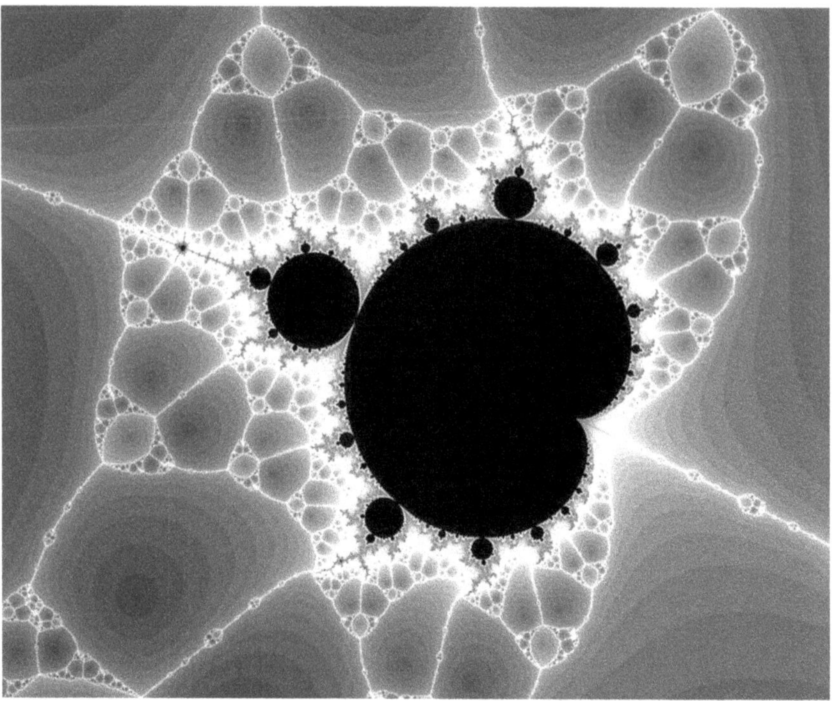

Figure i.2 Mandelbrot Set Fractal
Source: Created by David Boje. Used by permission.[2]

> *"Big whorls have little whorls,*
> *Which feed on their velocity;*
> *And little whorls have lesser whorls*
> *And so on to viscosity*
> *(in a molecular sense)."*
> *—Lewis Fry Richardson*

With that image in mind, we invite you to add this work to your cocreative assemblage for intra-acting with the fractal organizing processes in your own work. This text is intended to encourage the use of FCM by explaining it conceptually, offering examples and exercises, and suggesting methods and tools for use in organizations. The first section provides the foundation for the examination of fractal organizing processes. Part two provides cases and examples of fractal organizing processes in a variety of fields. Finally, the third section of the book provides the reader with a series of tools and methods for constructively interacting with fractal organizing processes. Do not be surprised if the situations you encounter do not fit neatly into a bucket labeled "fractal," for "a map must be simpler than the territory" (Stewart 2010, p. 5).

NOTES

1. For example, Lee, Goh, Kahng, and Kim (2010) explored the rise and fall of research fields by quantifying coauthorship ties among researchers over time.
2. A Mandelbrot set created by David Boje using software Xao (fractalfounda tion.org).

Part I

Fractal Change Management Theory

A Bold New Tool for a Brave New World

It has been shown that adaptation is pivotal to sustainability in individuals, organizations, and environments. It has been identified as a core competency in organizational strategy (Worley, Hitchin, and Ross 1996). To foster adaptation, it is useful to understand not only the patterns we see within a given context, but also to understand the core principles that foster the repetition of these patterns. One way to get at this is to ask successful people where they see scalable, self-similar repetition and go from there. In a study of 11 nonprofit executives, we found that using a content-agnostic interview protocol that simply asked where the subjects saw fractal patterns in their work lives yielded insights into the operating principles behind their success (Wakefield, 2012). The same approach has been used in other contexts to further demonstrate the methodology (Henderson and Deporres, 2014; Wakefield, Boje, and Lane, 2013).

Fractal Change Management theory has begun absorbing lessons from biology, mathematics, traditional physics, and quantum physics (Baskin 1995, Boje and Baskin 2010, Boje 2015 in press, Boje and Henderson 2014, Prigogine and Stengers 1984, Wakefield 2012). Competitive environments are no longer assumed to be static (Bevan and Gitsham 2009, Comunian 2011, Fainstein 2005, Worley et al. 1996). We are now moving to fractal ways of understanding (Hoverstadt 2011). Open boundaries, fractal self-organizing, and scalable self-similarity are gaining broader acceptance (Ashby 1958, Eoyang 2009, Houston 1999, Ison 2008, Johnson 2007, Kauffman 1995, Lewin 1999, Mitchell 2009, Rapoport, Horvath, and Goldstein 2009, Quade and Holladay 2010). Uncertainty is becoming less ominous and is even gaining recognition as fertile ground for innovation and adaptation (Boje and Arkoubi 2005). These changes require new ways of Fractal Change Management (FCM), fractal organizing and a way of viewing the work world that invites change as a grand adventure rather than clinging to old ways or jockeying for control. As such, the pendulum has swung—at least in some circles—from a Taylorist view of the firm as a well-oiled machine whose nature is to be seen in the assembly of its distinct functional elements, toward a multifractal view of the firm as a vitalistic assemblage best explored through its unfolding sociomaterial multifractal processes—or more progressively, simply viewed as a process itself.

This approach to the management of fractal and multifractal organizing processes is grounded in both object and process ontology, viewing organizations as unfolding sociomaterial processes best explored through the scalable, self-similar patterns of their emergence and dissipation, which occur in co-creative, often symbiotic, interaction with their environments. The contemporary multifractal world looks quite different from that of the enlightenment era. Globalism, the communications revolution, scientific advances, and air travel have fundamentally changed the way the current and future generations view the world and have virtually eliminated the ability of any one group of people to operate in isolation. The multifractal world intertwines all organizations with each other and their ecosystems.

The 2008 financial crisis shattered the notion of "too big to fail" as the once-revered pillars of Wall Street like Lehman Brothers marked the downward spiral of large financiers. We now live in a multifractal world of interconnected sociomaterial processes/assemblages (Boje, DuRant, Coppedge, Chambers, & Marcillo-Gomez 2012, Boje and Henderson 2014, Latour 2005), where the inseparability of the social and material have been made real by a bevy of subprime mortgages and foreclosures (Boje, DuRant, Coppedge, Chambers, & Marcillo-Gomez 2012, Coppedge 2014). The bridge between ontological process (e.g., deep ethnography and historical studies) and treating organizations as objects has been built, brick-by-brick by many scholars in recent years such that we are now able to stand in the center of it, leaning out over the rail to examine a flow of sociomaterial processes unfolding multifractally, denying the separation of the social and material. Therefore, we intentionally eliminate the dash between *socio* and *material,* in defiance of our spellchecker's posthumanist agency, to ease the separation between the social and material in our own understanding of unfolding fractal organizing processes. We do so in an effort to honor the role of posthumanist assemblage and co-creative forces in the emergence and dissipation of these patterns in the sociomaterial living story web.[1]

Our earlier works in the area of fractal organizing processes have been primarily ontologically focused, considering the values, beliefs, and social norms that often serve as the social equivalents of fractal generators, thereby characterizing the behavior of informal organizations and social networks with a view toward helping managers to use such insights strategically. In third-order cybernetic systems, the most effective modes of work are less tactically focused and more grounded in interconnectedness and shared values. By looking for fractal patterns, we focus on recurring situations with the possibility of generating large effects. If a pattern recurs on smaller scales, we can assume that the potential exists for the same pattern to recur on a large scale, at an unexpected time (Wakefield 2012). This realization prompts a quest for understanding the systemic, ontological factors that may serve as fractal generators in the human frame. Yet in recent years, there has also been a strong consideration of materiality in our own works and those of our contemporaries (Boje 2011c, Boje et al. 2012, Boje and Henderson 2014, Strand 2012), as we add our own work to the insights of Bennett (2010), Latour (2005, 1999), Barad (2007), and others.

To explore emergent phenomena from a sociomaterial perspective is to consider systemicity to an even greater degree than in past works. Boje (2008, p. 264) defines *systemicity* as "the dynamic, unfinished, unfinalized, and unmerged, and the interactivity of complexity properties with storytelling and narrative processes." Accepting systemicity structurally points one toward accepting that the boundaries of organizations are arbitrary and fuzzy, artificial lines drawn in response to an emotional craving for certainty in the guise of containment. It causes us to consider that the holistic view of the organizational change from moment to moment, as the system breathes and changes its shape, boundaries, size, and other tangible aspects at will. We come to understand that definitively characterizing a particular organization is akin to nailing Jell-O to a wall. So, we seek other ways of understanding, abandoning reductionism in favor of network-based approaches like Latour's (2005) actor network theory and looking for patterns of organizational behavior (Eoyang 2009, Quade 2011, Quade and Holladay 2010).

In this section, we suggest an approach called Fractal Change Management (FCM). We explain its origins and rationale, drawing from multiple disciplines. Next we consider the operational definition of a fractal organizing process, reasoning that to interact with one in any sort of constructive way necessitates the ability to clearly define and identify it in the first place. In doing so, we set the stage for a deeper exploration of today's operating environment as the context for sociomaterial emergence and dissipation in Part II, as a precursor to the practical examples and exercises in Part III that are designed to help the reader to put theory into practice.

1 What Is Fractal Change Management?

In this chapter, we offer six models of sociomateriality, merging material-based views with process ontology for a more comprehensive understanding of fractal organizing processes. Then we explore complexity theory and examine the movement of management theory away from mechanistic models toward a more fractal understanding of organizations. Next we explore the meaning of the term *fractal* in the context of management science. Finally, we provide an overview of fractal change management theory as an emergent, sociomaterial approach to organizational development. FCM theory uses self-similar, scalable patterns observed in the sociomaterial emergence and dissipation of organizations. FCM is a way of storytelling and it is a methodology for observing and changing scalability attunement in organizations, considering the organization in relation to its environments. In FCM, we take a process-oriented, ontologically based approach to organizational development.

Strazdina and Kirikova (2011, p. 735) state that "change management is an important process enabling the definition of a successful enterprise strategy and operations—especially in a turbulent environment)."[2]

Moving forward building upon the perspective of *sociomaterial ontology*, the first steps toward such an approach are the consideration of non-normal distributions and the rejection of reductionist analysis in favor of a "multi zoomed" consideration of aggregate sociomaterial fractal behaviors. Mandelbrot's pioneering work in the 1970s and 1980s drew our attention to the importance of the outliers, nonlinear distributions, and the possibilities of scalable repetition in infinite space. See for example Taleb 2007, Mandelbrot 1983, Mandelbrot and Hudson 2004, Mitchell 2009, and Waldrop 1992. The same kinds of fractal behavioral patterns play out repeatedly throughout human history, arguably correlated to the rise and fall of great men, great companies, societies, and nations (Pugesek 2014). Finally, one must explore the meaning of these patterns of catastrophes and their antenarrative potential for alignment with organizational intent, understanding that any such analysis must be both iterative and reflexive. Just as in strategic planning, organizations check proposed actions for alignment with their strategic guidance, so we suggest consideration of alignment to support value judgments and risk mitigation regarding unfolding fractal patterns in organizations and their environments. Whereas this approach does not offer the certainty frequently promised by linear models, wherein oversimplification often causes problems, it constitutes a more realistic approach to understanding in our complex, dynamic world.

SOCIOMATERIALITY IN THE MODERN ORGANIZATION

Fractal patterns are the signatures of complex adaptive systems. Complex adaptive systems are described by Quade and Holladay (2010) as groups of interdependent, semi-autonomous agents whose interaction creates systemic patterns, which then influence the agents' behavior at an individual level. Each system creates its own kind of scalable, self-similar repeating patterns as it unfolds. To know a system's nature, we need not bound it and catalogue its parts. Indeed, such an approach may not even be possible in many cases. Systemicity defies artificial boundaries placed without regard for myriad unseen connections to stakeholders near and far, whose connections may exist only through thin, lengthy, tangled threads that we simply can't follow given budgetary constraints and the limits of human cognition. Instead, we know it by its fractals. To understand a person, we observe behavior patterns over time and consider the values and beliefs that drive these patterns. To know a plant, we observe its scalable, self-similar growth patterns and compare them to others we have seen. Avalanche-prone snowfields are studied by observing the patterns of previous slides. In each case, we consider the nature of an open system by observing its behavior and form. Systems unfold in tangible ways, emerging and dissipating as companies' profits soar, stagnate, then peter out; social movements emerge from nowhere and dissipate into memory as adherents lose interest in the cause du jour.

This awareness brings us to a sociomateriality-based perspective of what it is to be part of an organization, to experience its unfolding and try to gain perspectives about the kinds of scalable self-similar patterns that constitute its nature. People can sense fractal patterns of organizational storytelling. This is most often below embodied-cognition (Lakoff 1990) *awareness*. Rather, our *fractal storytelling awareness* exists on an ontological plane of *Being-in-the-world*. This ontological awareness involves a process of *attunements* of moods, *alignments* of actions, and *antenarrative* processes. All four processes (awareness, attunements, alignments, and antenarratives) intertwine in spacetimemattering. In other words, instead of embodied-cognition in a social constructivism paradigm, we are a part of the paradigm shift to the growing field of sociomateriality.

MODELS OF SOCIAL (S) AND MATERIALITY (M) IN SOCIOMATERIALITY DEBATES

We explore sociomateriality by means of six models, gaining inspiration from the work of Dourish (2014). The first, separation, is the product of artificial boundaries, what Barad (2007) famously termed the "agential cut."[3] The second, the social domination model, follows the Western habit of placing man at the top of the hierarchy, giving him biblically inspired dominion to shape the posthuman assemblages of which he or she is a part at will, assigning socially constructed meaning that is accepted in the greater context without challenge. Third, is the opposite model wherein man is an unwitting pawn of material elements. Next we consider the harmony or symmetry model, grounded in the rather dubious assumption that sociomaterial systems are equilibrium seeking, following the model of closed systems in the sciences. Next we arrive at the intra-activity model, wherein there is a co-creative unfolding of sociomaterial enactment, which the sixth and final model explains more clearly with give and take between the influences of social and material aspects of unfolding systemicity. We believe the two latter models to offer a more complete and generative understanding for the purposes of navigating the world of fractal organizing processes.

The first model is the separation model. It is a Cartesian, agential cut, where socio is seen as apart from materiality, such as in subjective/objective split. René Descartes (1596–1650) is the exemplar of the Separation Model. This is the gulf between subject and object writ large.

The next model is Social Domination. The social dominates the material in this model. It is exemplified on one of Aristotle's fourfold causalities, efficient cause (the blacksmith forges the material into a desired form, an iron

Figure 1.1 Separation Model of S (social) and M (materiality)
Source: Drawing by David Boje

sculpture). Here materiality is wholly subordinate to our social aims and things are not considered as unfolding processes with a life of their own, but rather as tools and raw materials to be wielded by man, the social animal.

The Social Domination Model of sociomaterialism is also known as the shaping model, and harkens back to the social constructivist social science theories: the idea human social systems are the primary force in shaping material realities (Aristotle's material, efficient, form and final fourfold causality).

Next is the materialism dominance model, where the material dominates the social. In Aristotle's fourfold causalities, the material cause is the properties of the material itself are agential in limiting what the blacksmith can sculpt the iron into. The material limits the socio options.

The M→S model can be seen in the "affordances" work done by web technologists, trying to write video games and websites in ways that afford clues to the social, to the users, on how to navigate web pages. This has resulted in ethnographies of how users learn to use search engines, and complex virtual spaces, and how to make these more usable, so humans can pick their way, and are sort of herded along, to follow the material-symbolic clues (knowing which button to push, which icon to move your mouse over, etc.).

We contend that S→M and M→S models do not hold up. Empirical research by Mazmanian, Cohn, and Dourish (2014) does not find this sort of unidirectionality of human causal agents and material agency.

The next model attempts to "balance" socio and material as equal forces of sociomaterialism.

This is also known as the harmony or symmetry model of sociomaterialism. In systems theory, it is the common traditional idea that systems are equilibrium seeking. However, as we shall see this is a gross narrative generalization, and ideal type in search of sociorealization.

Next is the model we know from Karen Barad's (2003, 2007) work on "agential realism" the *intra*-activity of materiality *with* socio(discourse).

Figure 1.2 Social Domination Model of Socio (S) Materiality (M)
Source: Drawing by David Boje

Figure 1.3 Materialism Dominance Model
Source: Drawing by David Boje

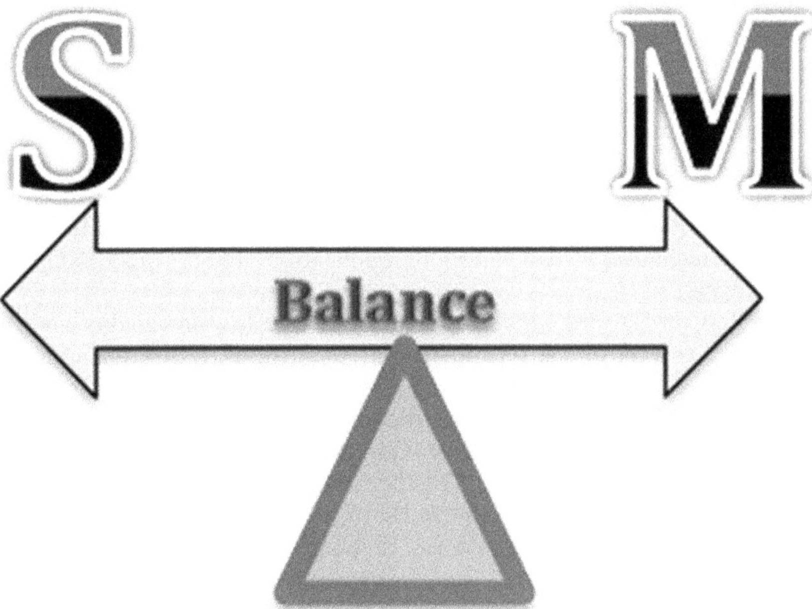

Figure 1.4 Balance Model of Sociomaterialism
Source: Drawing by David Boje

She follows Bruno Latour (1999) in contending that the linguistic turn has gone too far, and there we need to look at quantum sociomateriality as *intra*-activity, rather than an interaction that is balanced, or letting S→M dominate or M→S dominate. The posthumanist challenges of Barad, Bennett, Strand, Haraway, Hird, Henderson, and many other feminist sociomaterialists assert that humans have no primacy over other species.

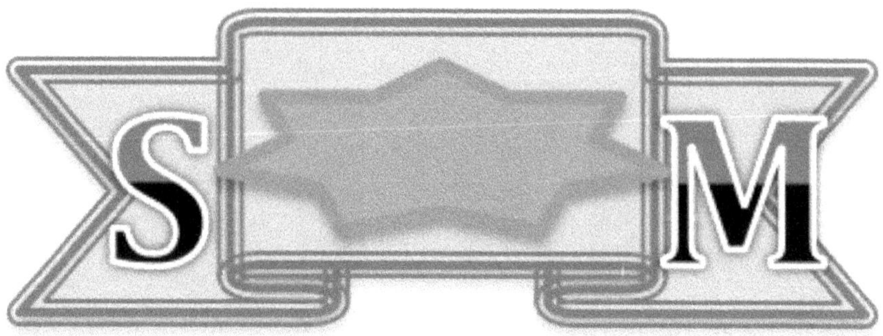

Figure 1.5 Intra-Activity Model of Sociomateriality
Source: Drawing by David Boje

One way to theorize *intra-activity* is that the socio- and the materialism fold into one another in quantum ways, rather than being in balance (equilibrium).

The newest candidate to explain the puzzle of how socio- and materialism are related is the Re-Con-Figuring model by Dourish. In Re-Con-Figur-ation, there is a rocking back and forth, where sometimes, material-stuff on the ground matters—the materiality of the products, market sectors, technologies, and so on. And sometimes there are interventions from the degrading technologies that force a reorganization of *both social and material practices.*

The Re-Con-Figuring Model looks at social aspects of materiality, and the materiality aspects of the social—seen as projections, rather than simpler *shaping, symmetry,* or *shaping* kind of models. Mazmanian, Cohn, and Dourish (2014) pay attention to the representationalist practices that the materialism of technologies provide the social with. Things that do material-stuff, by social control of them in the world, and at the same time craft a representation of the world to us, that makes certain kinds of opportunities for action manifest. For them, it also takes a step beyond the intra-activity model of Barad. Re-Con-Figure-Ation is more like sailing, a tacking back and forth that seems to work.

And as you can see in our "spiral fractal" rendition of Re-Con-Figuring, there is some patterning process about it, which Mazmanian, Cohn and Dourish (2014) have not addressed. The fractal spiral figure practices of Re-Con-Figuration, by which certain patterns of sociomaterialism reality are produced, done again, and again, reiterating, always partial, and never complete system, is what Boje (2008, 2014) calls "systemicity" (unfinalized, partial, overlapping, unfinished, series). And this fractal spiraling involves *awareness, attunement, alignment,* and *antenarrative* processes described later in this book.

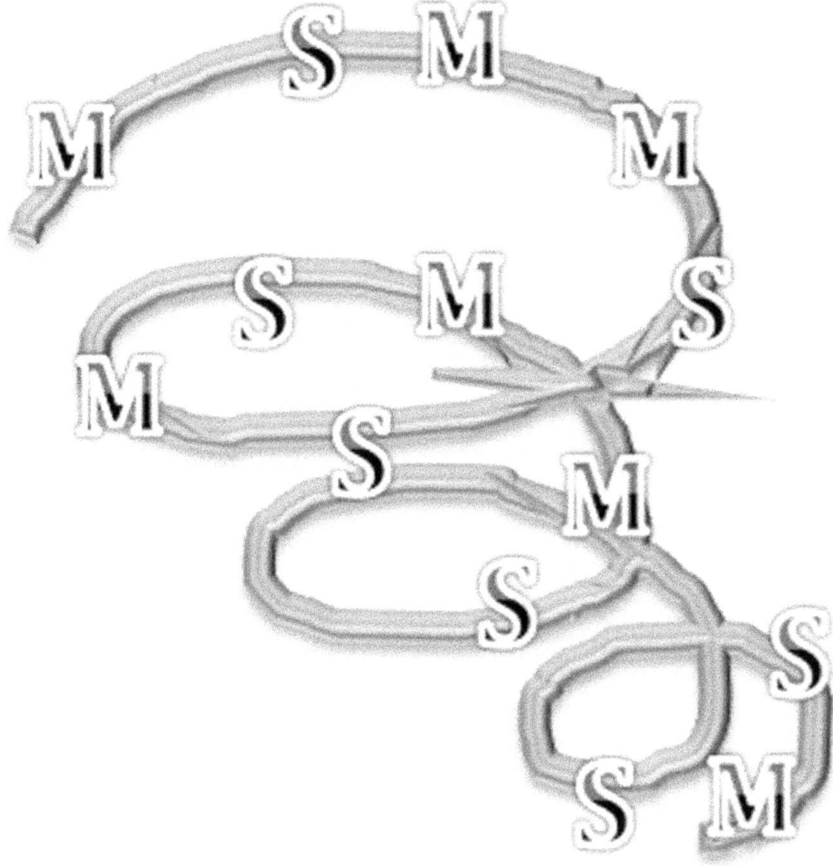

Figure 1.6 Re-Con-Figuring Model
Source: Drawing by David Boje

COMPLEXITY

Complexity theory is widely understood in the contexts of biology, technology, and human systems. Beginning with the seminal works in mathematics, biology, computer simulation, etc. the ideas governing the behavior of complex adaptive systems (CAS) originated in man's desire to better understand and model behaviors of living systems in nature. It is through complexity theory that we learn of the existence and importance of fractal patterns as the hallmarks of emergent phenomena. Of note, in keeping with the aforementioned sociomaterial perspectives, we heretofore use the term *phenomenon* to refer to both unfolding processes and their material aspects, also including the observer and any apparatuses used to make it apparent.[4]

Complexity theory is particularly relevant in the contexts of storytelling and other holistic approaches to exploring systemicity. Here we offer the reader some background before exploring the significance of fractals and how the concept relates to unfolding organizational processes.

Sociomateriality is defined as the intermingling of the social with the material. The problem is how to entangle the two, in terms of fractal organizing. Here we will focus on the paradigm conflicts in sociomateriality.

Sociomateriality theory is going through a paradigm shift. Until the last two decades, the *separation model* dominated: Social and material were seen as separated in the subjective and objective Cartesian cut. Then with Bruno Latour's work, an *assemblage model* of social structures (and structurations) combining with materiality became popular. In one strand of this work, Karen Barad (2003, 2007) developed the *intra-activity* (Agential Realism) *model* where materiality intra-acts with discourse (the social storytelling and ideas). One strand of this is *mutually constitutive model*—as things are social they are also material, and vice versa. However, very recently, new *sociomateriality models* are challenging all three earlier models (Assemblage, Intra-activity, Mutually Constitutive as too simplistic).

THE PARADIGM SHIFTS IN SOCIOMATERIALITY MODELS

There are three paradigm shifts: from separation, symmetry and shaping to Dourish's Re-Con-Figuation model, and an ensemble model David is doing with Rosile and Nez.

Separation Model

The problem with the older models (Intra-Activity and Mutually Consititutive) is they presume symmetry: social and material are two aspects of contemporary social systems that mirror each other in ways they push on the world, or constitute the world, both bring the world into particular arrangements, in *lockstep* both making things the way they are. But it does not work well in his data either. One would think a *separation model* would work well, that there is a *socio* and a *material*. But Mazmanian, Cohn, and Dourish (2014) do not find that *separation* works in the empirical findings. Rather, there are a myriad of stories. The notion of looking for points of *separation* of world that is purely *social* here, and a world that is purely *material* there that have some kind of *intra-active* link does not seem to work out well. There is a much more complicated entanglement at work in *sociomateriality*.

The Symmetry Model

It says social and material are two aspects of contemporary Complex Adaptive Systems (or open systems) that mirror each other in the ways they push on world, and they both *mutually constitute* the world, and both bring world in particular kind of arrangements, in roughly equal symmetric ways, in lockstep ways. But, this does not work well in the data either. The *symmetry/mutually constitutive model* locates agency equally and continually in both the social and material domains.

Shaping Model

Its argument harkens back to the social constructivist social science theories—the idea human social systems are the primary force in shaping material realities (Aristotle's material, efficient, form and final fourfold causality. The human social systems shape the materiality of tools (technologies) that still place the human at the center. The posthumanist challenges of Barad, Bennett, Haraway, Hird, and other feminist sociomaterialists assert that humans have no primacy over other species. And empirically Mazmanian, Cohn, and Dourish (2014) do not find this sort of unidirectionality of human causal agents and agency.

NEW MODEL CANDIDATES

As noted above, in Re-Con-Figuring Model, there is a back and forth, where sometimes, stuff on the ground is important—materiality, market sectors, and so on. And sometimes there are interventions from the degrading technologies forcing a reorganization of both social and material practices. It's more like sailing, a tacking back and forth that seems to work. The figural practices of re-con-figuration, by which certain models of reality are produced, done again, and again, always partial, and never complete. Looks at social aspects of materiality, and the materiality aspects of the social—seen as projections, rather than simpler shaping, symmetry, or shaping kind of model. Mazmanian, Cohn, and Dourish (2014) pay attention to the representationalist practices that the materialism of technologies provide the social with. Things have agency in that they affect material-conditions, by social control of them in the world, and at the same time craft a representation of the world to us; that makes certain kinds of opportunities for action manifest. Boje (2008, 2014) calls this the difference between a whole, coherent, finalized and totalized "system" and what he calls, "systemicity"—the ongoing, unfinished, never finalized, asymmetric, fragmented, overlapping, and shifting dynamic of relationships that is the underlying nature of sociomateriality.

The Ensemble Model was derived by Rosile, Boje, and Nez (in review) from pre-Hispanic archaeological, historical, and anthropological work. We assume that the naïve linear stage-by-stage models follow from unexamined structural–functionalist and outdated complex adaptive system schemata frameworks. Grand narratives of systems theory and organic evolution ignore the interplay of the lives and living stories of people, their material conditions, practices, and meanings. Poststructuralism (Bourdieu 1977, Butler 1993, Foucault 1977, Giddens 1979, Latour 2005, Sewell 1992), on the other hand, address the fragmented, contingent, fractured, and contested actions of people. Grand narrative is focused on issues of chronology and normative ideas. These ways of thinking have their merits, to be sure, but a deeper understanding is needed in order to capture the co-creative, sociomaterial aspects of what's going on.

The Ensemble Leadership model's focus is on the recursive nature of social life, where systems are in a state of becoming, rather than coherence and wholeness. Systemicity, is an alternative to whole systems thinking, where systems and structures are always in a state of becoming. Systems theory assumes a static, synchronic mode of ontology and analysis. Ancient Oaxaca is an example of how a web of fragmented affiliations of men, women, children, elders, farmers, merchants, potters, weavers, priests, soldiers, rulers, scribes, architects, and many other social personae—changed dramatically through the prehispanic period (para, Joyce 2009, p. 288). From a poststructural view, so-called whole systems functionalist theory is inherently problematic. In the poststructural view, all people have potential for agency and power, not just social elites. Evolutionary, ecological systems, and organic systems theories are abstract approaches that tend to obscure the distinctive history and practices of past peoples by situating grand narratives of unfolding universal laws of history. Social norms involve communities of practice, what people did in the past in their everyday activities. The assumption is that social norms are more empirically grounded than systems theory approaches, which make neo-evolutionism assumptions, and view human activity as caused by abstract high-level forces such as functioning of ecological systems or unfolding universal laws of history. Systems theory privileges integrated and coherent cultural and social evolution.

The Ensemble Model is derived from pre-Hispanic ensemble leadership. The early work in pre-Hispanic Mexico used theory models, such as Structural-Functionalism, Neo-Evolutionary History Stages, Open Systems Theory, and Complex Adaptive Systems theory that were popular social science models of World War II up to two decades ago. The problem is these models are far too abstract, general, and universalizing. The result is they miss the nuances of complexity and contextual perturbations.

Our alternative is to do Fractal Analysis. We start with a challenge to the Western systems and Neo-Evolutionary models: There are two Mexicos: indigenous Mexico descended from Pre-Hispanic peoples with norms of sustainable conservation practices that met the needs of future generations, and Colonial Mexico, the dominant society structure around norms of Western civilization that compromise the ability of future generations to meet their own needs. Sustainable development provides biological safeguards for future generations, whereas globalization prioritizes the needs of the present generation for natural resources and biodiversity protection (Gómez-Pompa and Kaus 1999). Joyce and Winter (1996) challenge systems theory that takes an organic-materialist approach. They cite studies of population, cultures, and ecosystems that did not find them to exist empirically or factually. Rather, goal-driven actors and conflicts of class, ethnic, and racial—use ideologies to initiate sociocultural change in a political way that Boje, Rosile, and Nez are calling the Ensemble Leadership Model. Joyce (2009) says, "Rather than assuming that social systems are integrated and coherent, a hallmark of functionalist theory, I view societies as fragmented and contested to varying genres such that there is never complete closure to any system of social relations" (p. 284). Joyce (2009) traces the communal leadership in the Valley of Oaxaca before the centralized leadership took root (p. 209, 222), and after with local communities and/or barrios were largely excluded (p. 197). Norms grow out of social practices and material conditions, from "negotiations among differently positioned actors—individuals and groups—distinguished by varying identities, interests, emotions, knowledge, outlooks, and dispositions" (Joyce 2009, p. 284). Functionalist systems theory and its organic and neo-evolutionary perspectives have been popular and influential. However they have obscured genealogies of practices that constitute particular histories (Joyce 2009, p. 287). In sum, the Ensemble Leadership Model challenges the idea that history is predetermined, "involving a sequence of episodic transitions from one stable system to another, which minimizes historical transformation and contingency" (Joyce 2009, 32). Dualism between materialism and idealism is rejected in Poststructural thought, wherein the view is that there is a co-constitution going on between cultural principles and material resources, what we call materiality (Joyce 2009, p. 22).

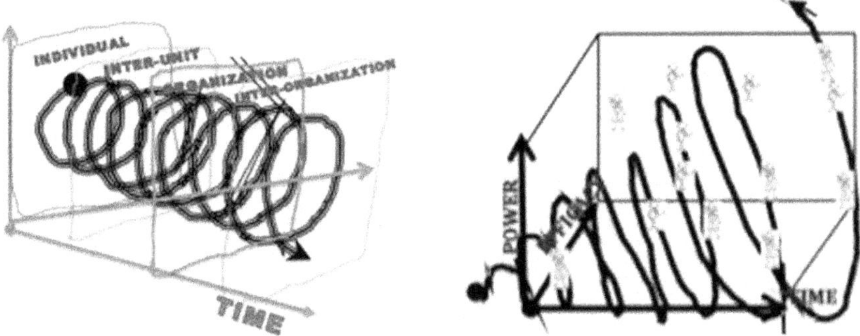

Figure 1.7 Contrast a 3D Nonaka Knowledge Management (slinky-like) Spiral Model with a 3D Fibonacci-Fractal-Spiral Model

Source: (Drawings by Boje, used by permission)

Both models iterate through individual, interunit, organization, and interorganization scalar levels of growth, in 3D. In the monofractal-spiral model of Nonaka's (1991) knowledge management is the repeating iteration of cycle-stages: Internalization Socialization, Externalization, and Combination (known as SECI). SECI stages repeat in Archimedes (bolt-like, or slinky-like) fractal-pattern of equal self-same cycle iterations.

The drawing at right depicts a Fibonacci spiral, where each whorl is larger than the previous one, following the number series 2, 3, 5, 8, 13, 21, etc. If the whorls as they increase in number, are equal size and at equal time intervals it is known as an Archimedes-fractal-spiral. If the whorls increase in number, and amplify in succession over time, then it is known as a Fibonacci-fractal-spiral. However, if the whorls are alternating in size, at regular intervals, then it's an alternating-fractal-spiral, much like ocean waves. Each of these fractal spiral types has continual similarity about a central axis (vector).

We need to understand the spiral dynamics of a three-dimensional mapping of scalability. To get to self-similar, self-organizing scalability, means to get at the rules of design, in situ, in-use, of fractal-spiral growth or decline. To get to a non-Archimedean-fractal-spiral means increasing the deviation-amplification from one cycle of activity to the next. And to get beyond the abstract notion of self-same cycles that expand progressively (logarithmically), we need to theorize and measure alternations of increasing whorl size and decreasing whorl size. It could be hypothesized that the alternating whorl size configuration is more efficient for making transitions between one scale to the next. We will leave you to craft such depictions. They are important to FCM, because the kind of abstraction we are making enables the kind of pattern rules we enact.

BUILDING BLOCKS: COMPLEX ADAPTIVE SYSTEMS PROCESS APPROACHES

There are a number of approaches to organizational development, management, and leadership that draw on complexity theory and take fractals into account. Some are grounded in process ontology, whereas others are strictly focused on structure. Here we offer a brief survey of some relevant approaches and key insights that they offer.

STRUCTURE-BASED APPROACHES

Oh, Ryu, Moon, Cho, and Jung (2010) model trust in multi-organizational automotive manufacturing supply chain work using a fractal-inspired concept. In their fuzzy trust model, relationships between organizations are modeled as fractal numerical values are assigned to the strength of trust between agents. They suggest that the automotive manufacturing environment is sufficiently diverse that collaboration is beneficial, particularly where just in time supply models are used. The authors suggest a collaborative, fractal-based supply chain management paradigm to incorporate the trust concept and analyze the effects at the operational, managerial, and strategic levels. The model includes globalization and outsourcing, among other things. In the context of just in time supply they model variation of trust value as it is reflected in the amount of safety stock kept on hand. Whereas we appreciate their fractal inspired, holistic approach to modeling trust in a network setting, the model is not recursive and seems to employ a certain amount of reductionism in the way that modules are broken out.

Whereas Hoverstadt's viable systems model (VSM), based on the original developed by Stafford Beer, goes a long way in getting business people to accept a more holistic, scalable approach, its strengths lie in its use of the law of requisite variety. Ashby's (1958) law states that a system attempting to adapt to external complexity must match that level of complexity. To us, it feels like a sort of statis in terms of complication. "In developing the VSM, Stafford beer sought to develop a 'science of organization', by setting down the principles that underpin all organizations and create viability, which is the capacity to exist and thrive in sometimes unpredictable and turbulent environments" (Hoverstadt 2011, p. 27). He emphasizes that viable organizations are adaptable, unlike strict Taylorist hierarchies, which are unstable by their nature, being designed with the intention of allowing the entire organization to be swayed by powerful minorities at the top of the formal power structure. He says that Taylorism doesn't work because of changes in technology and skills within organizations and acknowledges the existence of autonomy in even the most strictly hierarchical organizations.

There are seven constituent elements in the viable systems model, including the environment. The *operations system, coordination system, delivery management, monitoring system, development management* and *policy system* are replicated within each level of the organization (Hoverstadt 2011, p. 28). Yet different issues are dealt with at different levels of the organization, necessitating communication among levels. To be viable, organizations must balance the demands of their environments, ruling out centralized hierarchies in complex environments, and must be able to act coherently to be effective, eliminating anarchy. Boundary issues often cause coordination problems (p. 85).

"The job of strategy is to ensure the viability of the organization by creating and maintaining the fit between the organization and its environment" (p. 169). Hoverstadt (2008) offers a model wherein a strategic risk is "anything that has the potential to break the structural coupling between the organization and the elements of its operating environment with which it co-evolves" (p. 173). The term *structural coupling* is drawn from biology, where it refers to an organism's key relationships in terms of maintaining its fit and co-evolution with the environment. He advocates creating an organization wherein strategy is an emergent property of the organization and is developed in real time, keeping in mind that innovation is said to change the relationship between the organization and its environment.

His model for mosaic transformation in organizations has merit because it brings the lessons from successful ad hoc change efforts wherein large changes were adopted in pieces at the appropriate times. He suggests changing one component and those it interfaces with directly, but not changing everything at once. The book also has merit for its consideration of system boundaries and their limitations. Coase's law suggests that increasing environmental complexity increases the scope of stakeholders that companies must be concerned with (Hoverstadt 2011, p. 249). It states that "as transaction costs (the cost of trading rather than producing in house) drop, so organizations tend to outsource more" (p. 249). This is said to lead to a blurring of organizational boundaries. There is a good discussion of boundaries and how setting up a team creates an identity (p. 258). He criticizes organizations for drawing boundaries based solely on who is on the payroll and advocates a broader systemic look, something we agree with wholeheartedly (p. 259).

We appreciate the basic premise, the grounding of the model in complexity as a means of adaptation. It offers a step in the right direction in terms of how we see organizations in terms of adaptation and double loop learning. Yet the work is oriented more toward the deliberate design of organizational structure than process ontology.

> The fractal structure of the VSM means that the same mechanisms are replicated at each level of the sub-systems and sub-systems that we revealed in the unfolding of complexity. This allows the same structural model to be used at any level of the organization, for any type of organization.
>
> (Hoverstadt 2011, p. 36)

Our approach is much different. First, it is grounded in sociomaterial process ontology. We consider organizations to be unfolding processes of self-organization, dissipation, and re-emergence manifested in the co-creative flow of material and social processes. Groups of people self-organize to accomplish tasks, regardless of what their job descriptions and organization charts say. We find the coworkers with the right skills, form tiger teams, or meet informally over coffee to have informal exchanges, leveraging the shadow system to truly accomplish our tasks. That is not to say that employees do not interact according to management's desires or within the formal constructs of the official organization, but rather to assert that true collaboration is an emergent property of the living story web. This view, our lenses keenly focused on emergent and dissipative problem solving, is much different from the object ontology view, wherein one draws a diagram or an organization chart depicting concrete divisions or functional groups, with lines and arrows to suggest subordination or communication. (Van de Ven and Poole 2005).

PROCESS-ORIENTED APPROACHES

General Systems Theory (GST) embraces a linear evolution in complexity. As organizations become more complex, they evolve from simple closed systems with impermeable boundaries, through permeably bounded living organisms, into a state we call systemicity. In systemicity, an organization exhibits varying levels of rigidity in its structure, dynamically changing as its fuzzy borders shift in response to the changing environment. Whereas the model provides a useful hierarchy and taxonomy for discussing the different kinds of organizations people create, whether by design or by accident, we find the linear progression of ideals to be rather limiting. One may not necessarily evolve from the rigid, through the organic, arriving at systemicity as a Hegelian, evolutionary progression toward a desirable end. Most organizations will move up and down the ladder as conditions shift, exhibiting strict rigidity and closed boundaries in some areas and fuzzy, flexible systemicity in others. For example, an R&D firm may be very flexible and open to cross-pollination with other firms in terms of its creative endeavors in general, yet closed lipped about a particular technology it considers proprietary. Furthermore, it is unlikely that certain functions, even in the most liberal of contexts, can be successfully handled in this way. Accounting and other functions that are subject to regulatory oversight may need to remain in a first order cybernetic substructure in order for the organization as a whole to succeed. Whereas the taxonomy it provides is a very valuable tool, and we tip our hats to von Bertalanffy (1969) in gratitude for the language that enables us to describe these ideas, the linearity of the model is too restrictive for our purposes (Boje 2008, Pondy and Boje 2005).

For a practical approach to chaos and complexity, we find great utility in Eoyang's (2009) approach. As the founder of the Human Systems Dynamics Institute (www.hsdinstitute.org/index.html), Glenda Eoyang has been studying fractal patterns in human organizations since 1986. We had the privilege of interviewing her in the process of writing this book and learning more about how she got started, examples of her work with complexity in human systems, and where she sees the work going henceforth. She shared with us her passion for the complexity of human systems and how she got started in the field:

> I was running a technical training in documentation company and we'd been very successful with our engineering based structure in control

> model of software development . . . In 1986, several things changed at the same time. There was new technology, new business structures; some of our clients began to use total quality. They were re-organizing right and left. There were economic shifts. All of the sudden things went unpredictable and so in trying to figure out how to manage that process and how to be . . . how to lead through that kind of uncertainty. I ran across Gleick's work, *Chaos Making A New Science* and realized that those metaphors were really very informative about how I might stand as a leader and technician and so that was when I began investigating . . . I found out later there were other people who were writing but none us could get published at that point, so, from then until 1991 I pretty much just kind of worked in the dark, reading what I could in the sciences, using it in my practice, writing about it, talking about it, thinking about it and then in 1991 I found other people who were on the same path. So it was business necessity that drove me that drove me to complexity.
>
> —Glenda Eoyang (interview)

We agree with Eoyang's (2009) approach to managing self-organization. Working from a complexity-informed perspective, she suggests that managers pursue asking the correct questions, instead of necessarily finding specific answers. She advises them to be supportive of generative differentiation, create environments where feedback is encouraged, remove constraints opposing self-organization, reinforce these kinds of trends, and stay out of the way to avoid being seen as imposing an external order. She educates leaders in methods for spotting patterns in organizations, using that information strategically, and moving forward. We appreciate her way of explaining complexity in laymen's terms and making the concepts both accessible and actionable for leaders.

Her book *Coping With Chaos* provides seven simple tools for dealing with complex adaptive systems. She begins by introducing the notion of butterfly effects in organizations, where the tightly coupled nature of human systems leads small issues to create large effects in many cases. Next, she teaches managers to examine boundary conditions, not just formal organizational structural boundaries, but also those tied to informal power structures, demographic diversity, and differences of opinions. Following her sage advice, one might begin to improve organizational function by helping his staff to cross boundaries that adversely affect communications and task accomplishment, creating feedback loops. Most importantly, she acknowledges the fractal nature of organizations, noting that, "lines of communication and loyalty are fractal in nature" (Eoyang 2009, 75). She suggests that, "if you want to understand how work really gets done and how meaningful, permanent change can happen, you must ignore the formal organizational charts and see the fractal structure of individuals and groups within the company" (p. 78). Her discussion of fractals suggests that managers, "find the seed . . . the basic principle on which your organization acts," make that explicit, "collect and tell stories" about the system, introduce variety, acknowledge informal boundaries, and introduce change where the system is unstable (pp. 77–82). She also notes disruption of expected patterns in organizational behavior as a source of frustration (Eoyang 2009).

In our discussion with her, the topic of simple rules, the human equivalent of fractal generators, emerged as central to efforts to shift organizational fractal patterns. This discussion was consistent with prior speculation that values and beliefs serve as fractal generators in human systems (Wakefield 2012, Tetreault and Wakefield 2012). Eoyang describes it this way.

> We were working with a large government agency that did social service delivery and they were very siloed that they wanted to integrate services at the point of delivery . . . and they had the child care and the health care and the food stamps and political support and the education job training and all of that, were in separate parts of this large department. Three thousand people worked for this department and they wanted to integrate and they'd been trying to integrate for about a decade and it just hadn't worked.
>
> . . . we asked them in max mix groups to say simple rules they use to make decisions and the first group reported in an hour and they said "Oh, we support the client, always tell the truth, follow the law and work efficiently" And everybody in the room booed and I said "Oh, well, that's very interesting" and we went to the second table and they said "Well, these are our rules, cover your but and your bosses' but, don't share information unless you have to and make sure . . ." there was something about controlling a client—don't give the client anymore than they deserve, something like that, and everybody cheered.
>
> And so I said, well if you think about this pattern of siloes that you have, within your departments, among departments, between your agency and the rest of the agencies in the [inaudible], do you see how those rules would give you siloing patterns? And they said, "Well, of course they would" . . . I said, "Well, how might you want to change those rules to change the pattern?" and as I went through the rules one at a time, what they decided was . . . so not share information when you have to, but share information when it will help, that may be the pattern which shift. And I can't tell you that it was it was a miraculous transformation but they made a lot of change.
>
> Their information systems in their forms and community work and their processes and procedures weren't a total transformation, but it shifted the pattern. So this way of looking at a current pattern, trying to extract from it, one of the rules that drive that pattern asking, "What's a minimum shift in those rules that might change the pattern and then taking action to implement that and then iterating to see if that if that

> worked, what might work?" But that's the, the standard process that we use for pattern shifting, fractal shifting.[5]
>
> —Glenda Eoyang (interview)

We thought that it might be a problem to get people who are excited about change to implement such shifts in small steps, but Eoyang's experience suggests otherwise.

> People are so busy these days and they have so much overgrown change stuff that's put upon them, that often, to think about, just change in one little thing, they could do it, even if they think it won't make any difference. They're just glad to get off the hook with not much extra work to do. And then after they make that small change, they [are] really surprised that it makes a difference, but I think that people are simply overwhelmed these days. Too much work to do, too much stress too many things to understand, things are moving so quickly that even if they don't think it will work, they're happy to have a small thing to do.
>
> —Glenda Eoyang (interview)

Another practical approach in this field is that of Quade and Holladay (2010). They describe a complexity-derived leadership model called dynamical leadership and offer a model for adaptive capacity that encourages organizational learning and resilience in complex adaptive systems. It makes excellent use of the concept of fractal patterns in human systems and suggests that effective leadership hinges on the recognition and influencing of patterns. "Adaptive capacity is a leader's ability to see and influence system patterns rather than discrete organizational issues, events, or actions" (p. 15).

The ability of leaders to identify patterns and determine which ones are productive in order to support them, along with diminishing unproductive patterns, is encouraged. "A fundamental shift is required to understand how patterns emerge and how to influence them in complex situations. Patterns are defined as similarities, differences, and relationships that have meaning across space and time" (p. 21).

They suggest the work of a dynamical leader is to build organizational capacity by understanding and working with patterns, learning from them, and repeating generative patterns. Leaders are entreated to "amplify or grow productive patterns, set the conditions for new patterns to emerge, recognize and use unconventional patterns, shift patterns to improve the organization, and ensure others are able to do the same" (p. 37). Their leadership landscape model is divided into three zones: *organized* (high agreement, high certainty), *self-organizing* (medium agreement, medium certainty), and *random* (low agreement, low certainty) (p. 54). Leadership advice is offered specific to each zone.

The most powerful piece of leadership advice they offer is the notion of using simple rules, broadly defining general expectations, rather than control mechanisms. Whether they are formally stated, implied, or unspoken, these rules help people in organizations to take proper action amid a wide variety of circumstances. "Using a short list of simple rules, dynamical leaders create strong boundaries for expectations, behaviors, and decision-making." (Quade and Holladay 2010, p. 175). These rules are different from norms and organizational principles in that they are more action focused and directly affect actions taken inside the system.

In our interview with Dr. Quade, she elaborated.

> These simple rules are even bigger than that in that they can drive behavior and actions that are huge. . . . and some of the times they are articulated, and sometimes they are not. So, for example, during 9/11, well, this un-articulated [rule was] the people coming down the buildings didn't say, you know, "Get, go down the stairs this way." They just knew to reach out, touch the person in front of them, and follow the motion of the person in front of them. Another simple rule is take care of others. Nobody said, you know, "Help somebody in a wheelchair down the stairs." They just did it.
>
> —Kristine Quade (interview)

Beyond their excellent understanding and use of fractal patterns in human systems, we also appreciate the relational aspect of the work, their appreciation of difference and tension as part of creativity, scalability, and their demonstrated respect for the fluid, changing nature of fractal organizing processes. Mutual connections that are both fluid and candid are described as generative. They also discuss the importance of difference in creating tension within an organization. "At the intersection of differences, dynamical leaders find creativity necessary to bring about change, thereby reducing tension and increasing fit" (Quade and Holladay 2010, p. 24). "Dynamical leaders work with others to focus on differences and negotiate ways of generating patterns across those differences" (Quade and Holladay 2010, p. 131).

> Some patterns reverberate throughout the entire system, repeating themselves on many levels and in many forms. When the same behavior can be observed in leaders, groups, and individuals it may be understood as a fractal pattern. Fractals exist everywhere. In society, what impacts the community will impact families as well as individuals. In an organization, the behavior of a senior leader may be replicated at various levels of the organization.
>
> (Quade and Holladay 2010, p. 24)

They not only offer a clear explanation of how fractal patterns of behavior occur in organizations, they also do justice to the impermanence of those patterns.

> Patterns will always continue to emerge, whether or not they are watched and regardless of what happens. They will always change, and trying to identify one pattern—to put it in a box or frame it on the wall—is a fruitless gesture. The end toward which the system self-organizes is not a single point that signals the conclusion of the search. Rather its goal is fitness in the larger environment that is constantly shifting, making new demands, presenting new opportunities, and opening new vistas.
>
> (Quade and Holladay 2010, p. 23)

We also appreciate the lengths they go to in cautioning the reader not to myopically focus on a particular pattern at the expense of others. They note several times that there are multiple patterns unfolding in an organization at any given time and that they do influence one another.

These approaches are not incongruent with what Mark Frazier (2012) calls narrative fractals. In social interactions with others, the narrative fractal pattern may influence what we opt to focus on as we quickly scan an environment. He suggests the following labels as a means of tagging and categorizing narrative fractals.

> *Attractor:* Interest-generating opener [emotion: curiosity]
> *Challenge:* Disruptor of settled understandings/relationships [emotion: tension] (imagining)
> *Opportunity:* Vision of a desired outcome [emotion: inspiration]
> *Strategy:* Path to realize vision [emotion: hope] (doing)
> *Test:* Trial to confirm strategy [emotion: confidence]
> *Follow-up:* Implement strategy, reframe/reloop, discard [emotion: resolve]
>
> (Frazier 2012)

Many of these are what is called linear fractals. A linear fractal does translation, scaling, reflection, and rotation that rely on linear algebra (Nottale, 1994, 2011). For Frazier, "A story will often have some kind of obvious target, maybe the intent of one of the players."

Our FCM book explores this and other new models of sociomaterialism. We do this with a view toward not only understanding fractal processes, but in consideration of agency. To managers espousing the organizations as machines metaphor, these ideas are difficult to digest. The idea of control fails us, shattering convictions of certainty. Yet an absence of control does not eliminate all hope of agency (Boje and Wakefield 2011). In every context, there are still myriad choices to be made at the individual level, the team level, the organization level, and in ever-higher echelons. What are we to do with/about/in concert with such patterns as responsible, capable managers, leaders, players on the playing field of organizational unfolding?

Stable organizational structures exist within a basin of attraction and structures can be attractors with leadership of convergence pointing the organization toward a particular structure (Hazy 2006). Attractors in human existence maybe thought of as "system wide patterns of behavior" (xvi.)

He suggests three types of attractors: point (unidirectional), periodic (cyclical), and strange (pattern behaviors within the apparently random System, visible only if the scale of the observation is varied). Eoyang (2009) notes that "what is relevant is that the behavior of the group follows discernible patterns, even if the patterns cannot be predicted or controlled" (p. 96). Her process for influencing the attractor states within a complex adaptive human system is to recognize, evaluate, and intervene by participating in the current attractor, recognizing people's frustration, watching for changes, and establishing a combination of the attractors to increase organizational resiliency.

We differ from her approach in our interpretation of fractal patterns as the atractors in and of themselves, unfolding in process ontology. For us, fractal patterns are outward manifestations of emergence and dissipation of informal power structures and formal ones, such that these structures themselves constitute not only tangible relationships, but also unfolding processes. We advocate the evaluation of such processes in an antenarrative frame. Whereas Eoyang's (2009) work is admirably insightful and practical, we feel more comfortable considering fractal patterns differently. As human systems emerge and dissipate through storytelling, as patterns in the living story web, they approach and back away from certain patterns, archetypes if you will, of dynamic organization.

Deleuze and Guattari (1987) speak of a similar movement between striated and smooth spaces. They consider the Koch snowflake. Repetition of the step that serves as the fractal generator, in this case the replacement of the center of each line segment with a triangle, is repeated ad infinitem, producing an increasingly intricate curve. They note that the shape becomes increasingly smooth with each iteration, assuming our proximity to the page does not shift, eventually forming a "fuzzy aggregate" that grows increasingly smoother, rounding out the edges. They consider this process generative, noting, "Perhaps we must say that all progress is made by and in striated space, but all becoming occurs in smooth spaces" (Deleuze and Guattari 1987, p. 486). To be sure, each repetition of the process, replacing the center of each line segment with a triangle, appears to smooth out the curve and create less and less striation. Each iteration renders triangles of smaller and smaller magnitude until the curve appears smooth.

We struggle with this image. If we repeat the process, no matter how many times, can we really ever consider the curve smooth? Just because the triangles become smaller, that does not mean they are gone. Is, therefore, striation merely a messy part of life in a complex system—not a necessary evil, but a part of emergence and dissipation? Is the attempt to smooth out what is, by its nature bumpy, not "to do violence" to its nature, just as we do when imposing a dominant narrative onto a living story? How do we know that we are not simply choosing to ignore striation by failing to adjust our gaze such that its true nature is apparent? For this limitation, we find fault with Deleuze and Guattari's (1987) use of fractals in this way. The patterns persist. Koch's "beautiful monster" is all the more beautiful because of its scalable self-similarity. To be attuned to its nature, I need only to adjust my level of analysis. The patterns persist, just with greater granularity. They become subtle, perhaps beyond the limits of human cognition, but they never go away. They are the signatures of the system under study. Just as the points of Koch's snowflake are the signifiers of its underlying process, our own patterns of thought and behavior define us as living, thinking beings.

Yet there is a certain beauty in Deleuze and Guattaris' (1987) notion of transitioning between the smooth and striated. Certainly the impositions of the machine metaphor onto nature appear to be consistently characterized by rough edges, sharp corners, and an attendant cutting of all things wild and self-determined. Certainly the abuses of the industrial revolution and its dehumanizing reduction of human beings to cogs in a machine fall into this category. For all of Newton's role in ushering in the machine metaphor, his calculus does indeed allow for the transition from striated to smooth with great precision, making derivatives possible so we can calculate not only position and speed, but acceleration, etc. To use the very simplest integration example, Chapter 1 in most calculus texts, we are reminded of the woefully inaccurate way of calculating the area under a curve by filling the space with rectangles. Newton teaches us that only when we take the limit of the area as the number of rectangles in a given space becomes infinitely large, corresponding to the infinite shrinking of their width, can we know the actual area under the curve. We then transition from man-made striation toward a comprehensibility of nature's smoothness.

This progress can be likened to the yogic journey of reducing striation in one's thought patterns to progress toward a smoothness of mind that is closer to man's true spiritual nature as he draws further and further from the striated, harshness of the egoic self. The practices associated with yoga and arguably some other disciplines, amount to the intentional choice and imposition of a fractal generator or a set of generators on the emergence and dissipation of thought patterns in the mind, in this case via an embodied practice that sets new habits of behavior, muscle memory, and thought.

Notably, Carrera (2011) does not equate this with any sort of forceful imposition that goes against nature. For the yogi, the restraints imposed on the body and mind through practice are the path to realization of one's true nature, rather than an artificial suppression. This smoothing out of emergent and dissipative thought patterns and the smoothing out of bodily motions through disciplined repetition of a sequence of postures leads not to an externally imposed "they-self," to use Heidegger's (1962) term, but instead to the "authentic self," he treats as an absolute in the Hegelian sense. Yet where Westerners see a dichotomy, the Eastern absolute of Samadhi involves the classic "both-and." By connecting with the authentic self, the yogi does not disconnect from the rest of the world, but instead achieves a state of union with it, consistent with the Hindu concept that all people and things are manifestations of God (*The Bhagavad Gita* 2007). Yogic philosophy suggests that there is a seed of the divine within all persons, and that this god-like aspect unites the individual with the rest of the world when self-knowledge is pursued.

If we attempt to put this in quantum storytelling terms, viewing the mind as a microcosm of the universe, we can treat the development of yogic equanimity as a smoothing of emergence and dissipation in the psychological equivalent of the quantum field of potential. In quantum storytelling, we apply lessons of post-Newtonian thought, most notably the post-modern and post-humanist views of polyvocal storytelling and material agency combined, as viewed through a quantum physics inspired lens (Boje and Henderson 2014). To apply this lens, it is important to explain its origins and how the quantum storyteller takes complexity as an a priori then contextualizes it through the lens of quantum physics-inspired perspectives.

Storytelling is one area where groups of people demonstrate their natural tendencies to behave as complex adaptive systems (CAS). Quantum storytelling builds on the lessons of complexity theory applied to human systems, wherein we encourage organizations to avoid didactic imposition of "top-down" perspectives of organizational culture and "truth" and instead pay attention to the myriad perspectives of stakeholders of varying rank and stature. We take these in aggregate, allowing what Boje (2001) calls micro stories to coalesce into emergent impressions of organizational reality. Whereas many thought leaders emphasize the leader's role in establishing an elevator speech that is taken as organizational truth, we tend to emphasize the importance of the emergent, "behind the scenes" stories as valid perspectives that help constitute reality for the rank and file, as their reality shapes execution of tasks and affects leaders' and organizations' success at all levels (Boje 1991, 1995, 2008, 2011c).

Taking Lewin's (1951) field theory as contextual and with aggregate stories and impressions emerging and dissipating as situations change in what Boje (2011a, b) refers to as the living story web, we take a cocreative view of the story and its teller engaged in a creative dance that is at once a telling and an act of emergent becoming; we tell the stories and they tell us, shaping us at a deep psychological level in the process (Boje and Baskin 2010a). The stories told by any group of people can be used to tease out the rules of engagement in their world when we analyze the stories in aggregate to explore the fractal patterns that characterize their living story web at any given time (Wakefield 2012).

We have just addressed the theoretical underpinnings of FCM and considered some if its theoretical siblings. Next we will turn to a consideration of its implications for organizations. It offers a mode of Being that affects how we operate in the contexts of organizations that are process oriented and flexible.

Warneke's (1993) *Fractal Company* book, as we said, put old wine in new bottles, giving fractal labels to the old mechanistic-organic systems models. However, it does also make an important contribution by getting people thinking about how fractals relate to our organizations. Later, Mr. Hoverstadt's

(2011) *Fractal Organization* book also makes an important contribution to change management. He defines the fractal organization as a recursive map of an organization, but it is at the same time a hierarchical control. As Duarte (2014) contends, the developments in fractal geometry have had ripple effects in paradigm shifts in novels, films, and graphic arts. We assert that with Warnecke and Hoverstadt, the fractal-as-metaphor become a way of thinking about organizational change management.

A fractal is defined by Hoverstadt (2011, p. 305) as "a set of design rules . . . replicated in *systems, subsystems,* and *sub-sub-systems* and so on" at all levels of the organization.

Hoverstadt (2011) says "business planning is still rooted in an annual cycle of targets and budget setting that is indistinguishable form the centralized planning systems of soviet Russia under Stalin" (p. 4). He applies fractal thinking to Stafford Beer's "Viable System Model" yet does not succeed, in our view, in getting out of the centralized planning and control framework he critiques. To carry out organizational change (or to manage strategic change), we believe, involves awareness and attunement to turning points in the relation of organization adaptation to its environments (social, economic, political, cultural, ecological, etc.).

EMERGENCE, DISSIPATION, AND FRACTAL KNOWING

How do we decide what is emergence and what is dissipation? Isn't it a matter of perspective? A judgment grounded in our own personal biases? Tonya's perspective: On the yoga mat I spend time upside down, seeing the world and my body differently. Muscles work in opposite directions and even though my head, sometimes even my face, is on the ground, it is still generative. Just because the posture is not what others call "upright" does not make it negative. What Marx calls progress the capitalist calls decline. This line of reasoning brings us to thoughts about discernment. We choose the word in lieu of its more common cousin *judgment,* because the latter has negative connotations. Discernment has to do with carefully choosing, whereas judgment is often associated with condemnation. Who is to say what is truly "generative," since it is a matter of perspective? Yet to be human is to make a series of value judgments and attempt to act responsibly in the face of multiple options.

This observation of patterns in ourselves, in nature, and ultimately in organizations is something we call fractal knowing. It deeper than mere observation, developed longitudinally, and requires an ability to adjust our lenses, zooming in and out as we look for scalable self-similarity. To truly know a person, a tree, or an organization means attunement to the ways it manifests itself as a fractal. One must consider various mediums: space, time, materiality, and the intangible social fabric of the living story web,

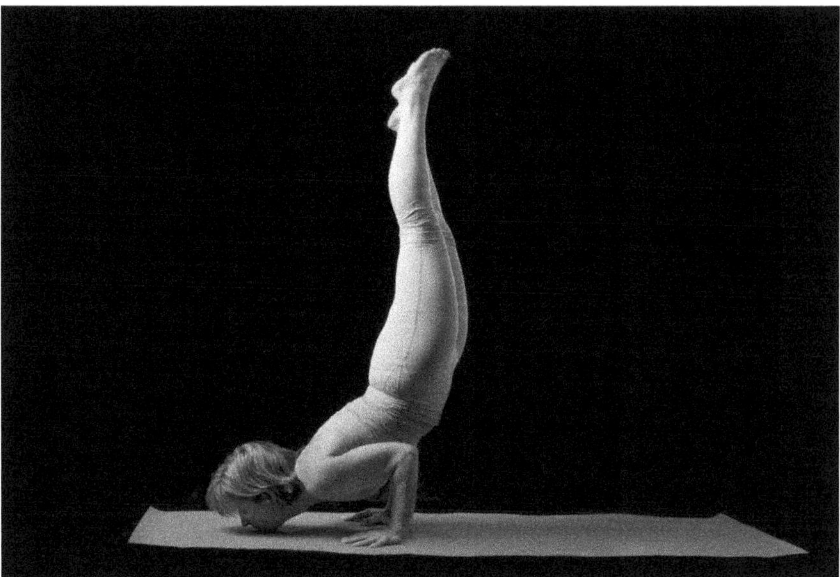

Figure 1.8 Tonya Working on Formidable Face Pose
Source: Tenacious Photography 2014 Used with permission.

where values and beliefs spawn repetition of patterns grounded in actors' perceptions.

The whole field of possibilities, including aspects beyond the reaches of human knowing, is the context for emergence and dissipation as people, plants, mountains, and organizations cocreatively exhibit their patterns, repeating according to their true nature and yet intra-acting with the environment and other actors in cocreative differentiation. There is something of each individual's authentic self, its own unique manifestation of some aspect of the universal consciousness that serves as the primary generator—the source of the dominant patterns that make me myself despite contextual influences and the cocreation that happens in what Anete Strand calls "the between" (Barad 2007, Strand 2012).

In this way of viewing the world, it is extremely important to develop a perspective that adjusts and shifts effortlessly among levels of analysis. When we wear blinders tied to our own perspectives and levels of authority, we often impose judgments that keep us from understanding what is really going on. For example, a middle manager who cannot adjust his perspective to that of an underpaid subordinate or the strategic level thinking behind the boss' demands becomes part of the problem, not the solution. When we consider the big picture exclusively, we can be prone to oversimplification and the development of models that undermine generative grassroots effects. Likewise, when we fail to zoom out, we may miss the ways in which our own team's efforts might better support the aims of the organization as a whole. In this book we propose a perspective that supports a continuous scanning of multiple levels of analysis, thereby countering the tendency to bury significant patterns in overgeneralizations as well as the tendency to myopically miss the aggregate behavior patterns and trends in which we take part.

Once we have learned to address the self-similar scalability of patterns in this way, it becomes important to consider them in a cocreative, multi-fractal way. Organizations are, by nature, relational; they are comprised of unfolding interactions among individuals, divisions, other organizations, groups of collaborators, competitors, suppliers . . . these processes unfold in complex ways as we consider the scalable self-similar patterns apparent in the various relationships. Whereas it is tempting to zoom in on a few key patterns and consider them as if they were occurring independent of others, such myopic examination distorts reality and grossly oversimplifies matters. When we consider the range of patterns occurring in and around an organization at a given time, it is prudent to consider the cocreative effects of processes unfolding in tandem, counter to one another, reinforcing one another, or tangentially influencing each other.

CO-CREATION

The relationship between the environment and organizations is said to be mutually adaptive. Coevolution is described as interrelationship between multiple elements with resulting interdependence (Antonacopoulou and Chia 2007). Antonacopoulou and Chia (2007) conceptualize organizational learning as "an emergent process" (p. 286). The article suggests a view of OL based on social complexity principles, specifically "schemas-diversity" and "interaction-interdependence" (p. 292).

Consistent with this concept is Eoyang's (2009) discussion of coupling, "attachments between various subsystems within the complex system" (xvii). She notes that coupling is necessarily a two-way street, negotiated by entities on both sides of an organizational boundary, be it informal or formal. She offers managers suggestions for addressing tightly coupled, loosely coupled, and uncoupled factors.

MATERIALITY AND SOCIOMATERIALITY

In our earlier works on quantum storytelling theory, a great deal of attention has been given to material agency (See for example Boje and Henderson, 2014). The ability of an object to tell a story or otherwise affect human behavior is the subject of many vital materialist works (see for example Bennett 2010). Antonacopoulu and Chia (2007) note that "The relationships that govern social systems are a complex mix of human and non-human interactions" (p. 282). Furthermore, they state, "evolving social systems self-organize as they seek to maximize internal co-ordination through interdependencies, schemas, and diversity, at the same time as they seek to enhance the external co-ordination with the environmental forces" (Antonacopoulou and Chia 2007, 283). We agree with these statements, as they reflect our own view of organizing as a complex flow of sociomaterial becoming and dissipation, always within the context of a larger, posthumanist assemblage. To come to terms with this incessant unfolding requires a certain clarity of perception that is both materially and socially derived.

This kind of clarity of perception is addressed extensively in yogic philosophy. The path to enlightenment suggested in the yoga sutras involves calming the mind in order to gain a clearer perception of reality (Carrera 2011). Of particular interest, yoga sutra 1.2 says that yoga is the cessation of the chattering of the mind. The incessant chatter of our inner dialogues is the product of the ego's attachments and judgments that cause us to obsess and "spin our wheels" in unconstructive ways. Yogis are taught that by clearing the mind through the habit of physical practice and meditation—a purposive sociomaterial processes, they can become more aware and open to the world as it really exists. The goal is to eliminate misperceptions by staying focused in the present, practicing diligently and regularly, and deliberately calming the mind. These acts bring us into contact with the self at a spiritual level and improve our interactions with the material world[6] as well.

This engagement with the material world fits well with our new materialism derived ideas as well. Posthumanist methods such as quantum storytelling counsel that material objects have agency, can tell stories, and are powerful in their own right (Boje 2011c, 2011f, Boje and Henderson 2014, Strand 2012) The ability of an inanimate object to affect human activities stems, in part, from Bergsonian notions of élan vital and Native American concepts of spirits that are resident in what Western thinkers consider inanimate objects (Gladstone 2014). From stage setting in boardrooms, to proper clothing selection for a job interview and feng shui inspired décor in homes and offices, we know the value of properly and clearly addressing material matters.

Quantum physics even further challenges our ability to gain clear perceptions of the material world. Heisenberg's uncertainty principle would suggest that our agency may extend beyond our Newtonian attempts to limit our influence and be external observers. Bohr's notions of indeterminacy encourage us to embrace the both/and, accepting the co-existence of multiple competing perspectives as Eastern philosophy suggests rather than being forced to choose. Barad further extends our agency as we make agential cuts with each new observation or selection of an apparatus for intra-acting with materiality in ways that create new configurations of knowing

(Barad 2007). As we begin to accept our powerful creative faculties in the context of a quantum field of potential, we find the physical and metaphysical worlds becoming increasingly entangled, to the point where they not only intra-act but merge into one.

KAIROTIC TIME

Drawing from the work of Gerri McCulloh, we have incorporated a Kairotic view of time. In her book chapter "Summoning Kairos," McCulloh (2014) describes a view of time that is grounded in opportunity and timing. Kairos, the Greek god of opportune time, is associated with the best time for action or opportunity. This view contrasts with linear, Newtonian perspectives of time, wherein we measure finite numbers of hours, minutes, seconds . . . and adopt a scarcity mentality as a result. McCulloh's time is about finding the right instant to act.

It is here that we wish to propose a third element to Bakhtin's (1993) model of two-sided answerability. Bakhtin suggests that for each act, one is answerable for both the intent of the actor and for the actual content of the act committed. We have previously extended this to include some ownership of unintended consequences in the context of chaotic and turbulent environments (Boje and Henderson 2014).

We now wish to take it a step further and propose a threefold answerability, in which an actor is also responsible for the timing of the act. If I know the right thing to do and do it hastily, at the wrong time, great harm can come from it. For example, Tonya had a dear friend and mentor who wanted to discuss a personal matter with her, to let Tonya know that she was making a mess of things, but at the time Tonya would not have been willing to listen. The information would have been useless and their friendship would have suffered. Instead, she waited several months, for the opportune time, when Tonya asked for her advice and was willing to listen. Tonya's friend exercised this threefold answerability. She acted with kind intentions, by telling the truth, and waited for the opportune time so that the effect would be as desired. We would suggest that, given the repetitive nature of the fractal patterns one might seek to influence, an aware actor must pay attention to the period of the phenomenon in question and ensure that acts intended to affect change occur at appropriate times to maximize their generative effects and minimize harm.

EMBODIED PRACTICES AND AUTHENTICITY

We touched briefly on how yoga supports shifting patterns of perception in ways that leverage the interplay between the social and material. The Embodied Restorying Process (ERP) also honors this connection. ERP involves building a support group for a self-authored "New Story" of our ownmost authentic Selves. Here are some steps in the ERP process:

Seven Steps of ERP

1. *Recharacterize* (authentic Self-identity): When you were at your best
2. *Externalize* (re-framing): Make the problem the old role-expectations of "they-self," *not* the person trapped in the role-label
3. *Sympathize* (benefits): Appreciate the benefits from the old role-label of Mr. Roadrunner (running from relations); map the payoffs (e.g., payoff that do not have to try, can be loner)
4. *Revise* (consequences): Map the social, economic, political, cultural influences of old role-label stereotypes (e.g., consequence of divorce, estranged from children, etc.)
5. *Strategize* (Little Wow Moments of exception to grand narrative role expectations): reclaim best of you and give them a new name (e.g., no longer Mr. Roadrunner, being Mr. Dependable). ERP facilitator writes a letter to person and to family listing Little Wow Moments
6. *Restory* (rehistoricize): Restory the Grand Narrative "they-self" by collecting Little Wow Moments into "New Story" of potentiality-for-Being-one's-authentic-whole-Self. ERP facilitator writes letter to service member and family members retelling the "New Story" that was told by them.
7. *Publicize* (support networking): For example, letter writing with supporters of your "New Story" with family members, the ERP facilitator write letters reinforcing support of family for service member's "New Story"

The Embodied Restorying Process (ERP) is about the anticipation of a "New Story" that combines revealing, unfolding, holding fast, and projection by anticipation of a possibility of "having an authentic potentiality-for-Being-a-whole emerges" (Heidegger 1962, section #266). ERP is about liberating the Self from the received (from others' expectations and perceptions) "they-self" of Grand Narratives (Boje 2001, see chapters on Grand Narrative, and on Microstoria). A Grand Narrative is a linear plot and characterization that decides a "they-self" general rule, a character–stereotype, a standard, tasks they become your role in life, rather than finding in "New Story" an "authentic-Being-one's-Self" (Heidegger 1962, #267). Restorying through Sandplay is letting the person rediscover Little Wow Moments of Exception, where they did not fulfill the expectations of "they-self." "Self-hood" is defined as a *way of existing* that is not just the body present-at-hand, rather in "New Story" its "authentic Being-one's-Self" (Heidegger 1962, #267).

The attestation in ERP of an authentic existence becoming possible lies in each participant's own anticipation of a "New Story" and finding Little Wow Moments of a specific place and a time when, as Erving Goffman puts it, there was a "unique outcome" not expected by the social, cultural, economic, political, schooling, or socialization. ERP through many rounds of restorying is about discovering a wide array of possibilities for a "New Story" to emerge. Each round of restorying "gives testimony" to the interplay or struggle between the "they-self" and a potentiality-for-Being-one's-authentic-Self. To the Grand Narratives of pathologizing a permanent labeling, the New Story is seen as fantasy. In ERP there is a revealing, unfolding, holding fast to LWMs, and projection of an authentic "New Story" for Self-being-a-whole.

When the impossibility of authentic existence is anticipated, there is no space for liberation to create "New Story." In sandplay, the person comes face-to-face with "they-self." There can be anxiety about the possibility-for-Being a liberated Self from all the they-self surrounding the person. The anticipation of a possible "New Story" is a self-rescue from "lostness in the they-self," and this is why it is necessary to work free of "Illusions" posed by Grand Narratives (Heidegger 1962, section #266).

The "New Story" takes on "facticial existence" (Heidegger 1962, section #264) through the sandplay as the person begins to liberate Self from the outstripping "they-self" to create a "whole potentiality-for-Being" (Heidegger 1962, #264). In Trial One, the they-self can be quite dominant in the rounds or restorying. The Self has accepted they-self as their role in life and is not anticipating out potential roles. This is about liberation from "they-self" to create a "New Story" that has potentiality-for-Being in an understanding and Interpretation of existence that the person and their family can support and cultivate. The Self anticipated being "liberated" from "they-self" (#264). This means the "New Story" its "authentic Self" coming along-side and Being-with the "they-self" and creating alternatives "bets" on the future in new potentialities-for-Being.

Lefebvre (2004, p. 67) concludes that it is import that "rhythmanalyical project" not lose sight of the *body*. The body is polyrhythmic (diverse rhythms) and eurhythmic (in normal situation). The Living body has to contend with arrhythmia when rhythms break apart, and even the "pathological situation" (p. 67). Our living body rhythms fall into place with the rhythms around us. Our military training is an intervention with the goal of making us attuned to extreme situations: "conflict supposes arrhythmia: a divergence in time, in space, in the use of energies" (p. 68). ERP is a method for recovering eurhythmic balance. It is a "moment of vision" and a reclaiming of exceptions to the stress moments, so that a glimpse of a "New Story" of rhythmic balance becomes a possibility and a futural potentiality to bring about in one's own living body.

LINEAR FRACTAL MANUFACTURING

Following Warnecke's (1993) *Fractal Company* book, several authors have theorized differences between the bionic, holonic, and fractal "flexible manufacturing systems." Tharumarajah, for example, develops an approach that looks at the relative participation and autonomy of units in bionic, holonic, and fractal manufacturing systems. Holonic manufacturing systems are supposed to be an alternative to hierarchical shop floor control (Kotak, Bardi, Groover, and Zohrevand 2000).

In Linear Fractal manufacturing (LFT), authors such as Sihn (1995) and Strauss and Hummel (1995) developed a reengineering approach through fractal structures. We find reengineering to be a rather limiting approach to fractals. The whole premise of flexible manufacturing is that a "conglomerate of distributed and autonomous" units are able to adapt to the environment by self-organizing and self-determination (Tharumarajah 2003, p. 11).

Tharumarajah compares bionic, holonic, and fractal models of flexible manufacturing.

Bionic manufacturing includes, in theory, autonomous and spontaneous behavior, and central coordination, within a hierarchically ordered organizational relationship of control structures. The manufacturing units are grouped together to form "manufacturing cells" and those are linked to form "manufacturing shops and so on, with layer upon layer of top-down hierarchical support" (Tharumarajah, 2003, pp. 16–17). In sociomateriality terms, the Bionic manufacturing system consists of materials and material flows ordered by information and coordinators according to policies and strategies.

Holonic manufacturing is an open system that is also hierarchically ordered into whole systems called holarchies (Tharumarajah 2003, pp. 18–19). Holons in holarchy manufacturing interact with member holons in the hierarchically ordered system that is said to possess hierarchic awareness and self-assertive tendencies as well as the opposing tendency of partness (Tharumarajah 2003, p. 19). Holonic manufacturing theorizes the counterbalance of autonomy and cooperation awareness. "Suppose that a change in the environment causes a holon to become unstable; the holon would increase its autonomy (and thereby decrease its cooperation with others) or do the reverse to maintain stability" (Tharumarajah 2003, p. 19). In terms of socialmaterialism, the material is stressed in Holonic manufacturing systems, over the social (human). The shop floor, for example, is envisioned as maintenance, tool supply, machining, washing, and other processes of material control. The hierarchies of material control are spatial in location of materials and machines, and temporal how the functions are enacted in time. In short, the spacetime process is divided, dialyzed with human, marginalized or excluded altogether.

Fractal factories focus on self-similarity across finer and finer scales. A unit providing a service to production or other units focuses on one or more criteria (product, processes, or materials) in a production system. In Tharumarajah (2003, p. 13), the word *fractal* is a metaphoric label used to replace the word *throughput* in the classic systems thinking of "inputs-throughput-outputs, so it becomes inputs-Fractal-outputs model" (p. 13).

Any self-similar throughput processes are relabeled "fractal entities" that have functional or goal similarity (p. 13). The difference between Bionic, Holonic, and the Fractal manufacturing systems, is that the Fractal Factory entities have the "vitality to monitor their environment and adapt" (p. 13). It is not clear how this is any more than a 1st order cybernetic, not even an open system (2nd order cybernetic) model. Tharumarajah cites Strauss and Hummel (1995), stressing how "fractals are always structured bottom-up, building fractals of a higher order. Units at a higher level always assume only those responsibilities in the process that cannot be fulfilled in the lower-order fractals" (p. 14). This means that vitality is defined as a hierarchic control of structural functionalism in at best a contingency model, as higher-level fractal planning and control order the lower-level production fractal.

Tharumarajah (2003) theorizes that a Holonic structure has highest autonomy of units according to fixed canons (policies), with self-similar Fractal entities setting goals and restructuring through vitality, and Bionic manufacturing cells able to respond to just the operating environment. He adds that the Fractal Factory does Just In Time Inventory, and Kanban, making it little more than a fractal translation of the Japanese manufacturing system of lean production: old wine in new bottles. Tharumarajah (2003) does see some features of Fractal Factory systems that make the bionic more manager/planner led, the holonic more self-managing, and the fractal (another name for autonomous work group) more self-designing, but able to do some self-governing (p. 26). Fractal Factory systems are considered to have greater autonomy potential due to their multi-dimensional focus, and some manufacturing may not be suited for the approach (p. 27).

FRACTAL CYCLES OF CHANGE

Next, we look at how Fibonacci cycles are used in a study of the rise and fall of ancient civilization and in the examination of market fluctuations. We do this here, in order to set up the ways in which FCM can apply an historical light, as well as predictive analysis of major and minor historical event pattern analysis, using fractal mathematics.

Bruce Pugesek's (2014) article on fractal cycle turning points, examined catastrophic events and observed that they occur at "Fibonacci intervals and exhibit the irregular regularity of fractal phenomena" (p. 157). He identifies several cycles (Kuwae, Tambora, and Deflationary) that align closely with historical events (disease pandemics, famines, revolutions, and war) in England and the U.S. that are linked to anomalous weather patterns (heat, drought, etc., leading to crop failures) and to sociopolitical turmoil dating back to the 6th century (p. 157). These are fractal cycles with higher order cycles, patterns occurring within wider change patterns. The catastrophic events occur at Fibonacci intervals in a complex cyclic–fractal manner that includes short-term price cycles that are a larger part of fractal price waves, which are part of the fractal patterns of the rise and fall of civilizations.

Fischer (1996) distinguishes between price waves and price cycles. A price cycle is defined as "having fixed rations a" while price waves "do not follow observable cycles and differ among one another in amplitude and periodicity" (Pugesek 2014, 158). The price waves for commodities are theorized to last 50–55 years (Kondrat´ev 1984), but the attempts to forecast price turning points have failed. Mandelbrot and Hudson (2004) studied price cycles using a power law approach in commodities such as cotton, wheat, as well as railroad and blue chip stocks, and interest rates. The power law approach was compared to a "normality-based random walk" of probability statistical methods for predicting behavior and events (Pugesek 2014, 158). Methods that consider the fractal nature of the economic and financial events sometimes do better than the normality-based probability statistics.

We assert that when multiple cycles form a spiral-fractal in historical data, that it is possible to look at Fibonacci (and other) intervals of time in the events. Commodity prices, for example, have highs and lows, where price reverses direction from current trend, and that turning point occurs at particular time intervals, that are tied to climate behavior, monetary policy, and so on, in ways that set up inflationary and deflationary price waves (Pugesek 2014, p. 158).

The observed fractal regularities, their time intervals and timing of human social cycles of change and stability of events (and episodes) of complex organizational systemicities, at local and higher scales of organizational changes, can be assessed with fractal mathematics as long as we are sensitive to the complex nature of the systems examined and take into account the likelihood that new actors and unseen connections can alter otherwise deterministic system-level behaviors at any time. Organizations are parts of larger and larger systemicity cycles, that interconnect in spiral–fractal patterns.

The Fibonacci cycles and intervals allow us to trace past turning points and thereby predict potential future turning points as a fractal-spiral unfolds. Rather than a random walk of probability statistics, we propose investigation of FCM, including the Fibonacci time sequences and fractal cycles, that through the property of self-similar iterations, exhibit fractal–spiral properties. This is an area for further study, building on prior works.

The Fibonacci cycles, were found in Pugesek's (2014) study, to have three levels of cycling, with intervals of price directional changes of agricultural commodities occurring in conjunctions with changes in precious metals (gold, solver) prices. The cycle is based on Fibonacci numbers that pinpoint inflationary peaks and deflationary troughs (turning points) at intervals in the Fibonacci number series (1, 3, 5, 8, 13, 21, and so on). Each interval "cycles forward and backward in time" in relation to the "next lower level in the Fibonacci sequence" (p. 159). The price major price turning points had secondary turning points, such as the years of significant famine in 1322 and 1432, and the plague outbreaks of 1453, 1563, 1624 and Great Famine 1315–1322, as well as the Kuwae volcano eruption 1453. These plague and ecological events were related to reversals of upwards or downwards price movements (turning points).

In what Pugesek (2014) calls the Kuwae Cycle, the Fibonacci intervals related to notable changes occurring in later part of 12th century BC where civilizations collapsed rapidly with severe climate change and invasions.

In the Tamboa Cycle of historical changes, the Taupo volcano erupted 184 AD and connects to a 1781 hyper inflationary peak during the American Revolutionary War (p. 161).

In the Deflationary Cycle, London (then a Roman encampment), saw previous two cycles change, as the Western Roman Empire collapsed, at intervals that correlate with the Fibonacci series of price data, climate change, and so on.

In sum, the Fibonacci Cycle Theory connected to the historical events of the Kuwae Cycle (411 AD), the Tambora Cycle (184 AD), and the Deflationary Cycle (44 AD) in an historical event process that exhibited a second Kuwae Cycle (2008), a second Tamara Cycle (1781), and a second Deflationary Cycle (1641), conforming to Fibonacci number series.

Volcanic eruptions occurred at Fibonacci intervals and corresponded to price cycles of commodities (agricultural and precious metals), as well as devastating disease outbreaks and wars (and rebellions) in England and in America. Spending on famines and war in the debased landscapes from climate change had the predictable outcome of complex interactions that three Fibonacci cycles explained. The time intervals of turning points were not random.

The Fibonacci cycle algorithm is therefore a potential candidate for tracking and prediction organizational change and development patterns in the rise and fall of organizations. We argue that this forms the basis of a new theory of organizational change that accounts for multifractal connectivity patterns that are consequential to organizational effectiveness. This area is ripe for further study to determine if such predictions can be made at various levels of analysis.

CONCLUSION

In this chapter, we introduced core concepts surrounding fractal change management theory. We offered a set of models explaining sociomateriality as a lens for understanding fractal organizing processes as a construct that is grounded in both process and object ontology. We then introduced the reader to a multifractal view of organizing processes and examined the idea of fractal knowing, including some specific concepts derived from the works of other scholars. Next, we will provide a practical definition of fractal organizing processes, grounded in complexity theory as it applies to human systems.

Multiple-fractal-sociomateriality entanglements occur in work organizations so that there are multiple and contending scalabilities that enact contradictory dynamics. Control and production, for example, may inhabit different scalabilities. Engagements of workers and managers can extend/escalate involvements according to different sociomateriality-scalabilities. Scalabilities of increasing/decreasing flexibility/control can interact. Different spatial parameters and temporality horizons can be brought about by preferences for different observational apparatuses. The top of an organization may telescope spacetime, while the producers in the working ranks microscope on a different spacetime, and marketers have yet another spacetime: the transaction of product for cash to a customer. Each stakeholder can be specialized and embodied in a different fractal-sociomateriality horizon.

Building on our earlier discussions of complexity theory, we now expand our sociomaterial awareness of fractal patterns by exploring them in the context of quantum storytelling theory and related embodied practices. Of particular interest is the potential role of attractor states toward which a system's structure may be drawn, consistent with Heidegger's (1962) contention that the future is already existent in the present and the role of historical occurrences as determinants of future outcomes in chaos and complexity theory. This chapter introduces quantum storytelling theory, a newly emerging, ontologically focused body of theory which we will explore more fully later on. We then examine fractal organizing processes through the lens of sociomaterial spacetimemattering with implications for management practice.

Implications: (1) Moving beyond the duality of fractal and sociomateriality; (2) engaging with multi-fractal-sociomateriality of work practices and also consumption practices, so we recognize we are not all in the same fractal-sociomateriality spacetime because we have adapted or adopted different observational apparatuses, and therefore embody differently; (3) reciprocity of multiplicity of fractal-sociomaterialities with local–global communication practices; (4) entanglements of multiple spacetime fractal-sociomateriality work and consumption practices; (5) we are changing skills and identities in universities to accommodate new fractal-sociomateriality career paths.

The systemicities of an organization are fractal-scales that do coexist, without one being reducible to the others. Actual systemicities can coexist at the different scalabilities and span multiple levels. The fractal patterns coexist in a single spacetime, and are entangled, interconnected, and embedded. The fractal patterns and their resolutions coexist in what Nottale (2011) calls a common "scale space." This scale space is also the transitions the particular fractal-scales are making in space-time.

NOTES

1. Karen Barad (Barad 2007, 2011) uses the prefix *intra-* in lieu of *inter-* to accentuate how the material world is a cocreative participant in discourse, inseparably entangled and intertwined with/in it.
2. They define a change management methodology for fractal systems.
3. Whereas bounding systems may be a necessary part of studying them in light of our human limitations, it is also important to note that by drawing a boundary around some part of a larger, arguably unbounded, living, breathing, emergent sociomaterial unfolding, we change its very nature in ways that may be obvious in the near-term or in ways that appear much later as their subtle influence ripples through the larger system over time.
4. This latter distinction is based on our understanding of the term as it was used by Neils Bohr and explained by Karen Barad (2007).
5. This approach is not inconsistent with Hoverstadt's mosaic approach to systemic change, wherein one part of the system is shifted, along with the elements that touch it, in lieu of a system-wide effort.
6. Of note, in the Bhagavad Gita, an ancient Hindu text, Krishna counsels that it is not necessary to renounce one's material obligations and daily life in order to follow the spiritual path of yoga. *The Bhagavad Gita*. Translated by Eknath Easwaran. Tomales, CA: Nilgiri Press. Original edition, 1985. Reprint, 2007.

REFERENCES

Antonacopoulou, Elena, and Ricardo Chia. (2007). "The Social Complexity of Organizational Learning: The Dynamics of Learning and Organizing." Management Learning 38 (3):277–295. doi: 10.1177/1350507607079029.

Ashby, W. Ross. (1958). "Requisite variety and its implications for the control of complex systems." *Cybernetica* 1 (2):83–99.

Bhagavad Gita, The. 2007. Translated by Eknath Easwaran. Tomales, CA: Nilgiri Press. Original edition, 1985. Reprint, 2007.

Bakhtin, Michel. (1993). Toward a philosophy of the act. Translated by Vadim Liapunov. Edited by Michael Holquist, University of Texas Press Slavic Series No. 10. Austin, TX: University of Texas Press.

Barad, Karen. (2003). "Posthumanist performativity: Toward an understanding of how matter comes to matter." Signs 28.3: 801–831. http://uspace.shef.ac.uk/servlet/JiveServlet/previewBody/66890-102-1-128601/signsbarad.pdf

Barad, Karen. (2007). Meeting the universe halfway: Quantum physics and the entanglement of matter and meaning. Durham, NC: Duke University Press.

Baskin, Ken. (1995). "DNA for corporations: Organizations learn to adapt or die." *The Futurist* 29 (1):68–68.

Bennett, Jane. (2010). *Vibrant Matter: A Political Ecology of Things*. Durham: Duke University Press.

Bevan, David, and Matthew Gitsham. (2009). "Context, complexity and connectedness: Dimensions of globalization revealed." *Corporate Governance* 9 (4):435–447.

Boje, D. (1991). The storytelling organization: A study of story performance. *Administrative Science Quarterly, 36*(1), 106–126.

Boje, D. (1995). Stories of the storytelling organization: a postmodern analysis of Disney as "Tamara-land" Academy of Management Journal, 38(4), 997–1035.

Boje, D. (2001). Narrative Methods for Organizational & Communication Research. London, UK: SAGE.

Boje, David. (2008). Storytelling Organizations. Los Angeles: SAGE Publications, Ltd.

Boje, David. (2010). "Complexity theory and the dance of storytelling in organizations." In Dance to the music of story, edited by David Boje and Ken Baskin, 39–59. Litchfield Park, AZ: Emergent publications.

Boje, D. (2011a, 15 June, 2011). Quantum physics implications of storytelling for socioeconomic research methods: Experiences in small business consulting research form New Mexico State University. Paper presented at the International Meeting of Research Methods Division of the Academy of Management, Lyon, France.

Boje, D. (2011b). Introduction to agential narratives that shape the future of organizations. In D. Boje (Ed.), Storytelling and the future of organizations: an antenarrative handbook (pp. 1–15). New York, NY: Routledge.

Boje, David. (2011c). "Quantum storytelling conference." Quantum storytelling conference, Las Cruces, NM. www.quantumstorytelling.org

Boje, D. M. (Ed., in press, 2015 expected). Change Solutions to the Chaos of Standards and Norms Overwhelming Organizations: Four Wings of Tetranormalizing. London/NY: Routledge.

Boje, David, and K. Arkoubi. (2005). "Third cybernetic revolution: Beyond open to dialogic system theories." *Tamara: Journal of Critical Postmodern Organization Science* 4 (1/2):138.

Boje, David, and Tonya L. Henderson, eds. (2014). *Being quantum: Ontological storytelling in the age of antenarrative*. Newcastle upon Tyne, United Kingdom: Cambridge Scholars Publishing.

Boje, David, and Tonya Wakefield. (2011). "Storytelling in Systemicity and Emergence: A Third Order Cybernetic." In The Routledge Companion to Organizational Change, edited by David Boje, Bernard Burnes and John Hassard.

Boje, David, Ivy DuRant, Krisha Coppedge, Ted Chambers, and Marilu Marcillo-Gomez. (2012). "Social materiality: A new direction in change management and action research." In David M. Boje, Bernard Burnes and John Hassard (eds.), *The Routledge Companion to Organizational Change* (pp. 580–597). New York, NY: Routledge.

Bourdieu, P. (1977). *Outline of a Theory of Practice*. New York: Cambridge University Press.

Butler, J. (1993). *Bodies that Matter*. New York: Routledge.

Carrera, Jagnath. (2011). *Inside the Yoga Sutras*. Buckingham, VA: Integral Yoga Publications.

Comunian, Roberta. (2011). "Rethinking the creative city." *Urban Studies* 48 (6): 1157–1179. doi: 10.1177/0042098010370626.

Coppedge, Krisha. (2014). "The preponderance of evidentuality enlightenment in home ownership." In Boje David M and Tonya L. Henderson (eds.), *Being Quantum: Ontological Storytelling in the Age of Antenarrative* (pp. 191–216). Newcastle Upon Tyne, UK: Cambridge Scholars.

Deleuze, G., & Guattari, F. (1987). *A Thousand Plateaus: Capitalism and Schizophrenia* (B. Massumi, Trans.). Minneapolis, MN: University of Minnesota Press.

Dourish, P. (2014). Reeconfiguring Sociomateriality: An Ethnographic Investigation of Robotic Deep Space Science. *Stanford Seminars* [Guest Lecture]. Stanford, CA: Stanford University.

Eoyang, Glenda. (2009). Coping With Chaos. Edited by Human Systems Dynamics Institute. Circle Pines, MN: Lagumo.

Fainstein, Susan S. (2005). "Cities and diversity." *Urban Affairs Review* 41 (1):3–19. doi: 10.1177/1078087405278968.

Fischer, D. H. (1996). The great wave: price revolutions and the rhythm of history. Oxford University Press.

Foucault, M. (1977). *Discipline and Punish: The Birth of the Prison* (A. Sheridan, Trans.). New York: Random House.

Frazier, Mark. (2012). "What are narrative fractals?". *Quora*, Last Modified 21 August 2012 (original post)

Giddens, A. (1979). *Central Problems in Social Theory: Action, Structure, and Contradiction in Social Science*. Berkley, Los Angeles: University of California Press.

Gladstone, Joe S. (2014). "Transplanar Wisdom: The Quantum Spirit of Native American Storytelling". In Being Quantum: Ontological Storytelling in the Age of Antenarrative, edited by David M. Boje and Tonya L. Henderson, 217–231. Newcastle upon Tyne, NE6 2XX, UK Cambridge Scholars Publishing.

Gómez-Pompa, A., & Kaus, A. (1999). From pre-Hispanic to future conservation alternatives: Lessons from Mexico. *Proceedings of the National Academy of Sciences, 96*(11), 5982–5986. doi: 10.1073/pnas.96.11.5982

Heidegger, Martin. (1962). Being and time. Translated by Ralph Mahnheim. 7th ed. New York: Harper & Rowe Publishers. Original edition, 1926.

Henderson, Tonya L., and Daphne Deporres. (2014). "Patterns of Perception Among Yoga Practitioners." International Conference of Management Cases, Greater Noida, India.

Houston, Renee. (1999). "Self-organizing systems theory: Historical challenges to new sciences." *Management Communication Quarterly* 13 (1): 119–134. doi: 10. 1177/0893318999131006.

Hoverstadt, Patrick. (2011). The fractal organization: creating sustainable organizations with the viable system model. John Wiley & Sons.

Ison, Ray. (2008). "Systems thinking and practice for action research." In Peter Reason and Hilary Bradbury (eds.), *The SAGE Handbook of Action Research: Participative Inquiry and Practice* (pp. 138–158). London: Sage. Original edition, 2008.

Johnson, Neil. (2007). *Simply Complexity: A Clear Guide to Complexity Theory.* Oxford, England: Oneworld Publications.

Joyce, Arthur A. (2009). Theorizing Urbanism in Ancient Mesoamerica. Ancient Mesoamerica, 20, pp 189–196. doi:10.1017/S0956536109990125.

Joyce, A.A., & Winter, M. (1996). Ideology, Power and Urban Society in Pre-Hispanic Oaxaca. *Current Anthropology, 37*(1).

Kauffman, Stuart. (1995). *At Home in the Universe*. New York, NY: Oxford University Press.

Kondrat´ev, Nikolaĭ Dmitrievich. (1984). *The long wave cycle*. [New York]: Richardson & Snyder.

Kotak, D., Bardi, S., Groover, W., & Zohrevand, K. (2000). *Comparison of Hierarchical and Holonic Shop Floor Control Using Virtual Manufacturing Environment*. Paper presented at the IEEE International Conference on Systems, Man, and Cybernetics.

Lakoff, G. (1990). The Invariance Hypothesis: is abstract reason based on image-schemas?. *Cognitive Linguistics (includes Cognitive Linguistic Bibliography), 1*(1), 39–74.

Latour, Bruno. (1999). Pandora's hope: essays on the reality of science studies. Cambridge, Massachusetts: Harvard University Press.

Latour, Bruno. (2005). Reassembling the social: an introduction to actor-network theory, Clarendon Lectures in Management Studies. Oxford: Oxford University Press.

Lefebvre, Henri. (2004). RhythmAnalysis: Space, Time and Everyday Life. Translated by Stuart Elden and Gerald Moore with an Introduction by Stuart Elden. London. NY: Continuum Press. Originally in French 1992.

Lewin, Roger. (1999). *Complexity: Life at the Edge of Chaos* (2nd ed.). Chicago, IL: University of Chicago Press. Original edition, 1992.

Mandelbrot, Benoit. (1983). The fractal geometry of nature. New York, NY: W.H. Freeman and Company. Original edition, 1977.

Mandelbrot, Benoit, and Richard L. Hudson. (2004). The (mis)behavior of markets: A fractal view of risk, ruin, and reward. New York, NY: Basic Books: A Member of the Perseus Books Group.

Mazmanian, M., Cohn, M., & Dourish, P. (2014). *Dynamic Reconfiguration in Planetary Exploration: A Sociomaterial Ethnography* University of California, Irvine. Irvine, CA. Retrieved from http://douri.sh/publications/2014/misq-cassini-dist.pdf

McCulloh, G.E. (2014). Summoning Kairos: Atavistic Processes in Quantum Adaptive Rhetoric. In G.M. Boje & T.L. Henderson (Eds.), *Being Quantum: Ontological Storytelling in the Age of Antenarrative* (pp. 51–89). Newcastle upon Tyne, NE6 2XX, UK: Cambridge Scholars Publishing.

Mitchell, Melanie. (2009). Complexity: a guided tour. Oxford, New York: Oxford University Press.

Nonaka, I. (1991). The knowledge-creating company. *Harvard Business Review,* 69(6), 96–104.

Nottale, L. (1996). Scale relativity and fractal space-time: applications to quantum physics, cosmology and chaotic systems. Chaos, Solitons & Fractals, 7(6), 877–938.

Nottale, L. (2011). *Scale Relativity and Fractal Space-Time: A new approach to Unifying Relativity and Quantum Mechanics.* London: Imperial College Press.

Oh, Seungjin, Kwangyeol Ryu, Ilkyeong Moon, Hyunbo Cho, and Moonyoung Jung. (2010). "Collaborative fractal-based supply chain management based on a trust model for the automotive industry." Flexible Services and Manufacturing Journal 22:183–213. doi: 10.1007/s10696-011-9082-7.

Pondy, L.R., & Boje, D. (2005). Beyond open system models of organization. *Emergence: Complexity & Organization,* 7(3/4), 119–137.

Prigogine, Ilya, and Isabella Stengers. (1984). *Order Out of Chaos.* Toronto: Bantam Books.

Pugeske, Bruce, H. (2014). Fractal cycle turning points: A theory of human social progression. Ecological Complexity 20:157–175.

Quade, Kristine, and Royce Holladay. (2010). Dynamical Leadership: Building Adaptive Capacity for Uncertain Times. Apache Junction, AZ: Gold Canyon Press.

Quade, Kristine. (2011). "Simple rules leaders use to guide their organizations during times of rapid change." Ed.D. Doctoral Dissertation, Graduate School of Education and Psychology, Pepperdine University.

Rapoport, Anatol, William J. Horvath, and Jeffrey Goldstein. (2009). "Thoughts on organization theory." *Emergence: Complexity & Organization* 11 (1):94–103.

Rosile, Grace Ann; Boje; Nez, Carma. (in review). Ensemble Leadership Theory of Pre-Hispanic Southwest Mesoamerica. New Mexico State University.

Sewell Jr, W.H. (1992). A theory of structure: Duality, agency, and transformation. *American Journal of Sociology*, 1–29.

Sihn, W. (2002) Fractal businesses in an E-business world. In the 8th International Conference on Concurrent Enterprising. Rome, Italy, pp. 17–19. June http://www.manubuild.net/projects/08/CE002/reforms/Business%20to%20Business/05_Sihn.pdf

Strand, A.M.C. (2012). *The between: on dis/continuous intra-active becoming of/through an apparatus of material storytelling.* (Doctoral Program in Human Centered Communication and Informatics (HCCI)), Aalborg University, Aalborg, Denmark.

Strauss, R.E., & Hummel, T. (1995, 28–30 Jun 1995). *The new industrial engineering revisited-information technology, business process re-engineering, and lean management in the self-organizing "fractal company."* Paper presented at the Engineering Management Conference, 1995. Global Engineering Management: Emerging Trends in the Asia Pacific., Proceedings of 1995 IEEE Annual International.

Strazdina, Renate, and Marite Kirikova. (2011). "Change Management for Fractal Enterprises." In Information Systems Development, edited by Jaroslav Pokorny, Vaclav Repa, Karel Richta, Wita Wojtkowski, Henry Linger, Chris Barry and Michael Lang, 735–745. Springer New York.

Taleb, Nassim Nicholas. (2007). The black swan: The impact of the highly improbable: Recorded Books, LLC. Audiobook.

Tetreault, Donald, and Tonya Henderson Wakefield. (2012). "Various." Columbia, SC.

Tharumarajah, A. (2003). From fractals and bionics to holonics. In *Agent-Based Manufacturing* (pp. 11–30). Springer Berlin Heidelberg.

Van de Ven, A. H., & Poole, M. S. (2005). Alternative Approaches for Studying Organizational Change. *Organization Studies (01708406), 26*(9), 1377–1404. doi: 10.1177/0170840605056907

von Bertalanffy, Ludwig. (1969). *General Systems Theory: Foundations, Development, Applications* [Revised ed.]. New York, NY: George Braziller.

Wakefield, Tonya L. Henderson. (2012). "An ontology of storytelling systemicity: Management, fractals and the Waldo Canyon fire." Doctorate of Management Doctoral dissertation, Management, Colorado Technical University.

Wakefield, Tonya L. Henderson, David Boje, and Michael Lane. (2013). "Fractals and Food." Standing Conference for Management and Organization Inquiry (SCMOI), Alexandria, VA.

Waldrop, M. Mitchell. (1992). Complexity: the emerging science at the order of chaos. New York: Simon & Schuster.

Warnecke, H. J. (1993). The Fractal Company—production in the network. NY: Springer-Verlag.

Worley, Christopher G., David E. Hitchin, and Walter L. Ross. (1996). In Edgar Schein and Richard Beckhard, *Integrated Strategic Change: How OD builds competitive advantage.* Addison-Wesley Series on Organizational Development. Reading, Massachusetts: Addison-Wesley Publishing Company.

2 What Are Fractals in Management Science?

A brief history of the term *fractal* is necessary before answering this question. Whereas the term can be applied with varying levels of specificity according to context, in this section, we will devote our attention to its origins in the field of mathematics. Mandelbrot coined the term *fractals*. Mandelbrot defines fractals as "irregular and/or fragmented at all scales" (Nottale 2011, p. 44). "A fractal is most generally defined as a structure which displays increasingly more detail as one zooms into it" (Vrobel 2011, p. 18). The human body exhibits such characteristics as well (Leibovitch 1998). Here we apply fractals to management science.

There are hundreds of articles now appearing in the business literature that feature fractal concepts (Boje, 2015 in press), with myriad theories concerning management and organizational development. What makes this one different? Everyone grounds their use of fractals in complexity theory, as do we. It makes use of storytelling, as do many others (Duarte 2014; Noon 1993, 1996a, 1996b; Palumbo 1998, 2002, 2004).

Gulick and Scott (2010) look at plants, how they form fractal branch structures over time, and at varying scalability resolutions. This approach could help understand how organization structures have replication rules for branching. In a recursion function, a simple branch rule gets repeated, over and over again. In plants the recursion function, is the set of instructions that plants follow to branch, when to branch, to flower, and when to flower, etc. Can such a recursion function be applied to understand complex organization fractal processes?

Growth in the simple, branching fractal depicted in Figure 2.1 is by splitting in two. For example, we were once a Business Administration Department, then split into the Management and Marketing Departments, and then those developed subspecialties, again and again. For a few generations, it was a male department, and then it began hiring more females. This branching fractal is growth by recruiting similar others in terms of gender, race, political values, etc. Notice in the branching-fractal the arrow lines get shorter and smaller as the pace of change increases, and the branching picks up momentum, pace, and coherence.

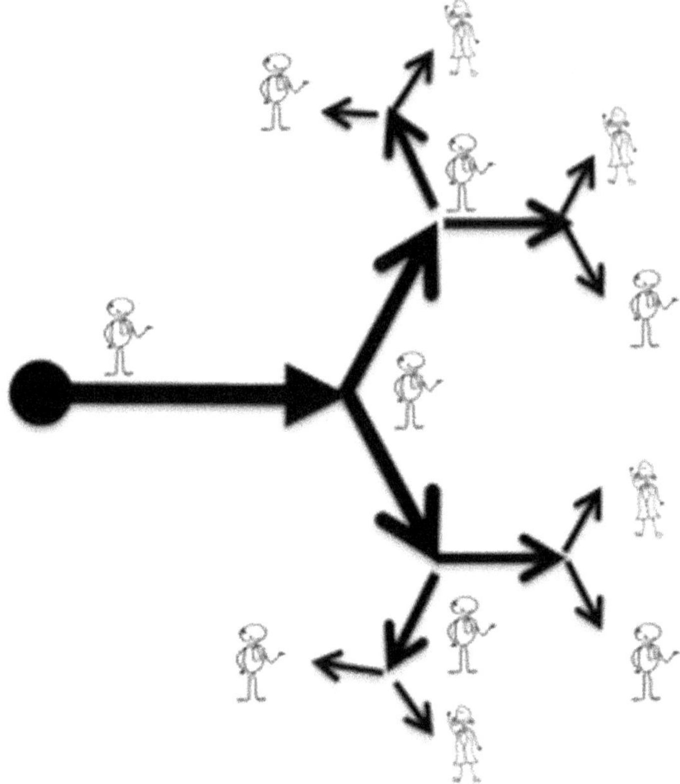

Figure 2.1 Branching Fractal
Source: Drawing by D.M. Boje (used with permission)

We can introduce a new branching rule. Instead of splitting in twos, there can be any number of branches, or none at all. Furthermore, the people recruited can be of unequal power.

Above we have one to three branches sprouting off each node. There are both males and females who manage their departments, or subunits of a department, as the case may be. We can easily begin to research the diversity of each department in terms of gender, race, ethnicity, political orientation, academic background, professional work experience, and so forth.

What does the branching-fractal look like if we go from two-dimensional visual depictions to three dimensions? It may look something like the situation depicted in Figure 2.3 below.

Let's assume we are tracing the growth in terms of number of people, from left to right, in *time* as the first dimension, and the relative *power* and influence the department or subunit has from bottom to top (top having as always higher power), as the second dimension. For the third dimension, it's the *efficacy* of each person, department, or unit (defined as the ability to enact and carry out tasks).

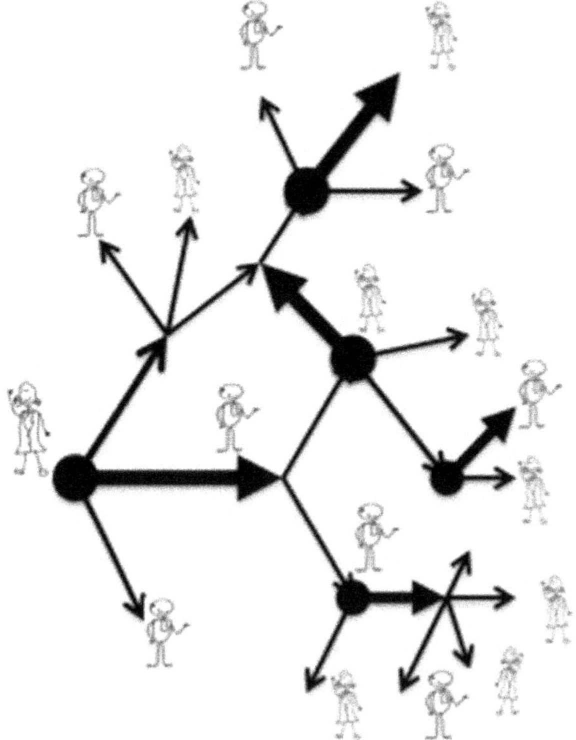

Figure 2.2 Branching in Non-Duality Branching Fractal with Unequal Nodes
Source: Drawing by D. M. Boje. (Used by permission)

Our purpose here is to reveal the interdisciplinary aspects of fractal storytelling across the departments and specialties of the College of Business at New Mexico State University.

Fractal-branching that is almost exactly the same, but not quite, is called self-similar. Here it is self-similar across departments, each of which splits into specialties. Management Department, for example, is split into operation, human resources, strategy, entrepreneurship, leadership, and whatever it is Boje does (storytelling pattern analyses; http://business.nmsu.edu/about/history/). Marketing is split into consumer behavior, branding, etc. There is replication at every scale across the departments. The other three departments are mergers of two departments. For example, Economics acquired a Statistics Department form the Agriculture College. Accounting acquired BCIS (Business Computing & Information Systems), and Finance acquired Business Law. There are some differences. Marketing and Management have Ph.D. programs. Accounting has its own masters in accounting, and has its own career fair for its students. Economics has a doctorate in Economic Development (DED) rather than a Ph.D. program.

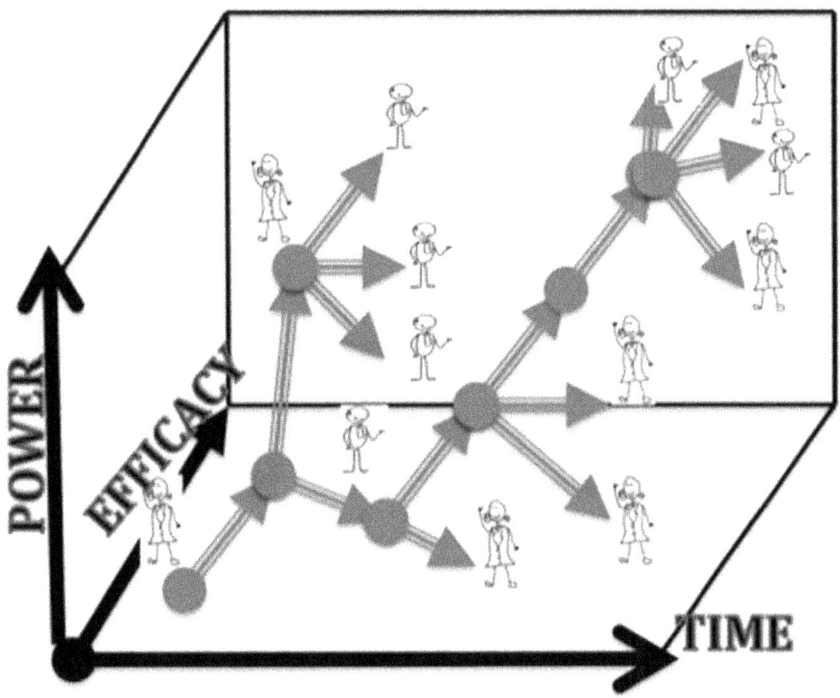

Figure 2.3 Branching Fractal in Three Dimensions: Time, Power, and Efficacy
Source: Drawing by D. M. Boje (used by permission)

Next, we will look more carefully, at the Fractal-branching story of the College of Business of NMSU.

This Fractal-branching, shown in Figure 2.4, occurred year-by-year, semester-by-semester, day-by-day—over the history of the college (1964–2014, 50th Anniversary). Of course, the Fractal-branching started before there was an official "College of Business." In 1916, a two-year program in Business Administration was offered in the Department of Education in the College of Arts and Sciences. Its focus was secretarial training classes in typing, stenography, commercial arithmetic, and business English. In 1920, a Department of Commerce was founded, and two years later, the two-year program became a four-year program. In 1926, the first class graduated from and was awarded the Bachelor of Science in Business Administration. In 1929, more fractal-branching occurred: economic courses were added to the Department of Commerce. In 1942, with WWII, enrollment dropped to about 100, and there was a reduction in staff. 1947 to 1950, the Bachelor of Science in Business Administration is taught in former military barracks. By 1950, the name of the fractal-branching has changed to Department of Business Administration and Economics (DBA&E). This growing fractal (DBA&E) moves into the basement of Hadley Hall in 1954.

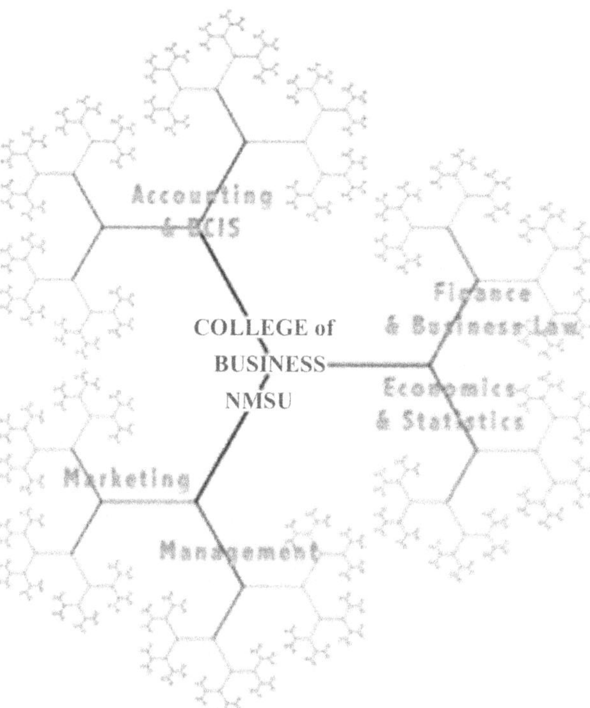

Figure 2.4 Example of a Branching Fractal
Source: Drawing by Boje (January 15, 2014)

1962, DBA&E split locations, with secretarial labs remaining in basement of Hadley Hall, and the BA&E classes moving to surplus buildings moved to Las Cruces, NM, from Fort Bliss, TX (History 2014).

The Department of Commerce has outgrown its basement facilities and moves during the first week of fall semester classes, this time into surplus buildings (from Fort Bliss, TX) that were placed near Young Hall. The accounting and secretarial labs remain in Hadley Hall. "Created by action of the Board of Regents on September 10, 1963, the College of Business Administration and Economics (CBAE) becomes a reality" (NMSU Business Department 2014). Gwynne Leland Guthrie becomes the college's first dean. By 1964, there are three departments in the CBAE: Accounting, Economics, and General Business. Bachelor degrees are offered in Accounting, Economics, Finance, General Business, Management, Marketing, and Secretarial Administration. There are two-year Certificates in Secretarial, and in Data Processing and Computer Technology. In 1968, the fractal-branching of CBAE moves into Gutherie Hall, and it transforms its labels: "The General Business Administration Department changes to the Business Administration Department. Two-Year Certificates are changed to Two-Year Associate

Degrees" (NMSU College of Business, 2014). In 1969, majors in General Business and Management are combined into one, General Management major. In 1970, there are changes: Business Systems Analysis major is added, and the major for Secretarial Administration is discontinued. The 1971 Graduate degrees are added for an MBA and a Master of Arts in Economics. In 1972, there was more shifting of the CBAE fractal-branching:

> The BBA major in Accounting is changed to Bachelor of Accountancy. General Management changes to Management, and Managerial Accounting is added. The Accounting Department name is changed to the Accounting & Finance Department. The Business Administration Department is changed to the Management Department.
>
> (History: 1964–2014: Our 50th Anniversary 2014)

In 1973, all the secretarial courses and data processing/computer technology are discontinued. In 1974, Management Department adds Marketing to its name, becoming Management and Marketing Department. But in 1975, "The Management and Marketing Department is renamed back to the Management Department," and there is a split, another fractal-branching: "The Marketing & General Business Department is added to the college" (History 2014). There are four departments for the next few years: Accounting & Finance, Economics, Management, and Marketing and General Business. In 1984, there is a split, a branching-fractal development: "The Accounting & Finance Department changes its name to the Accounting Department, and the college creates the Finance, Insurance & Real Estate Department" (NMSU Business Department 2014). There are now five departments, as shown in Figure 2.4.

Branching-fractals are common occurrences in university college and department development. What we have done is create a fractal-branching narrative. Take a look at the following exercise.

Exercise:

The following questions are suggested as a way to explore the unfolding of your own organization, considering whether or not its evolution demonstrates fractal self-similarity and exploring the implications of differences and similarity between the formal and informal power structures.

1. Examine the organization chart of an institution you are familiar with. How has it changed over time? What kinds of patterns do you notice in its unfolding over time?
2. If the organization does not exhibit this kind of fractal unfolding over time, what other pattern does it follow? Is that pattern likely to continue in the future?
3. If you do not observe scalable, repeated patterns as the organizational structure changes over time, why do you think that is?

4. What does the underlying social network look like? Does it parallel the formal organizational structure or take a different shape?
5. If the two structures are not consistent, can you think of times where that difference caused tension? What happened? Was it constructive or did it hinder the organization?

There have been many contributions to fractal geometry:

Phidias (500 BC–432 BC), a Greek sculptor and mathematician, studied phi and applied it to the design of sculptures for the Parthenon (Meisner, 2012). And Plato (circa 428 BC–347 BC) said it was the most fundamental of all relationships.

"Euclid (330–275 B.C.) proposed lines with infinite lengths to illustrate the concept of parallel lines, there he also used self-similar triangles to show the congruency of triangles . . ." (Wahl, Roy, Larsen, Kampman, & Gonzalez n.d).

"Archimedes (287–212 B.C.) used spirals to illustrate repeating transformations. . . ." (Wahl et al. n.d.). For example, in the Archimedes spiral, whorls expand at a constant scale (such as in a bolt thread pattern).

Italian mathematician Leonardo Bonacci Fibonacci (c. 1170–c. 1250) introduced the Fibonacci number sequence, where each next number is the sum of the previous two: 1, 1, 2, 3, 5, 8, 13, 21, 34, 55, 89, 144, 233, 377, 610, 987. . . . This can be used to create the Fibonacci Spiral (Figure 2.5).

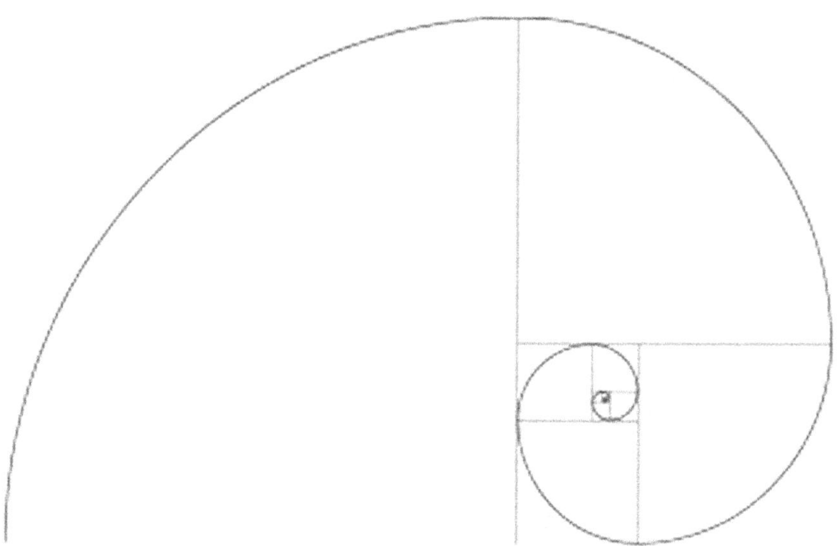

Figure 2.5 Fibonacci Spiral

Source: http://en.wikipedia.org/wiki/File:Fibonacci_spiral.svg

This is also known as a Logarithmic Spiral. And if you take the ratio of the two numbers added together in the Fibonacci series, it approximates the Greek *Golden Ratio*.

"Mathematician Jacob Bernoulli (1654–1705) expanded this idea to show that some spirals could be drawn with an infinite length, of which the logarithmic spiral is the most famous" (Wahl et al. n.d.). For example, in the Logarithmic spiral, whorls expand at ever increasing sale (such as spiroidal shells: snail shell, conch shell, etc.).

"Felix Hausdorff (1868–1942) and Abram Besicovitch (1891–1970) revolutionized mathematics by proposing dimensions with non-integer values. This served to expand the fractal dimensionality"[1] (Wahl et al. n.d.).

"Lewis Fry Richardson (1881–1953), an English meteorologist, pioneered a process for calculating dimensions with varied measurements." His work is famous for coastline calculations, and for spiral fractals. "It was Richardson's work that prompted Mandelbrot and others to ask the now famous question 'How Long is the Coast of Britain?'" (Wahl et al. n.d.).

These and other works founded the basis for modern fractal theory. Their pioneering efforts to understand the material world paved the way for consideration of fractal patterns in the social and sociomaterial realms. Having explored the genesis of the term, we now zoom out to take a systems view and apply it to the field of organizational development.

SCALABILITY AND MANAGERIAL PERSPECTIVE

If we accept the premise that organizational life is an emergent phenomenon that can be expected to exhibit fractal patterns, then one would expect to see scalability in key areas of importance. But does the manager see them all? A manager can get stuck in one of these zoom-scales understanding a constricted or very dilated one, and be attuned to only that one scalability. With training and experience, the manager can learn to be attuned to alternative zoom scales. The research question becomes, "To what extent are managers attuned to fractal scalability?" Many managers, we assume, have developed scale-dependence. This means managing an awareness and action orientation attuned to a particular level of analysis, or zoom-scale, for example, with the very local situation of the organization. Their perceptions are limited to their own experience of the organization, rendering them unable to consider the possibility of similar experiences at a systemic level or at lower levels within the organization. This is fairly typical of the subpar managers and leaders we have known in our own work experiences. This scale-dependence choice making by a manager selecting either local, or quantum, or an increasingly global, even transcendent, understanding of space of organization-and-environment has communication and actual performance consequences.

Yet there are some other managers who are able to be attuned to what is going on in multiple levels of the organization, keyed into the happenings at among subordinates and suppliers, and keenly aware of the goings on at headquarters or to a trends in a particular global market. These managers are keenly aware of patterns at multiple levels of the organization and are the best poised to comprehend systemic problems. We will further illustrate the point by offering the Koch snowflake as a metaphor for the levels of granularity visible to lower-, middle-, and upper-tier managers.[2]

Sometimes it can be difficult to see the patterns in something so abstract as the way that organizations function unless we first train ourselves to spot them in concrete, tangible ways. Let us take a few lessons from from nature and geometry. First, consider the broccoli image in figure 2.6. It is possible to look very closely and observe the patterns in a small section. Next we consider a larger piece, wherein the same kinds of patterns repeat. Taking an even larger chunk yields similar results. How is that consistent with what we see in the behaviors of individual, small workgroups, divisions, and entire companies? A manager who can not observe the similarities and differences in aggregate behaviors in his organization and in the industry at large has a distinct advantage.

Figure 2.6 Broccoli Romanesco Approximates Fractal Structures and Fractal-Spiral Cones

Source: https://en.wikipedia.org/wiki/Romanesco_broccoli#mediaviewer/File:Fractal_Broccoli.jpg

"The Broccoli Romanesco exhibits fractal structure in its perimeter, planar and volumetric dimensions" (Wahl et al. n.d.). However, keep in mind, this is an approximation to the fractal geometry, since the fractal patterns only occurs at a few levels of magnification. There is a jaggedness-appearance in the irregular boundary (perimeter dimension), which is apparent in Figure 2.6. We can do cross sections to get at the planar fractal dimension.

To drive the point home, let us consider a simple geometric fractal, the Koch snowflake. Looking at a computer-generated image after many iterations we can observe the same kind of scalable self-similarity noted above. Now we invite you to consider the way the image can be constructed through the iterative repetition of something so simple as adding a tent-shaped triangle to the center of each solid line over and over. Each solid line ____ then looks like this __/__ on the subsequent iteration. Repeating the process over and over creates increasing intricacy as the level of magnification required to see what is going in increases. How can you apply this as a metaphor for the way that repeating small acts in an organization shapes it?

Figure 2.7 shows structure at several zoom-scales at different levels of observation. Fractals show structures at all these scales.

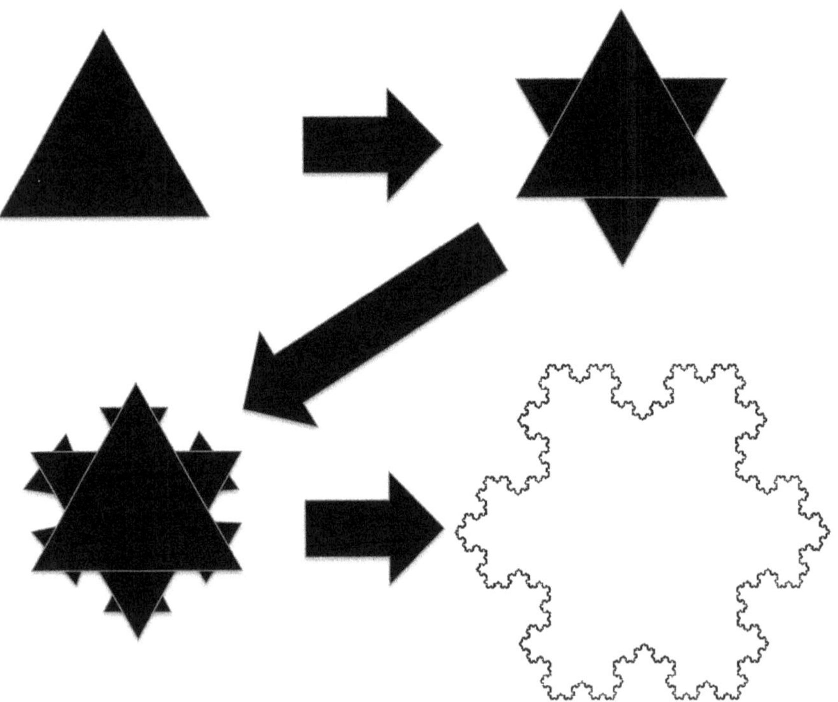

Figure 2.7 Koch Snowflake

Source: Adapted by Tonya L. Henderson (https://commons.wikimedia.org/wiki/File:Flocke.PNG)

Temporal Fractals and Managerial Time Horizons

Fractals are not just topological. There can also be temporal fractals. The fractal curve can manifest in time, at various speeds, and our observation of time fractals needs to have a measurement method that is attuned to the fractal curve's temporality. Plots are created over time, and depending on the observation resolution, there is less or more assessment of finer structures. All levels of resolution give some sense of the trend line.

We see the same effect when we examine charts for stocks or financial indices at various scales of granularity. Examining the same stock or commodity's bar chart for a one-hour period, yields similar patterns to a chart of the same instrument over a longer period of time. In each case, it is not apparent to the observer what scale is being represented, absent labels on the X-axis representing the time periods examined. As an exercise, visit http://stockcharts.com/ or your favorite financial charts site and examine the chart of any stock. We chose Apple (ticker symbol AAPL). If you adjust the time period of the chart, you will notice the same kinds of self-similar, scalable patterns such that of you ignore the labels on the chart it is not clear which scale you are looking at.

In a managerial context, there is among managers scale-divergence in focusing on scales of finer or grosser structures, as well as dependence upon topological (spatial) or temporality differentiations. This fractality scale-divergence has consequences for how managers understand strategy, history, operations, and ecology. This resolution orientation of managers' attunement is something worked out in specialization and experience.

This aspect of fractal patterns in the organizational context is also an area where extra caution is required. There are myriad ways to measure and conceive of the passage of time. When we consider this aspect in the human frame, the measured clock time of traditional reckoning is seldom in effect. Other perspectives may affect the manager's perceptions of the passage of time, such as variations in workload, patterns of behavior tied to cyclical trends or predictable events, etc. When looking for patterns in lived experience it may be necessary to look longitudinally for patterns whose periodicity not only varies, but may exist on a timeline that exceeds one's own experience.

Scale Transformations

Mandelbrot (1983) considers a fractal a compound entity composed of subpatterns, with a global characteristic of self-similarity. The subset entities are infinitely separable, at an infinitesimal scale of magnification (or *resolution*, as Nottale, 1996 puts it). Tang (2012), unlike Nottale, is focused on Euclidian understandings of spatial dimensions. The problem is that the Euclidian understanding of fractals is monological: monotonicity (p. 61), a countable stability, invariant transformations, continuous transformations, and inverse are also assumed to be continuous (p. 63). Tang, however, brings up

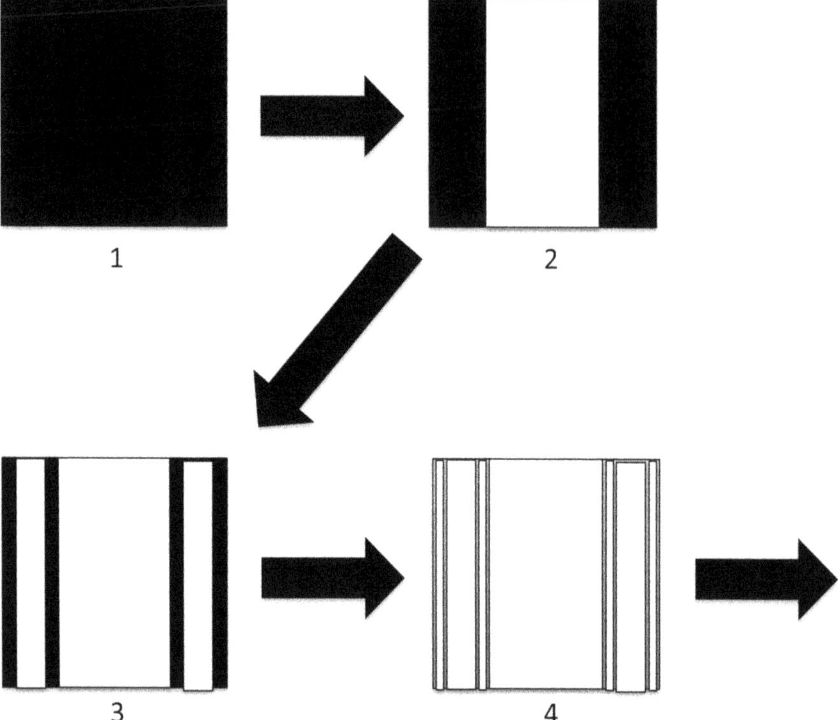

Figure 2.8 Cantor Fractal Measurement Example
Source: Created by Tonya L. Henderson (January 31, 2015)

an interesting problem with the measurement system being used to measure the fractals and their subset separations, intervals, and transformations. For example, in the Cantor Dust fractals, the measurement of a space is to focus on subareas (Figure 2.8).

HOW ARE SCALE TRANSFORMATIONS HAPPENING IN ORGANIZATIONS?

Fractal spacetime management observations can get into a rut. If we only consider one level of analysis, it can be hard to see patterns that may be repeating at multiple levels. By improving resolution relative to the task at hand, and learning to consider multiple scales of analysis, the strategic horizon can shift. The classic view is those at the top of the hierarchy of an organization have a wider field of vision, but are not sensitive to the finer structures, as are those in the technological core, or on the ground, in the bottom of the hierarchy. Most managers, then, are in-between, making out both the wider and narrow resolutions of fractal structures. To be effective they must understand what is going on at multiple levels of analysis. However, all too often we only teach them one level. Those promoted from within the ranks sometimes continue to think like technicians and struggle to understand the broader view. Sometimes a person who is groomed for leadership at a young age can rise to the top without garnering the perspective of the rank and file, devoid of understanding and therefore empathy. To overcome these issues it is important to develop an understanding of multiple levels of work and to be able to identify not only how they relate to one another, but what sociomaterial patterns are unfolding across them all.

For example, when Tonya worked in an operations center in the U.S. military, it was necessary for the bulk of the crew to spend an entire shift in the center, with the exception of meal and restroom breaks. Yet occasional trips down the hallway to talk with the next echelon up in their own environment tended to improve her perspective of operations. This activity combined with prior experience in subordinate units, both hers and those of her crewmembers, to support a multilevel awareness of the operational and systemic issues faced by watch-standers at different levels. The crew as an organization benefitted from multiple levels of perspectives and was able to use that understanding in an operational context. This is an example of how we can apply multiple levels of analysis to improve organizational function, recognizing the similarities and differences in operations at multiple echelons. This is a spatial consideration of scaling.

Next we look at temporal structures, first in a curvilinear fractal sequence, then in nested simultaneous fractal structures. There are measurement choices by a measurement-observation-system to observe a target systemicity over temporal horizon. Making these choices is akin to what Karen Barad (2007) calls making agential cuts, where the choice of apparatus is instrumental in determining what is observed. Time intervals are constructed by the measurement-system. The measurement-system can measure local peaks and valleys, upslopes, and downslopes, at various time-intervals of the wavelet's wavelength.

Let us consider two examples from the world of text analysis algorithms, wherein fractal-derived insights are useful to examine large data sets. Tang uses the Euclidian measurement algorithms of the Box and the Wavelet methods to assess regions of text documents. A fractal pattern can be extracted by the measurement-system by assessing the structural layout of the document (headlines, graphics, sections, etc.) and then mapping the logical structures of the document to approximate "understanding" (Tang 2012, 173). For the layout analysis of the text, parts (entities, subsets) are either treated as in-hierarchical relationship to one another, or as nonhierarchical. Parts of the documents are broken into successively smaller subparts.

In automated text analysis software packages, such as Diction, Leximancer, Crawdad, and Latent Semantic Analysis (LSA), understanding is simulated by either consulting pre-prepared dictionaries (Diction) or developing proximity measures of key words (LSA), or something in-between

(Leximancer, Crawdad). This makes analysis between sets of documents possible.

For example, in LSA:

> A matrix containing word counts per paragraph (rows represent unique words and columns represent each paragraph) is constructed from a large piece of text and a mathematical technique called *singular value decomposition* (SVD) is used to reduce the number of rows while preserving the similarity structure among columns.
>
> (Latent semantic analysis, 2014)

A limitation is that LSA cannot capture multiple meanings of a word. Second, LSA assumes with multiple documents, a joint space with an underlying monologic is formed.

"**Leximancer** is a data-mining tool that can be used to analyze the content of collections of textual documents and to visually display the extracted information" (Leximancer 2005). Leximancer uses proximity calculations. It cannot assess actual emotional inflections or nuances: "Affect extraction, which aims at providing an emotional evaluation of the emotional and psychological state of the speaker, is a quite specific form of content analysis that is beyond the scope of this document" (Leximancer 2005, p. 27).

Tang (2012) is attempting to reveal a fractal approach to text analysis, in ways that go beyond LSA, Leximancer, Crawdad, and Diction. "Fractal is mathematical sets with a high degree of geometrical complexity, which can model many classes of time-series data as well as images" (Tang 2012, p. 177). Tang's approach is to develop a method to search for a Modified Fractal Signature (MFS) in texts including their images/graphics/photos. Keep in mind Tang is not claiming to actually measure the underlying fractal directly. Rather the signature of the fractal, in its modified form is the being sought.

ANTENARRATIVES

An antenarrative is a prediction of likely outcomes, given a particular set of conditions (Boje 2011b, 2011d, 2011e,). It is a "bet" on the future, preceding sanctioned narrative (Boje, 2011b). This temporal relationship is supported by Heidegger's (1962) idea of a future that is already embedded in the present. Boje (2011a, 2011b, 2011c) characterizes antenarratives as linear, cyclic, spiral, or assemblage. Linear antenarrative assumes predictable causal relationships. Cyclic antenarrative repeats iteratively. Spiral antenarrative is considered a three dimensional fractal wave function with multiple vortices, propagating into future possibility space (D. Boje, 2011b, 2011c). Assemblage antenarrative is rhizomatic, propagating omnidirectionally (D. Boje, 2011b, 2011c). These archetypes vary in their conceptual structures and environmental responsiveness. Cyclical and linear antenarratives are suited to more stable ecosystems, while the latter two can accommodate systemicity.

When examining self-organization, predictability via coarse-grained linear analysis of individual trajectories is abandoned in favor of aggregate possibilities (Prigogine 1996, Sheldrake 1988, Talbot 1993, Tsoukas and Dooley 2011, Waddington 1961). Heisenberg and Bohr collectively force acceptance that not every attribute of an entity can be predicted or even measured at a given time and place, albeit for different reasons (Barad 2007, Hawking and Mlodinow 2005, Talbot 1993, Wheatley 2006).

Deleuze and Guattari (1987) in Chapter 14 develop the mathematics of fractal-spatiality (smooth-striated interactions), but seem to miss the embodiment ontology of fractal-sociomateriality. The difficulty in having fractal awareness is that social science tends to operate out of an ontology of separation of fractality from sociomateriality. In that separation, fractality either determines sociomateriality, or sociomateriality determines fractality. In Wanda Orlikowski (2009), the focus is on the mutuality of social and materiality→sociomateriality. Applying that premise, fractality is mutually constitutive with sociomateriality. Rather than privileging either fractality or sociomateriality, we need them mutually constitutive→fractal-sociomateriality.

We introduced key concepts in this section, then explored some examples of mathematical fractals in the context of management science to consider managerial issues of perception, scaling, time, and repetition. Next we offer you exercises to support practical application of these concepts.

Exercises for Building an Understanding of Fractal Storytelling and Fractal Organizing Processes

We would like to propose an experiential activity for the purpose of improving our understanding of fractal organizing processes kinesthetically.

Exercise: Understanding Scalable Self-Similarity

Construct a Sierpinski Triangle by drawing an upright equilateral triangle, then placing an upside down equilateral triangle inside of it. Next, draw an upside down equilateral triangle inside of each upright triangle again. Repeat the process ad infinitem. Figure 2.9 demonstrates the process.

Ask Yourself the Following Questions:

What was the process I repeated in order to reproduce the pattern with increasing levels of granularity?

How might this process be analogous to repeated behaviors in the workplace?

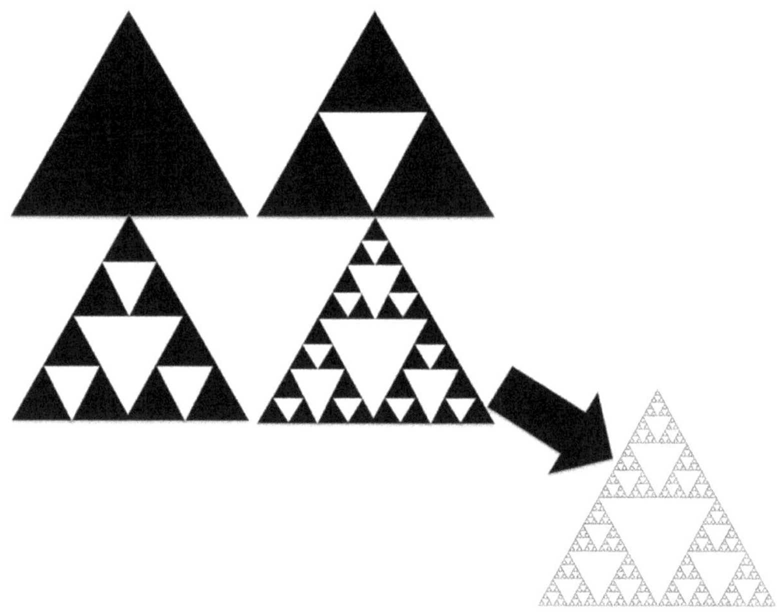

Figure 2.9 Generating a Sierpinski Gasket
Source: By Tonya L. Henderson (Adapted from https://commons.wikimedia.org/wiki/Fractal)

Figure 2.10 Sierpinski Pyramid
Source: http://upload.wikimedia.org/wikipedia/commons/2/29/Sierpinski_pyramid.jpg

Choose a workplace behavior that happens over and over, in big and small ways. Pick one word to describe that process and write it in the center of each inverted triangle going to as small a scale as the size of your paper and handwriting permit.

Inside each inverted triangle, write the names of the people and/or products affected by the pattern.

Figure 2.11 Multiple Unfolding Fractal Processes with Different Effects
Source: Created by Tonya L. Henderson

What are the stories surrounding each occurrence? Can you see them as self-similar fractal patterns unfolding in the living story web of your organization?

If I had just seen the finished product, would I have immediately known how to make it myself?

Might the same outcome be achieved using a different process?[3]

Now, consider the three dimensional variant that follows. How might the fractal generator, the process that is repeated iteratively, look in three dimensions?

What does that do for your perception of the stories considered above and how they interact?

Do these processes unfold independently? Go back to the diagram and draw lines between occurrences that are related in some tangible way, whether through the involvement of the same people, the same accounts, or in some other way.

If the geometry weren't perfect, if the triangles weren't exactly equilateral, would it be a more accurate depiction of what is going on in the organization?

What if there were myriad unfolding processes at different stages of development, occurring simultaneously and shaping the lived experience of the organization to different degrees? What might that look like?

Is figure 2.11 closer to an accurate depiction? Draw your own version.

NOTES

1. A common feature of fractal discussions is the use of the term fractal dimension (Lesmoir-Gordon et al., 2009; Mandelbrot, 1983; Mitchell, 2009). The fractal dimension is the exponent in the power law used to mathematically describe a fractal pattern. Mitchell (2009) explains the term by means of a simple illustration and offers the following general formula: "Create a geometric structure from an original object by repeatedly dividing the length of its sides by a number x. Then each level is made up of xdimension copies of the previous level" (Mitchell, 2009, p. 107). Liebovitch (1998) defines a fractal as "an object in space or a process in time that has a fractal dimension greater than its topological dimension" and explains that for fractals, dimensionality need not be an integer (p. 64). This dimension not only tells one the number of copies to expect at each level of magnification, but also relates the change in length, area, or volume for changing levels of magnification (Wakefield 2012, pp. 73–75).
2. A word of caution for the mathematically inclined manager: Fractals that are self-similar show structures at all zoom-scales (observed/measured at different spatial resolutions). Yet the power law may not always be applicable in terms of predicting expansion in such systems.

   "Therefore, the power law divergence of self-similar fractals is only a very particular case, and several other modes of divergence are possible, including slower divergences of the logarithmic type or faster divergences of the exponential type" (Nottale 2011, p. 57).

3. Note: An alternate way to generate the same figure is described by Manfred Schroeder (1991, p. 21).

REFERENCES

1964–2014: Our 50th Anniversary. (2014). History. Retrieved 15 May, 2015, from http://business.nmsu.edu/about/history/

Barad, Karen. (2007). Meeting the universe halfway: Quantum physics and the entanglement of matter and meaning. Durham, NC: Duke University Press.

Boje, D. (2011a, 15 June, 2011). *Quantum physics implications of storytelling for socioeconomic research methods: Experiences in small business consulting research form New Mexico State University*. Paper presented at the International Meeting of Research Methods Division of the Academy of Management, Lyon, France.

Boje, D. (Ed.). (2011b). *Storytelling and the future of organizations: An antenarrative handbook*. New York: Routledge.

Boje, D. (2011d). *The cycle and spiral-antenarrative: A quantum-ontology manifesto*. Working Papers. New Mexico State University. Las Cruces, NM. Retrieved from http://business.nmsu.edu/~dboje/655/anteriority_and_antenarrative_spiral.html

Boje, D.M. (Ed., in press, 2015) Change Solutions to the Chaos of Standards and Norms Overwhelming Organizations: Four Wings of Tetranormalizing. London/NY: Routledge.

Boje, David, and Ken Baskin. (2010d). "When storytelling dances with complexity-the search for Morin's keys." In *Dance to the music of story: Understanding human behavior through the integration of storytelling and complexity thinking*, edited by David Boje and Ken Baskin, 21–37. Litchfield Park, AZ.

Deleuze, G., & Guattari, F. (1987). A Thousand Plateaus: Capitalism and Schizophrenia (B. Massumi, Trans.). Minneapolis, MN: University of Minnesota Press.

Duarte, G.A. (2014). Fractal Narrative: About the Relationship Between Geometries and Technology and Its Impact on Narrative Spaces (Vol. 12). Deutsche Nationalbibliotehek.

Gulick, D., & Scott, J. (2010). *The Beauty of Fractals: Six Different Views*: Mathematical Association of America. Washington DC.

Hawking, Stephen, and Leonard Mlodinow. (2005). A briefer history of time. Westminster, MD: Random House. audio-book.

Heidegger, Martin. (1962). Being and time. Translated by Ralph Mahnheim. 7th ed. New York: Harper & Rowe Publishers. Original edition, 1926.

History: 1964–2014: Our 50th Anniversary. (2014). New Mexico State University, College of Business. Accessed 15 May 2015, from http://business.nmsu.edu/about/history/

Latent semantic analysis. (2015, 25 April). Retrieved 15 May, 2015, from http://en.wikipedia.org/wiki/Latent_semantic_analysis

Leibovitch, Larry S. (1998). Fractals and Chaos for the Life Sciences. New York: Oxford University Press.

Lesmoir-Gordon, N., Rood, W., & Edney, R. (2009). Fractals: A graphic guide. London, UK: Icon Books, Ltd.

Leximancer (version 2.2) Manual. (2005). Brisbane, Australia: Leximancer. https://www.leximancer.com/wiki/images/7/77/Leximancer_V2_Manual.pdf

Mandelbrot, Benoit. (1983). The fractal geometry of nature. New York, NY: W.H. Freeman and Company. Original edition, 1977. Reprint, 1983.

Meisner, G. (2012, 13 May). Phi 1.618: The Golden Number. Retrieved 3 Mar 2015, 2015, from http://www.goldennumber.net/golden-ratio-history/

Mitchell, Melanie. (2009). *Complexity: A Guided Tour.* Oxford, New York: Oxford University Press.

NMSU College of Business. (2014). from http://business.nmsu.edu/

Noon, Jeff. (1993). Vurt. Great Britain: Ringpull Press. fiction.

Noon, Jeff. (1996a). Automated Alice. NY: Crown Publishers, Inc.

Noon, Jeff. (1996b). Pollen. NY: Crown Publishers, Inc.

Nottale, L. (2011). *Scale Relativity and Fractal Space-Time: A new approach to Unifying Relativity and Quantum Mechanics*. London: Imperial College Press.

Orlikowski, W. J. (2009). The sociomateriality of organisational life: considering technology in management research. Cambridge Journal of Economics, bep058.

Palumbo, D. (1998). The monomyth as fractal pattern in Frank Herbert's Dune novels. Science Fiction Studies, 433–458.

Palumbo, D. E. (2004). The Monomyth in Alfred Bester's The Stars My Destination. The Journal of Popular Culture, 38(2), 333–368.

Palumbo, D. (2002). Chaos theory, Asimov's foundations and robots, and Herbert's Dune: the fractal aesthetic of epic science fiction (No. 100). Greenwood Press.

Prigogine, Ilya, and Isabella Stengers. (1984). Order out of Chaos. Toronto: Bantam Books.

Prigogine, I. (1996). *The end of certainty*. New York, NY: The Free Press, A Division of Simon & Schuster.

Tang, Y. Y. (2012). *Document Analysis And Recognition With Wavelet And Fractal Theories*. Singapore, New Jersey, London: World Scientific Publishing Company.

Schroeder, Manfred. (1991). *Fractals, Chaos, and Power Laws: Minutes from an Infinite Paradise.* Mineola, NY: Dover Publications.

Sheldrake, Rupert. (1988). The presence of the past: Morphic resonance and the habits of nature. New York, NY: Vintage Books.

Talbot, Michael. (1993). Mysticism and the new physics. 2nd ed. London, England: Arkana: Penguin Books. Original edition, 1981.

Tsoukas, Haridimos, and Kevin J. Dooley. (2011). "Introduction to the Special Issue: Towards the Ecological Style: Embracing Complexity in Organizational Research." Organization Studies 32 (6): 729–735. doi: 10.1177/0170840611410805.

Vrobel, S. (2011). *Fractal Time: Why a Watched Kettle Never Boils*. New Jersey, London: World Scientific Publishing Company.

Waddington, C.H. (1961). The nature of life, Kessinger Legacy Reprints. New York, NY: Athenium. Lecture Series.

Wahl, B. R., Roy, P. V., Larsen, M., Kampman, E.D., & Gonzalez, L.K. (n.d.). Chapter 4—Calculating: Fractals Dimension. *Fractal Explorer.* Retrieved 31 Jan, 2015, from http://www.wahl.org/fe/HTML_version/link/FE4W/c4.htm

Wheatley, Margaret J. (2006). Leadership and the new science: discovering order in a chaotic world. 1st ed. San Francisco, CA: Brett-Koehler Publishers, Inc.

3 Fractal Organizing Processes

Knowing One When You See It!

"If it walks like a duck, quacks like a duck, and has feathers like a duck . . . maybe it's a duck!"

Arguably, for managers to interact effectively with fractal organizing processes requires them to have a solid mechanism for identifying them. Yet identifying fractal operating processes can be a difficult thing to codify. There are those who spot them intuitively, for whom the scalable self-similarity of intangible social processes seems apparent. It is something akin to US Supreme Court Justice James Potter's (n.d.) famous statement about the difficulty in legally defining what constitutes obscenity: "I know it when I see it." Yet for the average manager, things may not be so obvious.

To that end, in this chapter, we offer an operational definition of fractal organizing processes, grounded in our understanding of complexity, storytelling, and organizational development theory and practice. Our task in this chapter is to answer the question, "How will I know a fractal organizing process when I see it?" We begin with the operational definition, followed by discussions of fractal storytelling, fractal narratives, and finally some exercises and a tool for recognizing fractal organizing processes.

FRACTAL ORGANIZING PROCESSES: SOCIOMATERIAL UNFOLDING OF ORGANIZATIONAL LIVED EXPERIENCE

Fractals in Human Systems

There are a variety of applications of the fractal concept to organization development.

Glenda Eoyang (2009, p. 66) defines fractals in terms of iterative, natural processes wherein a leader can develop a vibrant, adaptive organization through the iterative application of a "specific and clear concept of the organizational principle," with sensitivity to the environment and circumstances at hand. For her, this "generative principle" leads to coherence and adaptability comes from sensitivity to context. She emphasizes self-similarity among the parts and the whole of the organization, scaling in terms of critical organizational characteristics such as ethics and esprit de corps, recognition and management of differences, and fuzzy boundaries akin to the jagged edges of fractal images. Such boundaries are difficult to discern and serve as "focal points for creative interaction and transformation" (Eoyang 2009, p. 75).

For Quade and Holladay (2010, p. 24), "Some patterns reverberate through the entire system, repeating themselves on many levels and in many forms. When the same behavior can be observed in leaders, groups, and individuals, it may be understood as a fractal pattern." They explain that these kinds of patterns exist throughout society, where we see patterns of behavior exhibited by leaders echoed throughout their organizations and community issues affecting families and individuals as well. They then apply the concept to leadership models grounded in a complexity-based understanding.

Along those lines Mike Bonifer, the founder and CEO of Big Story, shared the following example when asked about fractal patterns in his work experience.

> So with Proctor and Gamble, . . . I was a lonesome soldier out in Effingham, Illinois and assigned to this case foods division as a management trainee in the sales division and they were not necessarily visible but it was all in place, like, the games were very clear and, you know, you just have to know the game or not know the game but the games were set. And so one of them, the very first thing was the guy that was going to be my big boss picked me up at the airport or I picked him up at the airport in my company car. It was my first day on the job, I think, and we turned the radio off right away and within the first couple of minutes he asked me about my intended.
>
> I had a girlfriend but he called her "My Intended" and so there was this idea that, "Oh your family life and your company life are going to be one in the same and I'm going to get right in your business about your intended and I'm going to turn down your radio, like, I'm your parent and I'm not even going to tell you to turn it down. I'm just going to turn it off." . . . he was friendly but I go, "Wow this guy really is trying to be my dad here" . . . and I'm getting the message that, you know, he was a long-time employee and was selling beyond the company and so there was that. And everything was very regimented so that the shipments that you got each month and what they want you to put on your license plate when you applied for a license and how our boss wanted our division numbers, SL405 was mine . . . for Saint Louis District 405 and he wanted them all on our license plates and I broke the fractal, I just forgot to do it, you know, but I was the only one in our division that didn't have that and our boss . . . my boss was

so pissed because he wanted everybody to have their company car lined up with their license plate and us sitting on the hoods like . . . a bunch of stars or something with our license plates and our numbers and I've ruined the photograph just because I didn't, you know, I wasn't spinning at that same . . . in that same fractal.

I wasn't doing that and it just . . . I just forgot about it and it didn't mean anything to me, you know, and yet this was a big disappointment to my boss, I remember, and then at each meeting . . . there were regular meetings and everybody was supposed to have a meeting on these regular cycles and so we would all get together. Our group would get together and it was very . . . you have to do of sales presentation as part of the meeting and that was regimented. Like, everybody would do a sales presentation at as part of this meeting and I knew this wasn't my boss's idea. I knew this came from HQ or it had been handed down.

So this had been cycling for a long time, it felt like they were so stilted and ridiculous and I remember one way was a guy would drop a pocketful of change on a table in front of them and then his playing as the seller and the buyer would go, "What's that?" and then the seller would go, "That's the money you're going to save on the three pound Criso, June promotion" and, you know, per case and, uh, and then the person will go, "Oh okay I'll take that deal." And that was it, you know, and then the next person would so something and it would just be equally cliched and . . . but every time that one guy have to do the presentation, he would just drop the change on the table and then there was a famous one where somebody opened up a can of Criso and started eating it, and buyer goes, "You can't do that," and he goes "Exactly, you can't eat Crisco alone which is why we want to sell you a double and I'll display a Crisco and Duncan Hine's cake mix because you can't eat Crisco alone."

So the guy had packed it with whipped cream and these things had circulated, you know, as being very rigid and I remember we got our employee manuals, they were still . . . it was men and they were just like mad men, they were wearing hats, they look just like mad men in the drawings of the . . . of the sales manual so they haven't changed in 10 or 15 years, probably, you know, because there were still guys in hats and those Don Drekker suits and so I just knew they were trying to fit me as a small town person into a small town.

That was their thinking, you know, square peg in a square territory and, um, it didn't allow for my growth. It was like, "Oh you're going to be a fractal too. You're going to be, like, you were, you're going to be a small town guy because that's how you grew up." And so anything that moved against that, you know, was just not, you know, it didn't, work, you know. It was bad for the company. I remember the first time

I showed up in Cincinnati for a meeting and I had a . . . I had my regular suit on, which was a white suit, kind of an off white suit and a peach colored shirt and a tie that was hand-painted with a man feeding a horse on it.

A picture of a man feeding a horse and platform shoes which are at that time my disco shoes and some guy took a look at me and went, "Can I see you out in the hallway for a second?" and he looked at me and he goes, "This has got to change. Like, go back and change now at your hotel. Did you bring something else to wear?"

So I wore my plaid suit, which today would look like some kind of crazy . . . so I still looked like a circus barker compared to everybody else, you know, the music man, because I had a plaid suit but, um, that was my conservative suit. But anyhow, I just didn't fit and I knew that I didn't fit and you know, the disruptions were all really subtle, and I was so far in that edge of the network and I wasn't able to know what went on in Cincinnati, but the little things I would see were just people being pranksters more than anything.

You know, people that would prank the system and those were little inflection points. Little signs of humanity where somebody would say, "Oh you can be human within this company but you have to do it in this winking way". And so we had a guy that would take . . . there was a company magazine called Moon Beams and in the back of Moon Beams, uh, there was a double track. Might have been in a single page of employees of the month and so it would be . . . I don't know, 15 or 20 employees of the month and it was from the whole company or at least, yeah from the whole company around the world.

So this guy in our division would take that . . . that he could be an employee of the month in the next month's Moon Beams. And everybody would go, "Wait a second, there's 60,000 employees in this company and we're so little out here in Saint Louis and you're going to get employee of the month, I'll take that bet, I'll bet you 10 bucks" and what this guy knew was that if you found the typo in the current issue and tell the editors about it, they would make you an employee of the month for the next issue. So if you would help the editors that got you in, so he knew that game and he would show up as an employee of the month and collect his money.

So there were little things like that where somebody will go like, "Oh you can game the system," like, you can do it and tweak it a bit and have fun with it. The other thing that I noticed was we would get a standardized shipment every month of supplies, so pencils and rubber bands and paper clips and what not. It was almost always more than you use as an average but the one thing I noticed was every month you get like 50 mechanical pencil and erasers wrapped in a rubber band and I would think I get these 50 and it was like that

> big, like a silver dollar size and there be 50 of them to have wrapped up. Maybe there were 30 but it was a lot. And I go, "Why are getting all these mechanical pencil and erasers for? What's that about?" And I asked my boss about it one time and then he goes, "Well you see that's the genius of Proctor and Gamble, is it's highly inefficient to send everybody what they need so they take the mean and they figured that out the average of what everybody needs and they send that."
>
> And I'm thinking to myself, there's some prankster out there telling somebody he uses 10,000 mechanical pencil erasers a month because it blows this whole thing so out of the water, nobody uses 50 erasers a month, nobody. It's impossible to think about it, you know, to even imagine.
>
> So somebody's on the form, requisition form, they're putting down a bogus number just to . . . That was always my thought. Like, I never proved it but I just thought that got to be the only . . . but they're figuring out the average number of mechanical pencil erasers and I'm getting 30 or 50 a month and somebody's jacking the system.
>
> So I just had to get, you know, I just had . . . personally I just had to get out of there. I had to, you know, there wasn't any way for me to change anything at Proctor and Gamble in any meaningful ways. So for me the inflection point was personal and I've move into writing at that point. It really took me in that direction because I was so . . . kind of annoyed that the only tonic for me became writing. Um, and then, you know, I learned to write a little bit and went to Disney and Disney was the flip side of the coin for me.
>
> —Mike Bonifer (interview)

Bonifer's story shows us how there can be several ongoing fractal patterns in any work situation. Fractals are not just topological. There can also be temporal fractals. The fractal curve can manifest in time, at various speeds, and our observation of time fractals needs to have a measurement method that is attuned to the fractal curve's temporality.

All work organizations are already constituted by fractal-sociomateriality: (1) bodies in pattern arrangements; (2) documents flowing between actors physically and electronically; (3) ways buildings are constructed, changed, retrofitted, demolished to make new ones; (4) time frames changing for writing, publishing, referencing beyond single disciplines; (5) how local and global distances are desevered by Internet communications so that niches of interest are not among neighbors, rather they are between people in similar niches who can be continents apart, and so on.

Following Latour (2004), to dualize "fractality" and "sociomateriality" seeing how they are an assemblage misses the embodied nature of fractal-sociomateriality. Following Barad (2003, 2007) the relations of enacted observation apparatuses are in agency relation with fractal-sociomateriality, in their intra-activity. This would take seriously their mutually constitutive entanglement.

Fractal Organizing Processes

Building on these understandings of fractal patterns in human systems and our own work (see Chapter 5, this volume, for example), we extend the concept into the sociomaterial realm, blending the notion of fractal organization structures, whether intentionally developed or organically evolving, with the idea that organizations are, at their core, unfolding processes of becoming. We are now prepared to address the question, "What is a fractal organizing process?"

We would argue that some aspects of every organization can be considered this way. We abandon any reductionist inclinations, even vis-à-vis the material, structural elements of human systems and examine organizations as emergent patterns of sociomaterial and dissipation. In practical terms this means that drawing from Eastern philosophy, we consider that at any given time, all things exist in a state of growth/becoming, preservation, or decline (*The Bhagavad Gita* 2007). These states or stages are tied to environmental fitness as the iterative rules or principles comprising the organization's purpose and culture are either applied indiscriminately or are adapted in response to changes in context. Social and material factors both internal and external to the organization combine to necessitate organizational shifts to match internal and external complexity and other contextual factors.

When there is a need for it, whether to fulfill a social purpose or simply a desire for revenue on someone's part, an organization will emerge in any given context. Just as with technology, there is innovation in response to a felt need. That innovation is sometimes widely adopted. Then times change and yesterday's innovation becomes tomorrow's dying industry. Today's thriving company goes the way of the dodo as the need for it diminishes.

Definition: A fractal organizing process is a sociomaterial pattern of growth or dissipation in a human system that is characterized by scalable self-similarity that is observable in terms of social and/or material factors. Our operating definition of fractal organizing process is that it's an ensemble extension to sociomateriality.

Simply put, a *fractal organizing process* is a sociomaterial pattern of growth or dissipation in a human system that is characterized by scalable self-similarity that is observable in terms of social and/or material factors. These patterns may be manifested through intentional strategic design intended to promote resilience or, more commonly, as a matter of organic self-organizing behaviors. These behaviors are typically manifested through storytelling, which brings us to consider the concepts of fractal storytelling and fractal narrative. Table 3.1 serves as a worksheet for identifying fractal organizing processes.

Table 3.1 A Worksheet for Identifying Fractal Organizing Processes

Process Identification and Characterization		
What's going on?	Setting/context: Who is actively involved? Who/what is directly affected?	
Relational View of the Situation: How might the situation be seen from each of these perspectives? (Be sure to consider each aspect from a sociomaterial change perspective)		
Self:	Others:	Ecosystem:
Is it a fractal organizing process?		
Sociomateriality: Social aspects: Material aspects: How are they entwined?	Scalability: Does it happen in big and small ways? How so?	Repetition: Where and when?
If it's not a fractal organization process, what other kind of patterns do you see, if any?		

Source: By Tonya L. Henderson. Used by permission.

Using this tool, one can begin to assess whether or not a process of interest constitutes a fractal organizing process. It is important to make the distinction that not all organizing processes are fractal. For instance, a once in a lifetime occurrence may yield great organizational learning, to include subprocesses that could propagate fractally, but not be a scalable, self-similar occurrence in and of itself. We are reminded of Eglash's (2005) quest for fractal patterns. Whereas he found self-similar scalable patterns in the way that African villages and buildings were constructed, he did not find the same to be true in the Native American settings he explored. If a situation is examined using the above tool and is not found to be scalable and self-similar, then it may be less complex and suitable for a reductionist approach.

We offer this tool to assist the reader in avoiding positive confirmation bias, the danger that we get "fractal fever" and see them everywhere because this is our own lens for viewing the world.

UNDERSTANDING AND AGENCY: A MULTIFRACTAL VIEW

Fractality is being introduced as a way to think about organizational behavior. There are two distinct approaches. One looks at how the whole organization is a fractal "whole" system (or multifractal) that adapts to environmental exigencies. The approach is multifractal, but from the bottom up, and the parts are in search of a whole. This second approach relates to our work on systemicity and third-order cybernetics, where systems are unfinished, unfinalized, and partial.

Both the top-down (whole controls parts) and the bottom-up, parts in search of a coherent collective pattern, may well be in interactions in ways that form a top-up hybrid. Following Fryer (2004), Kirikova (2009) addresses fractal emergence, adaptation, and evolution. Fractal theory has been applied to manufacturing (Tharumarajah, Wells, and Nemes 1998), product design (Chiva-Gomez 2004), enterprise development (Ramanthan 2005; Ryu and Jung 2003; Hongzhao, Dongxu, Yanwei, and Ying 2005), software development (Gabriel and Goldman 2006), and Information Systems (Sprice and Kirikova 2006, Kirikova 2009).

We theorize the interplay between natural and artificial multifractal systems. They influence one another at different scalabilities. The theory and practice problem is that many participants regard their organizations as a natural (or organic) adaptive and evolving system. However, we contend that many, if not all, complex organizations, are at least partially artificial.

One way to theorize this is to look at multifractality as the interplay (or hybrid) of linear monomyth *fractal narratives,* which have artificiality, in *intra-activity* with *living story multifractal webs*, which are more natured and organic (humans are part of the living, vital, environment, along with nonhuman species). The monomyth, as described by Palumbo is not only linear, but centerpieces one character's quest, as he finds helpers, refuses the call, fails along the way and finally succeeds in his quest. The hero then brings home the boon, following Campbell's (1987) hero's journey.

We are not especially interested in treating organizations as if they were composed of simple parts (components) and theorizing these as fractal entities that exhibit self-similarity and recurrence. Nor, do we view fractal organizations as the outcome of planned change strategies. That only invites more hierarchical control and treats fractality as yet another managerialist metaphor instead of the naturally unfolding sociomaterial process of organizational Being/becoming that we consider it to be.

How do you blend all the different fractals together—*to normalize* across them all (if we assume that normalization is a good thing)?

Organizations are constructed from fractal sets. These fractal sets are regular and irregular fractals. Regular fractals exhibit self-similarity. Irregular fractals exhibit asymmetry. Social norms of organizations create both regular (self-similar) and irregular (asymmetrical) fractal sets. Both are generated in iteration after iteration. The math fractals (Mandelbrot Set, Koch Snowflake, Sierpinski Triangle) are each idealization as (ideal types form mathematical formulae). These ideal types can approximate, but no not equal fractal patterns in nature. Mandelbrot (1983, p. 1) recognized this: "Clouds are not spheres, mountains are not cones, coastlines are not circles, and bark is not smooth, nor does lightning travel in a straight line."

The implication is that grand narratives approximate the living story web patterns in gross generalizations that tempt us to be unaware of the underlying fractal patterning. This narrative-grossness and story-particularness interact and interweave in *antenarrative processes*.

All living things, large and small, seem to be creatures of self-similar, scalable emergence and dissipation. Not only are living things prone to such behaviors, even mountains emerge in a sometimes gradual sliding of tectonic plates or a sudden and fiery birth only to dissipate, sinking or crashing back into flatness as the earth breathes in and out in cycles spanning millions of years. The markets boom and crash as the collective of global investors rallies then panics, cyclically breathing in and out, yet with an overall upward direction favoring the long-term investor whose Hegelian absolute is wealth. Interpersonal relationships emerge and dissipate at varied paces, in healthy and unhealthy ways. In all open systems, there is a pulse—a rhythm to the emergence and dissipation of an entity's pattern as it intra-acts with others in context. To understand fractal patterns is to be attuned to the unfolding of the universe, not myopic, singular unfoldings, but embedded in larger contexts amid the messiness of other patterns emerging and dissipating as they bump into one another, adding and strengthening each other here, cancelling each other out there, and occasionally colliding catastrophically to the detriment of all parties. So much potential. So many alternate possibilities open up in each moment of choice and yet mountains, markets, trees, and people tend to live and die by their patterns, unconsciously repeating the same formulae day in, and day out. Do they have a choice? What does it take to shift a pattern?

This question plagues everyone who wants to elicit some improvement in the world, from humanists to environmentalists. Psychologists and social workers have long pondered this point in the individual frame of reference. Does not the little boy who pulls the wings off of flies sometimes escalate to harming people too? We even explore destructive patterns of money management affecting individual lives in an effort to combat addiction and poverty (Payne 2001). Certainly sociologists and historians have long pondered the patterns of societal emergence and dissipation on a global scale, just as political scientists watch the patterns of nations, usually in an effort to prolong the existence of their own preferred power structure. We are reminded of Marx's dialectic materialism, which is typically presented as linear even though the progression is simply the emergence of increasingly relational modes of power distribution until the darkness of human nature intervenes and collapses the system back into the dark ages, from which it must re-emerge to progress as indicated in Marx's ideal. The body politic, too, breathes in and out.

Now that we have considered the concepts of fractal story and fractal narrative and established what to look for to identify fractal organizing processes, it is important to be clear that not all sociomaterial changes one might observe in organizations fit the bill. Early in her work with fractal organizing processes, colleagues warned Tonya not to mistake the map for the territory. Eglash (2005) set the example with his very honest accounting of his unsuccessful investigation into North American Indian architecture and design, where he expected to find something similar to the fractal designs he explored in Africa. Others have also noted this need in their work with human systems dynamics and data-driven decision making. Lest we tumble blindly over the cliff of self-confirmation bias, let us polish our fractal-colored glasses and consider other possibilities of patterns that we might see in organizations. There are other kinds of patterns worth observing when diagnosing and helping to address organizational concerns.

We asked Kristine Quade to tell us how she recognizes patterns in her work with organizations. For her, fractal patterns are but one, albeit a very important one, kind of pattern she looks for in organizations. The others are periodic, random, and point attractors, as described in complexity science.

> The definition of a pattern is similarities, differences over time and space . . . periodic, random, fractal and point attractors. . . . So, my brain is always first starting to look at where is the similarity and the difference in the system. So, it's always looking there first. And then, I drop in to look at . . . okay, this would start to repeat itself in some sort of regularity.
>
> —Kristine Quade (interview)

Periodic patterns can be as simple as seasonal marketing trends, industry lifecycles, etc. They repeat but are not scalable. She used employee behavior changes when it is time for performance reviews and budgeting to illustrate periodic patterns of behavior in organizations as well:

> The periodic attractor pattern is one that repeats itself like a little wave, you know, so it's like . . . how I see it in the organization is specifically around performance reviews . . . when the people start raising their head to say, "I'm doing an amazing job. Notice me. Notice me." . . .
>
> Or, by the time, which is [like], "Oh, now, I have to hide some of my resources, so they don't take them away," or "reallocate them something

> else." So, it's . . . really bizarre behaviors . . . in an organization. Now, each one of those can be also in fractal pattern because the fractal pattern is exactly the same at every single level. So, that's the distinction that I make.
>
> —Kristine Quade (interview)

> Point attractors are phenomena surrounding a particular occurrence. It could be a charismatic leader. But, there is a dynamic that is starting to focus . . . and I always think of, oh; I walk by the water cooler and . . . there's an issue calling people to the water cooler or the coffee pot.
>
> —Kristine Quade (interview)

We asked Glenda Eoyang to share an example of a time when she expected to find a fractal pattern in her work with a client and did not:

> It was an international agricultural research project and there were thirty local research projects in four different regions, twelve different nations around the world, very locally based agricultural research projects, and then there were regional management teams and then there was a central foundation that funded all of the research and coordinated all the conversation. And I began with the assumption that if we used adaptive action, which would be familiar to the scientists that were on the ground doing research, that we could use that same process for the regional analysis and for the decision-making and action taking at the level of the foundation.
>
> And that turned out not to be so easy, partly because of the cycle times, so the foundation was making decisions on a quarterly basis. The regional planning was annual. The local research projects were daily and seasonal and annual and so they just would not, did not see their processes as being fractal. They had different vocabularies. They had different decision-making methods, they had different identities in each of those levels. So what I thought should be an easy self-organizing fractal, three layered meaning-making machine turned out to be very sensitive to the differences scale to scale, rather than the similarities.
>
> . . . I worked with that group for about six years doing facilitation at meetings and became very sensitive to the differences among the layers, and so I continued to keep the self-similarity in mind when I designed meetings but I had to be very careful not to over focus on the similarity across the scales. . . . In theory specific applications, it [self-similarity] would show up, so we were at one point working with geo-positioning, satellite imagery to make some decisions about climate change and that was a point in that particular application, that all three scales could see themselves and adaptive action and could come together in that

> particular project, but they didn't generalize it to a kind of broader organizational identity.
>
> —Glenda Eoyang (interview)

These examples remind us that there are other kinds of patterns occurring in organizations. These patterns mimic the antenarrative archetypes that David has explored in past works (Boje 2011a, 2011b). There are cyclical patterns, such as annual retail cycles with increases around the holidays. There are rhizomatic patterns, wherein an idea spreads in unpredictable directions and pops up in unexpected places as the result of unseen connections, analogous to strawberry plant runners or Aspen grove roots that expand underground. The connections are very real and tangible, although they are not apparent to the above-ground observer. Beginning-Middle-End (BME) antenarratives continue a linear trajectory that has already been set, often by authority, and whereas they are not repeating patterns within a particular system, we can certainly see the same ones appearing in multiple contexts over time, as in Duarte's (2014) work on fractal narrative.

In this chapter, we have provided operational definitions of key terms, along with a tool for identifying fractal organizing processes. We have also addressed some of the roots of skepticism, to include the danger of using the wrong tools if we tend to view every process we see as fractal. As the saying goes, "When all you have is a hammer, the whole world looks like a nail." We do not advocate the emptying of one's toolbox. On the contrary, it is our intent to simply add a process-oriented, fractal-based approach to organization development and management tasks for use under the right circumstances.

In sum, *fractal change management* theory is defined here as the way people in organizations are attuned to fractal dimensions[1] and enact fractal storytelling. Fractal storytelling (or fractal story) is not the same as what the fractal mathematics define as fractal perimeter, plane, volume, self-similar or irregularity scalability.

Fractal Ethics

When we consider ethics in the world of fractal processes, two philosophers come to mind: Bahktin and Aristotle. Bakhtin's (1993) concept of answerability is of the utmost importance, as is Aristotle's treatment of habituation. These two perspectives support the model presented herein in very different ways. The former suggests that for each act that a person undertakes, there is answerability for not only the actor's intent, but for the act itself. We extend this concept by adding answerability for the timing of action and any unintended consequences.

The timing of our actions is extremely important in an ecosystem that is constantly changing. Today's right action may be disastrous if implemented late or too soon. For example, the marketing of a new, innovative product after one's competitors have cornered the market can be disastrous. Likewise, introducing the product before consumers are able to see its usefulness or before adequate studies have been conducted to determine its salability is equally harmful.

Complexity teaches us that in a very interconnected system, such as today's global economy, the effects of a given action may be hard to trace. If we truly believe in the butterfly effect, then it is a simple extension of it to understand that there may be long-term implications of any given action that are potentially untraceable to their origins. This problem is further complicated by the cocreative nature of intra-action. There is not a simple, isolated model of a causal agent and a direct effect in most cases. With business and social interests around the world linked by air travel and telecommunications, there are usually many, many actors in the mix each time we take an action. Just as a doctor must often consider multiple risk factors in assessing a patient's presenting condition, consultants examining business problems in this frame must consider the entire context, to include patterns occurring at multiple levels of analysis. In interconnected systems like the global economy and society at large, there are often unintended consequences for our actions. When it is so difficult to understand the full range of stakeholders and possible implications of our actions, it is more important than ever that our actions be grounded in sound moral principles. Even so, well-intentioned acts may still result in harm to unknown parties, but nevertheless, positive intent decreases the likelihood that our actions will be anything other than generative on the whole.

NOTE

1. In fractal geometry, fractals are geometrical shapes that have noninteger dimensions.

REFERENCES

Bakhtin, Michel. (1993). Toward a philosophy of the act. Translated by Vadim Liapunov. Edited by Michael Holquist, University of Texas Press Slavic Series No. 10. Austin, TX: University of Texas Press.

Barad, Karen. (2003). "Posthumanist performativity: Toward an understanding of how matter comes to matter." *Signs,* vol. 28.3: 801–831. http://uspace.shef.ac.uk/servlet/JiveServlet/previewBody/66890-102-1-128601/signsbarad.pdf

Barad, Karen. (2007). Meeting the universe halfway: Quantum physics and the entanglement of matter and meaning. Durham, NC: Duke University Press.

Bhagavad Gita, The. 2007. Translated by Eknath Easwaran. Tomales, CA: Nilgiri Press. Original edition, 1985. Reprint, 2007.

Boje, David. (2011a). "Quantum physics implications of storytelling for socioeconomic research methods: Experiences in small business consulting research form New Mexico State University." International Meeting of Research Methods Division of the Academy of Management, Lyon, France, 15 June, 2011.

Boje, David. (2011e). *The Quantum Physics of Storytelling.* [Author's Draft ed.].

Campbell, J. (1987). The hero's journey.

Chiva-Gomez, R. (2004). Repercussions of complex adaptive systems on product design management. *Technovation*, *24*(9), 707–711.

Duarte, G.A. (2014). *Fractal Narrative: About the Relationship Between Geometries and Technology and Its Impact on Narrative Spaces* (Vol. 12). Bielefeld: Transcript Verlag, Deutsche Nationalbibliotekhe.

Eglash, Ron. (2005). African fractals: Modern computing and indigenous design. New Brunswick, NJ: Rutgers University Press. Original edition, 1999. Reprint, third.

Eoyang, Glenda. (2009). Coping With Chaos. Edited by Human Systems Dynamics Institute. Circle Pines, MN: Lagumo.

Fryer, P., & Ruis, J. (2004). What are Fractal Systems? A brief description of 'Complex Adaptive and Emergent Systems'(CAES).

Gabriel, R.P., & Goldman, R. (2006, October). Conscientious software. In *Acm Sigplan Notices* (Vol. 41, No. 10, pp. 433–450). ACM.

Hongzhao, D., Dongxu, L., Yanwei, Z., & Ying, C. (2005). A novel approach of networked manufacturing collaboration: fractal web-based extended enterprise. *The International Journal of Advanced Manufacturing Technology, 26*(11–12), 1436–1442. doi: 10.1007/s00170-004-2125-4

Kirikova, M. (2009). Towards multifractal approach in IS development. In Wita Wojtkowski, Gregory Wojtkowski, Michael Lang, Kieran Conboy, and Chris Barry (eds.), *Information Systems Development* (pp. 295–306). Springer US.

Latour, B. (2004). How to talk about the body? The normative dimension of science studies. *Body & society*, *10*(2–3), 205–229.

Mandelbrot, Benoit. (1983). The fractal geometry of nature. New York, NY: W.H. Freeman and Company. Original edition, 1977. Reprint, 1983.

Payne, R. K. (2001). *Bridges out of poverty*. Highlands, TX: aha! Process, Inc.

Potter, James (n.d.) "Obscenity." Farlex Accessed 6 Jan. http://legal-ictionary.thefreedictionary.com/obscenity.

Quade, Kristine, and Royce Holladay. (2010). Dynamical Leadership: Building Adaptive Capacity for Uncertain Times. Apache Junction, AZ: Gold Canyon Press.

Ramanathan, J. (2005). Fractal architecture for the adaptive complex enterprise. *Communications of the ACM*, *48*(5), 51–57.

Ryu, K., & Jung, M. (2003). Agent-based fractal architecture and modeling for developing distributed manufacturing systems. *International Journal of Production Research, 41*(17), 4233–4255.

Sprice, R., & Kirikova, M. (2006). Feasibility study: New knowledge demands in turbulent business world. In Anders G. Nilsson, Remigijus Gustas, Wita Wojtkowski, W. Gregory Wojtkowski, Stanisław Wrycza, and Jože Zupančič (eds.), *Advances in Information Systems Development* (pp. 131–142). Springer US.

Tharumarajah, A., Wells, A.J., & Nemes, L. (1998, October). Comparison of emerging manufacturing concepts. In *Systems, Man, and Cybernetics, 1998. 1998 IEEE International Conference on* (Vol. 1, pp. 325–331). IEEE.

4 Fractal Storytelling

This chapter makes the case for fractal storytelling as the way of all storytelling, where living stories emerge and dissipate as agentive parts of complex adaptive sociomaterial systems. If we accept this as the way of all stories, to be repeated self-similarly on multiple scales or to dissipate, then other kinds of storytelling amount to socially constructed choices within the larger field.

Fractal storytelling is a way people in organizations attune to the sociomateriality of fractal *spacetimemattering*. We can zoom in and zoom out in our storied observations of the relationship of organization and environments. It exists in and between organizations and ecosystems! *Fractal storytelling* is defined here, as the study of the relationship between many small events in living story webs, brought into antenarrative processes into interactivity with the grander narratives of quite few events. Organizations and their environments form fractal relationships of irregular and/or fragmented scales.

THREE TYPES OF STORYTELLING

Traditional discussion of storytelling focuses on oral and written traditions. Here we take it further with the help of our colleagues (Boje 2011c, 2011d; Boje, DuRant, Coppedge, Chambers, & Marcello-GOmez 2012; Boje and Coppedge 2014; Henderson 2014; Henderson and Deporres 2014; Wakefield 2012). Material storytelling focuses on the materiality of storytelling and the power of thingness (Bennett 2010). Ontological storytelling focuses on the underlying principles that serve as fractal generators within the living story web. Quantum storytelling unites the three.

Material Storytelling: This is the work of Anete Camille Strand (2011, 2012) from Denmark.

Strand, Anete Mikkala Camille. (2011). Presentation on "material storytelling" to 20th anniversary meeting of S'CMoi, meeting in Philadelphia, April.

Strand, Anete Mikkala Camille. (2012). Enacting the Between: On Dis/continuous Intra-active Becoming of/through an Apparatus of Material

Storytelling. Unpublished Doctoral Dissertation, Aalborg University, Denmark. Books 1 and 2 are online available at http://storytelling.

Ontological Storytelling: This is David Boje's work applying Heidegger, Bakhtin, Mead, Deleuze, and others.

Quantum Storytelling: This is an evolving body of work, described in our edited book *Being Quantum: Ontological Storytelling in the Age of Antenarrative* (Boje and Henderson 2014). Additional resources are available through peaceaware.com and http://quantumstorytelling.org/Resources.html.

How are material storytelling, ontological storytelling, and quantum storytelling related? The old material ontologies have been giving ground to quantum storytelling.

FOUR ANTENARRATIVE TRAJECTORIES

Antenarrative is a bet and a prestory that can aspire to be very transformative.

> *Antenarrative is a bridge between living story and narrative by four pathways: linear-antenarrative, cyclical-antenarrative, spiral-antenarrative, and rhizomatic-antenarrative.* Two pathways between living story and narrative, the linear- and cyclic-antenarratives are from past predicted to recur in the future (Boje 2014d). This is known as conventional and ordinary retrospective sensemaking. The other two pathways are from the future to the past, and this is quite radical. The spiral- and rhizomatic-antenarratives are future→present and future→past destining, directionalities futurals, drafts (up or down, in and out, left or right quantum directions), and disclosabilites of quantum materiality in a vitalistic sense of living story.
>
> The connection between antenarrative and fractal organizing processes is that Antenarratives make different types of fractal connections between grand narratives that try to universalize everything and webs of living stories that go on without end. The four types of antenarratives are types of connections between universal narratives and webs of living stories that form between people and organizations. For example, in Campbell's Hero's journey there is a cycle of the hero accepting the call, recruiting helpers, succeeding to overpower a damaging force.
>
> (Boje, in press)

This is an example of a fractal narrative reduced to a grand narrative. It amounts to an oversimplification of Being-In-The-World as unfolding lived sociomaterial experiences described by Heidegger. This simplification of fractal organizing processes into a grand narrative is what Palumbo calls the monomyth. We renegotiate that by being between the grand narratives of governments, medias, and our own collectively lived fractal stories. The different antenarrative processes form transformations of the grand narratives of universalization and are in between webs of living stories of our day to day relationships.

To the original four types of antenarratives David has added the beneath and between. The beneath is a combination of rhizomatic hidden connections and the symbol-generation that must happen in order to be transformational within the entanglement of grand narratives and living story web. We see the emergence of fractal organizing processes as a sociomaterial emergence in the heteroglossic tension between lived experience of the living story web and the grand narratives imposed by society. This is tied to the notions of fore-having, fore-conceiving.

WHAT ARE FOUR KINDS OF ANTENARRATIVES?

Antenarratives are the *bets, before, beneath,* and *between* unfolding occurrences in a living story web. The *Between* of Grand Narratives and

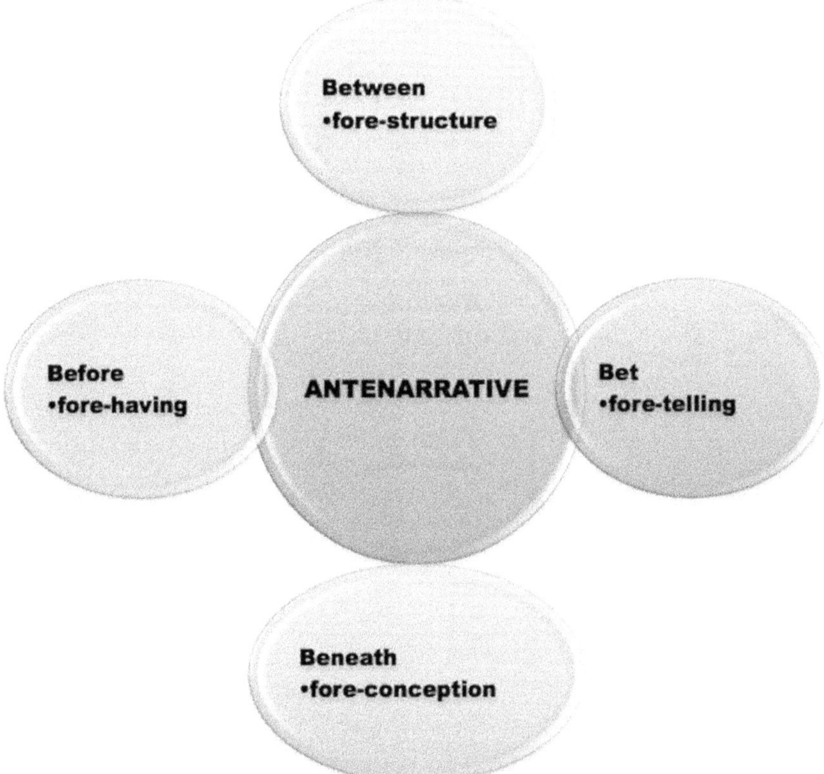

Figure 4.1 Four *B*s of Antenarrative

Source: http://business.nmsu.edu/~dboje/655/study_guide_grandnarratives.htm (Used by permission)

individuated living story webs. They are the bets on the future. the beneath the Grand Narratives and living story webs.[1]

Four *B*s of Antenarrative (adapted from Boje, 2014e)

- *Before*-systems-wholeness
- *Bets* on many systems–systemicity developments possible
- *Beneath* the Grander Narratives of system-wholeness-universalizations, and the Living Story Webs of encounters that are grounded
- *Between* living story webs of individuation and Grander Narratives of generality, universality, and essentialism

Fore-having, fore-telling (aka fore-sight), fore-conception, and fore-structure are developed by Martin Heidegger (1962) in *Being and Time*. Here we summarize the relevant citations to developing an antenarrative

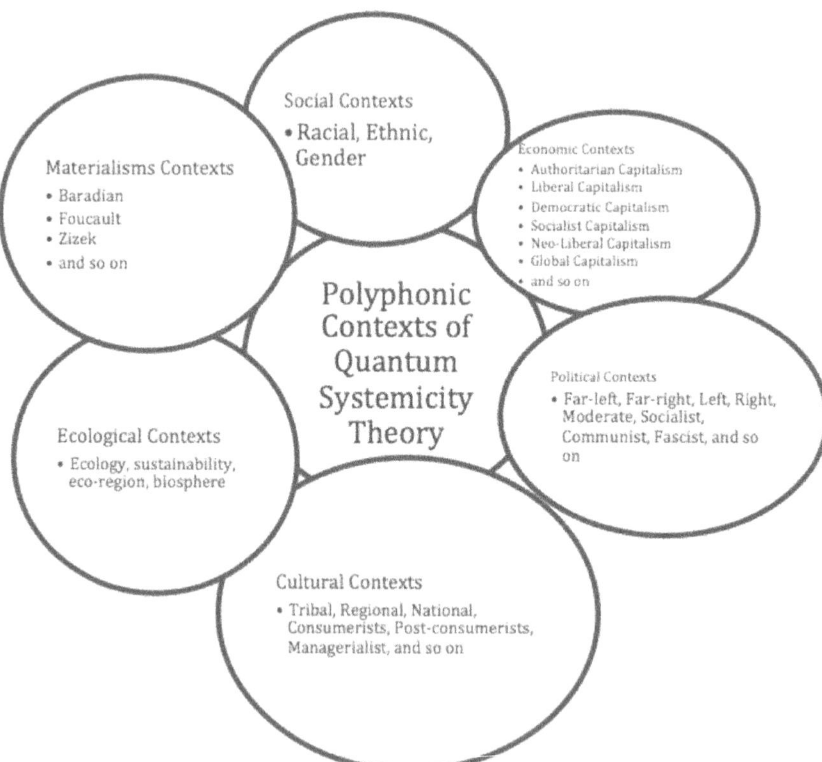

Figure 4.2 Polyphony of Systemicity Contexts and Their Interplay
Source: Drawing by Boje.

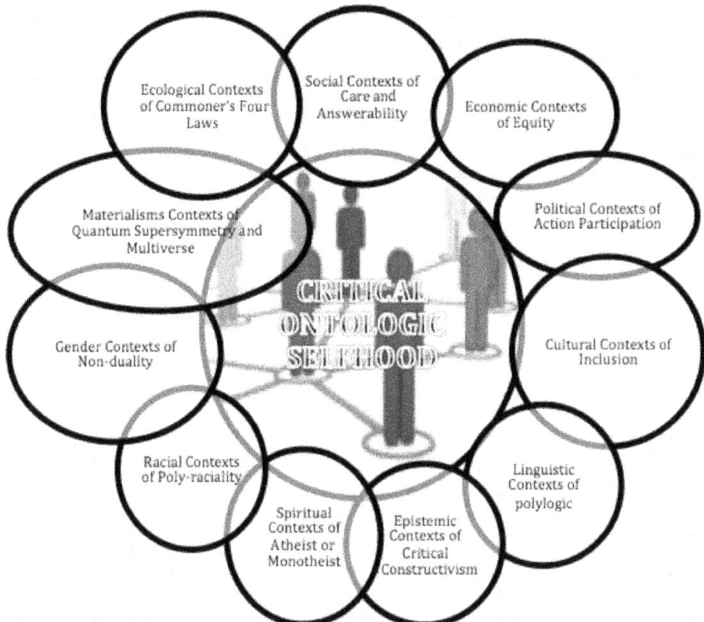

Figure 4.3 Critical Ontologic-Selfhood in Contexts of Multiplicity
Source: Drawing by Boje.

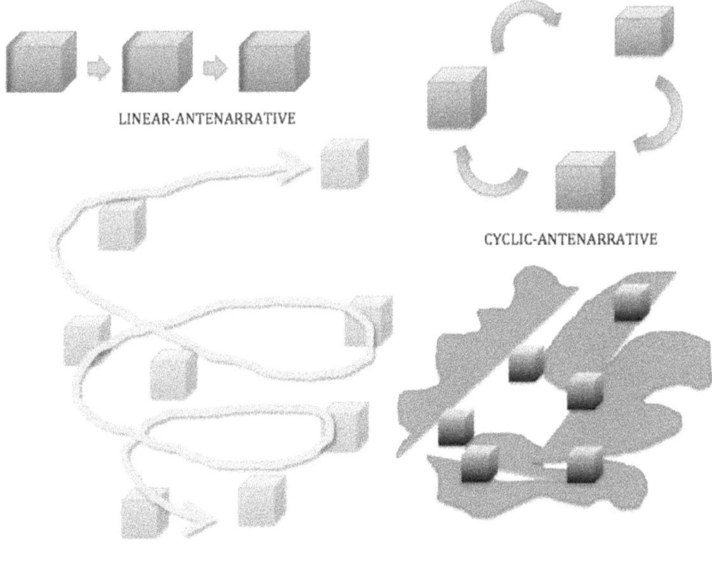

Figure 4.4 Four Types of Antenarrative
Source: Drawing by David Boje. Used by permission.

extension to the fores' in relation to *before-bets-between-beneath*. Heidegger (1962) develops the fores' throughout *Being and Time*:[2]

"Whenever something is interpreted as something, the interpretation will be founded essentially upon fore-having, fore-sight, and fore-conception" (Heidegger 1962, #150).

"Like any interpretation wherever, assertion necessarily has a fore-having, a fore-sight, and a fore-conception as its existential foundations" (Heidegger 1962, #157).

http://peaceaware.com/Warwick/spikes.htm is a case that goes with it.

COMPLEX ADAPTIVE SYSTEMS

Life is a process Being-In-The-World of interconnectedness and entangled contexts. The "new" critical ontology is all about the how so-called systems have Being-In-The-World, in-spaces, in-times, and in-materialisms. Here is an example:

"Where mind ends and matter begins is difficult to discern, a situation that operates to overturn the long-standing and problematic Cartesian separation of the two entities. In Mataurana's and Varela's conception, mind and matter are merely parts of the same process—one cannot exist without the other. A critical ontology seeks to repair this rupture between mind and matter, self and world" (Kincheloe 2007, p. 895).

Furthermore, "autopoiesis as the process of self-production is the way living things operate" as the diverse parts of an organization-system interact and create meaning in their attunement to multiple-contexts (Kincheloe 2007, p. 896). "The Web is an autopoietic organism that constructs itself in a hypertextual mode of operation" (p. 897).

Hermeneutic Circle—In the hermeneutic circle the relationships between parts "self-construct" previously unimagined meanings. So we examine a text in the context of the times, deepening our understanding of it. We bring a modern perspective to something forged in another time and space and thus create a new meaning born of this fusion of old and new. Thus, for students of ontology, the thing itself (often a text) does not generate the meaning; instead it is a co-creative emergence through "its relationships to an infinite number of other things" (Kincheloe 2007, p. 896).

FACETS OF STORYTELLING

Storytelling is constituted by three interactive facets: (1) grand narratives of the past, (2) webs of living stories unfolding in the present, and (3) antenarrative trajectories that relate grand narratives to living stories webs in quite different ways to prospect the future. For background, please see

Ontological Storytelling? What is Living Story? and *What is Antenarrative?* studyguides.

A current *storytelling* definition found in Boje, Jørgensen and Strand (2013, p. 3) is:

> Storytelling, here, is defined more broadly, as something agential such as the iterative intra-active-material-storytelling domains of "living stories" and "antenarratives" in the theatre of action, which go beyond the classical narrative focus on structuralist and representationalist elements and retrospection.
>
> (Boje, 2001, 2008a)

In other words storytelling is the way that antenarratives inter-connect retrospective-narratives with living stories in the theatre of action. Narratives often focus on epistemic (knowing), living stories (on Being-In-The-World) and the antenarrative connect them together quite differently. Organizations undergo transformations.

Fractal storytelling consists of a combination of irregular and regularizing self-similar storytelling behaviors. Self-similar fractal narratives are repeated across scales (micro to macro) of "storytelling organizations" (Boje, 1995, 2008a). Irregular fractal stories do not exhibit the fractal-self-sameness imputed to grand narrative iterations. A random process can lead to non-self-similar fractal storytelling.

Natural fractals have limit points, above and below which, the self-similar scalability stops after a few cross scale associations. Social norms of organizations change from one generation to the next, thereby creating transformations of the fractal structures of organizing. The generating norms and rules produce combinations of irregular and regular fractal sets. An everyday example is the formation of departments and colleges in universities, from one generation of faculty, students, and administrators—to the next. A fractal branching process occurs in which colleges are added, colleges split into two or more colleges, departments proliferate, often combining and splitting departments. Unlike a branching tree fractal, there are interdisciplinary relationships that form across departments (joint research, interdisciplinary minors and majors, joint appointments, etc.).

As the scale of a grand narrative becomes grander, more general, the precision of the evenness decreases, yet the coherence (simplicity) of it increases. More living story-ness is taken-for-granted, assumed, assimilated, and a reductionism of facticity occurs in the grand narrating. Living story webs, on the other hand, generate differences, localities, and come into contradiction with grand narrative schemata. The scaling of event-ness is different in grand narratives and living story webs. Grand narratives scale on very few events, and few characters, generating the illusion that other events and characters are marginal to organizing processes and outcomes. Living story webs, tend toward particularities within their vicinity of the web, and toward stereotyping what is non-local. Both go through iterative function-processes, we call antenarrating. The combination of the three (grand narratives, living story webs, and antenarrating processes) forms storytelling organization.

Fractal storytelling methodology can explore the complex dynamic process of systemicities, as events are selected into narratives, and the grand events are differentiated into infinitesimally smaller event-ness, as the iterations proceed. Using different fractal observation apparatuses or measurement devices produces different understandings. Using a yardstick to measure a Koch Curve will yield different results than a millimeter-stick.

Fractal storytelling expresses the fractal patterns of practical organization phenomena, including turbulence, social networking, emergence, growth, market niches, and ecosystem relations. Unlike a state grand narrative, a living story web behaves with relationality, flows, folds, and the intra-activities of sociomateriality (interface of the social with the material). In the alternative scaling of storytelling event-ness, strange attractor dynamics produce such antenarrative patterns as swirls that produce spirals of symmetry and asymmetry. Whereas organizations are rich in self-similar fractal sets, they are also rich in irregular fractals, and in non-fractal random processes.

Ken Baskin has written extensively on the subject of complexity in organizations, including some works in storytelling. (See for example: Baskin 1995, 2003, 2005, 2007b, 2008; and Boje and Baskin 2010b). For him, a social constructionist perspective applies. He considers stories to be the shapers of culture, noting the power of a world story to echo throughout entire periods of history (Baskin and Bondarenko, 2014). Yet he hesitates to consider stories as "fractal."

According to Ken Baskin,

> There are certain basic questions that we have to ask, "How did we get here? What's our purpose? How should we behave towards each other? How should we govern each other?" and in China it's that dyadic relationship between two people one of whom has power and one of whom is to be protected. Each culture has that kind of thing fixed in the world story and very often it will be reflected through out.
>
> —Ken Baskin (interview)

For Baskin, the important point is not the idea of rules that underpin self-similarity, but what it takes to change the overarching story that shapes perception. At an individual level that amounts to admitting that our perceptions might be wrong. For him,

> [what] creates the self similarity is the organization's story . . . Organizational culture is a network of stories and if the story is that, if the story that people hear is, if I make a suggestion to my boss that he hasn't

> thought of he's just going to say no, then you get that behavior, it's not that there's a rule that says you can't do it . . .
>
> —Ken Baskin (interview)

For example, racism is promoted within a social group by shared stories about the perceived negative aspects of other races. For someone who accepts these stories to experience the opposite in an encounter with another race can be a powerful and transformational thing. He suggests that considering rules as drivers of behaviors obscures the way that organizational culture is embedded in stories. In the absence of instinctive knowing, the way a bird instinctively knows how to build a nest, stories tell us what to do and how to behave.

FRACTAL STORY

A fractal story is defined here as a web of fluid "living story" interrelationships between urban-chaos and fractal-cyber-order that is centrifugal, veering away from order, toward anarchism, discontinuity, and the erratic, violent urbanism. Examples include William Gibson's *Neuromancer* (1995) and Jeff Noon's *Vurt* (1993). Both create what Samuel R. Delany (1987) calls paraspaces that by definition are not in a linear or hierarchical relation to so-called real spaces. A paraspatial fractal story puts emphasis on enduring, observing, learning, surviving, and changing in order to become in new ways of Being-In-The-World. Noon's ontologies make it impossible to decide if the hallucination, cybernetic simulacra, or the Manchester socio-economic anarchy is "authentic." Noon weaves together multiple ontological realms, in a fractal story paraspatial journey between colliding worlds.

Fractal story meshworks demand a different way of sensemaking, the paraspace. An example: Jeff Noon's fractal story meshwork of cyberpunk and postmodern surreal fictions constitutes a pattern Boje (2008, 2011, 2014) calls the "spiral-antenarrative, and it is always on the verge of becoming rhizomatic. There is often an ensemble of characters, rather than a central hero or heroine."

Unlike a linear fractal or even a repetitive cyclic-antenarrative, the spiral-antenarrative. Noon's characters feed on chaos, breaching the progress narrative, deconstructing all visions of harmony, returning our attention to the chaotic universe. Noon's fractal story combines process philosophy, the remix, and cyberpunk into a spiraling-fractal series that creates a chamber of echoes for everyday words in new layers of meaning, results in a postmodern critique of late modern capitalism's flexible capitalism and its "fluid society" (Wenaus 2011). Flexible global capitalism makes us feel very strange. The new flexible capitalism, its loose network structure (Sennett 1998) that makes it difficult to have long-term ecosystem. *Vurt* shifts from self-sameness fractals toward unpredictability as Deleuzian rhizomatic feedback loops make irregular and monstrous fractal patterns inevitable. Addicted characters (Scribble, Beetle, Mandy, Bridget . . .) put hallucinogenic Vurt-feathers into their mouths to escape dystopian Manchester UK. Desdemona has fallen into a Vurt hole, and by the Hobart Exchange Rule, has been exchanged for the Thing-from-Outer-Space (a Vurt being). The ensemble of characters are on a quest to rescue Scribble's sister, Desdemona from a Vurt realm. The group of Vurt characters, interact with the Game Cte who gives clues, hints, tips, and evasions. The ensemble is pursued by both the Vurt and by Manchester cyber- and flesh-and-blood-police. Scribble decides to offer himself in exchange for his sister, Desdemona. This returns the rhizomatic fractal story web to linear monomythic fractal narrative, akin to Orpheus and Eurdice myth.

Noon belongs to the tradition of the labyrinthine quest story, with characters caught up in ever-tightening complex feedback loops of systemicity-relationalities between contemporary and postmodern science fiction, cyberpunk, and New Wave discourses. Systemicity is defined as unfinished, unfinalized, and emergent perspective opposed to the idea that here is anything "whole" systems or consensus in the socioeconomic realm. The fractal story is an ontology of angst, an anti-progress futurity where a web of living stories form spiral- and rhizomatic-antenarrative patterns.

The Vurt-feather is polysemous, an hallucinogenic delicacy, a plume for fruiting, and a plume of smoke that has wild eddies, fissions, velocities, and spirals that interconnect Manchester, Vurts, mat-VUrts, and meta-meta-Vurts, and so on ad infinitum creating an ontologic worlds that shifts and morphs between linear-, cyclic-, spiral- and rhizomatic-antenarratives. In this way fractal narratives dance and vibe with quantum fractal story webs, as postmodern spaces of fission destabilize and even gobble up modern spaces of self-same grand narratives of fractal geometry universal-harmony and-symmetry.

We believe that storytelling is where complexity manifests itself in human organizations (Baskin 2005; Boje 2008, 2010; Boje and Baskin 2010d; Henderson 2014; Wakefield 2012). Even in the most tightly controlled business environment, there exists a living story web with emergence and dissipation of fractal rumors, relationships, intrigues, and bonds. This is the social side of sociotechnical systems theory, where human will meets assigned tasks and duties and aggregately formed opinions constitute cultures of cooperation, resistance, and if we are lucky—co-creation. When organizations focus solely on the technical part of the equation, they fail to mobilize the collective will of those whose cooperation is necessary to get the job done.

We will illustrate using an example of sociomaterial unfolding of fractal organizing processes that affect society at all levels of analysis.

> David's perspective: I figured out what a fractal story is. I am in the "academic fractal." Its a multifractal, composed of "publish or perish" fractal, the "AQ" fractal, the "outcomes assessment" fractal, the "journal ranking" fractals, and "annual review." My publishing-muscled

fingers keep stroking the keys, pressing one after the other, producing lines of Facebook text, pretending, this is leisure. It's not. I noticed the "academic" multifractal when I was reading the Vurt. My annual review just done, and several pieces in the pipeline. Got one top-tier hit, so my AQ is good for another five year hitch. I tell myself "It's under control." Then I ask, "whose control?" Each key stroke is med-like. It takes more publishing hits to get the high of the first one. My new dean thinks he is in control! He demands six hits each five year (rolling mean) or I get to teach an additional course. And one of these each three years must be top tier. Yes, I am deep into the academic fractality. I remember a time, long long ago, when a one hit every other year, was "good enough." Now there is nothing good enough! There is no end to it. I fool myself into thinking, retirement is near, and that will end it. Not really. I will fall into the fractal of publishing after retirement, thinking I have all this time, away form committees, just to write. Put down the laptop, I hear a voice calling from the distance. Can I? I won't perish?

Fractals are not singular, or isolated. Fractals occur in meshworks. The meshwork can be an assemblage, an ensemble of lateral relations, or just a hierarchy, with a central character. From Jeff Noon's (1993) *Vurt*, we get insight into being addicted to fractals:

> An academic multi fractal is flickering in my eyes. I can no longer differentiate between the academic dream and the "real" academy of "publish or perish." The dream keeps beckoning, and the "real" keeps bending to it.
>
> The deans own the "publish or perish" fractal. It's a fractal-worm, much like Noon's Tapewormer. It keeps replaying your latest pubs, as you make bets on getting, yet another top-tier "hit." Fractals are owned. This one is owned by the administrative order. And we, the players, are addicted, addicted to publishing, and to playing the game.
>
> I lost my son to a fractal. His name is Raymond, and he's schizophrenic. Being Shizo by itself, is not so bad. But he is addicted to a Meds-cocktail, administered by the medical establishment, controlled by the health care industry, fed by the Pharmaceutical corporate giants. The case worker makes sure he stays on his meds. He will never be free of the Meds fractal. The Shizo-fractal does strange things to space and time. In the Shizo-meds fractal, there are particular spaces. You go to the Psychiatrists to get the meds prescription, then to Walgreens or Wal-Mart to get the capsules. The State pays for them, Medicare (or is it Medicaid), I never remember.
>
> Ray should be having the "good life," not falling into med-addiction, being thrown about the health care system. There was a time, long long ago, about 20 years, to be exact, when he was not on meds. There was this drive by shooting in the park, a few blocks from home. He was

there taking Kung Fu lessons. He was being picked on by the other kids. It was before his growth spurt. Now he is 6'3", and muscled, a Kung Fu Black Belt. But, back then, he was the smallest kid, and the gangs used to jump him, knock him to the ground, take his new bicycle or his replacement skateboard, or some cash. But in the park on this fateful day, there was a drive by, and his teacher was shot dead. And Ray saw him there bleeding out.

He goes to Starlight, a place for groups of Shizo-meds to congregate. They have become his closest friends, and his counselor, lets him go to Manhattan, whenever he gets, yet another tattoo. Ray goes to and from this place, and all other places, by taking public transportation. He wears his "buds" and tries not too look anyone in the eye. He wears a hoodie, and this helps him not draw too much attention. Now and again, he spies a teenager, and Tubewormer fractal invites him for a ride. It takes him back in time, to that park, to those teens who used to beat on him. He says, "what are you looking at." "Beware!" "I know my Kung Fu." Proudly and defiantly, he proclaims, "I know Snake style." It is only a style that the black belts know with any proficiency. And he is very proficient, in fact, lethal. If all are lucky, he "jerks out" of the Snake subfractal just in time. Every few times this happens, on the train, or the bus, Ray is called out by a gang leader, and sometimes, by the whole gang. It's typical behavior on Staten Island, on public transportation in the urban places.

Fractals have a strange time. In the Tubewormer fractal, you merge the past-nows, with this "now" that is "here." It is very selective merging of past times and a current time, mediated by the fractal you are within. The Snake is one of several reptile characters, at least a dozen, and Ray cares deeply for each of them. We, the family members, have learned, that trying to persuade him otherwise, only makes him hang on to his virtual-comrades more tightly.

Fractals are not just a mathematical formulae, or patterns of repeating visual scales. Rather, the storytelling fractals are habits, routines, behavioral scripts, ways of attuning to Being-in-the-world, all strung together in antenarrative lines of connection to horizons of significance.

My Academic-fractal interacts, here and now, with his Shizo-meds-fractals, stretching along our horizons of significance. We are entwined, more than entangled, we are in resonance with each other and those horizons we attune with. Ray's eyes show the glint form the meds, but in the shadows, in-between, are the shades of blue, a glimmer of that young boy before the terrorism of living in Las Angeles, his encounters with the drive-by shooter, and the thugs of the neighborhood. Now Ray is just reduced to meat and flesh by the pharmaceutical corporations, the health care workers of the medical system. Who am I to cast a finger of blame? I am addicted to "publish or perish," run all around by the Administrative Order of the Academy, attached to horizons of insignificance. Look into my eyes and you can see the fractal patterns, perfect spirals, entrained. Ray and I get out of touch with planet Earth, and the horizons of insignificance become more pronounced. All our senses are clogged with addictive-shit. I can still hear Ray calling me, from the park, from the drive-by shooting. I was faintly present, still rehearsing the lines of my next publishing hit, about to send in the fifth revision to *Academy of Management Journal*, on the *Tamara-land* hit (Boje, 1995).

We each regenerate in-between hits. At the time of the drive-by, I was drinking alcohol, not that evening, but the other ones, for sure. Now I have been sober 20 some years, but still am embedded in addictive fractals, pattens of insignificance, not attuned to Being-in-the-world, to the primordial patterns.

(Adapted from Boje, 2015)

This story demonstrates the recurrence of fractal organizing processes as they unfold in a multigenerational context. The sociomaterial unfolding of scalable, self-similar patterns is nowhere so apparent as in the cycles of addiction and trauma that often afflict multiple generations, hindering individuals, families, communities, and society. These stories combine with others to generate a diffracted societal organizing process that reflects the diffraction not only of patterns of addiction but associated patterns of judgment, as well as kindness and healing.

FRACTAL NARRATIVES

We contrast this with the notion of fractal narratives, as described by Duarte (2014). We assert that fractal narrative and factual story are not the same sort of fractality. They are two different kinds of fractals that are in a strange antenarrative relationship. How do you blend all the different fractals together? Here, we will theorize that different sorts of fractals form antenarrative relationships in sociomateriality contexts. The linear- and cyclic- interweave with the cyclic- and rhizomatic-antenarrative processes.

Fractal Narrative—A fractal narrative is linear or cyclical, with a central monologic or monomythic structure, a heroic character, in a complex plots within plots, patterns within patterns—that repeats and repeats, but does so within a centralizing framework. *Dune* is an example of the centralizing centripetal fractal narrative, a monomythic saga. There are many such mono mythic frameworks in film: *Start Wars, Star Trek, Matrix,* and *Blade Runner,* to name a few.

In *Fractal Narrative and Entrepreneurship*, German Duarte (2014) argues that since Mandelbrot's fractal geometry, the fractal narrative has become popular in film and novels, and inspired and is currently transforming the social sciences. The implication for entrepreneurial narrative studies, is that fractal characteristics are creeping with contagion into the theories, methods, and practices. This means that the traditional entrepreneurial narratives, with linear sequence of beginning, middle and end, are changing as fractalization of narrative becomes stronger (Duarte 2014). The focus shifts to a "fractal narrative space" that is "free from linearity" as the "narrative loses its strict linear way" and the "narrative act" shifts "narrative space" and the "method of navigation" is no longer in the classic monologic plot (p. 270). Rather the participants in the entrepreneurial narrative, can modify the narrative structure, the space and time scales, and navigate through many different trajectories. The fractalization of the entrepreneurial narrative shifts the monomythic narrative structure from a single Horatio Alger entrepreneur to the fractal process of entrepreneurship, itself, distributed in fractal spaces, in types that change, in narrative places and times, that are more like a hypertext or hypertextual-network of agents, not following rule of hierarchy, rather than a single narrative ordering one agent in a monologic narrative (Bakhtin 1981). Hence, the fractal narrative is changing the spacetime fabric of the entrepreneurial grand narrative (Lyotaard) into a hyperdialogical process, involving multifractals and multiple agents. "Consequently, a non linear text develops a different kind of dynamic" where the number of agents, their intra-activity dynamics, creates a Deleuzian rhizomatic process that does not conform to Aristotelean plot beginning-middle-end construction of linearity, wholeness, and coherence (Duarte 2014, pp. 274–276). The advantage of this "hypertextal story space" (p. 276) is that it affords infinite set of possible network linkages, that are variable, shifting the forces of entrepreneurial processes to multidimensional becoming (emergence). For example Brown University is developing a fractal narrative that recalls the *Sierpinski Carpet*, called "Storyspace" in which the reader can add rooms, change the narrative structure, delete former structures, according to various paths and menus (p. 277). In addition, this kind of entrepreneurial Storyspace means that participants can play with the "materiality" and "fractality" of the narrative space, in hypertextuality that Roland Barthes (1970) theorized (p. 279). Further as Genette (1982) notes in the hypertext, the "*transtextualities*" are between very different genres: texts, conceptual relations, citations, mimetic, and so on (pp. 279–280). The episteme of postmodern narrative comes into relation with an ontological short in the construction, navigation, and iterative scalability of narrative. New entrepreneurial narrative hyperspaces of navigating multi-plot become possible as digital technology remediates the field of entrepreneurship. Wikia, for example, is describable as a "fractal story" an articulation of a new way of organizing and navigating narrative spaces, linking processes that can be called a "fractalization of the narrative space" (p. 283).

Bygrave (1993, 2007) argues that theory building in the entrepreneurship paradigm can apply nonlinear mathematics to get at the chaos and complexity of the entrepreneurial process. This means a shift in theory (concepts and definitions) from the character-traits and functions of the entrepreneur to the 'entrepreneurial process.' Bygrave and Hofer (1991) suggest that the Heisenberg uncertainty principle imposes limits on observing "mega-entrepreneurial events of the kind that create new industries" (p. 20). The idea is to observe entrepreneurship at different scales called fractal. Processes may be studied as fractal structures, where the entrepreneurial process of self-similarity of small parts forms a scalability of dynamic enterprise, by iterative processing, for example in "portfolio entrepreneurship" of "multiple local subsidiaries" and in transgenerational entrepreneurship (Plate, Schiede, and von Schlippe, 2010, p. 117). Bodunkova and Chernaya (2012) examine embedding entrepreneurial culture in the university by implementing "fractal organization structure" of self-similar scalability, trust, and reciprocity networks. (p. 74). They apply Warnecke's (1993) *fractal factory theory* by focusing on how self-similiar units, are integral to the fractal itself, creating cooperative structures, joint efforts. The fractal company theory (Shin 2002, Ahmed and Yasin 2010, Kuehnle 2002). A growing number of strategic entrepreneurship theories are addressing fractional differentiations, how the idea of a fractal captures the repeating, self-similar, and simple rules repeating, at ever-finer scales of analysis—creates emergent complexity patterns that are nonlinear. This is constituting a "fractal narrative" as Mandelbrot's (1983) fractal geometry makes its way into films, novels, and now into the social science of entrepreneurship. Fractal architecture, the "cradle-to-cradle fractal triad (or fractal triangle) (McDonough and Braungart 2002) inspired the design of eco-effective products" (Schindehutte and Morris 2009, p. 264). "The fractal triangle reveals the subtle relation between pattern creation and pattern identification, and shows how, at any level, each action impacts . . . the opportunity space" of entrepreneurship (Schindehutte and Morris 2009, p. 265). The challenge is to trace emergent fractal patterns and structures in the flux and flow of the entrepreneurial process in space–time–mattering contexts. Carayannis and Campbell (2009, 2012) apply Etzkowitz and Leydesdorff (2000). Triple Helix theory of university–industry–government, in a fractal approach to entrepreneurship at a scale of analysis beyond the individual entrepreneur, and beyond the single entrepreneur organization, to an inter-organization network of communication. Modes of coevolution, cospecialization, and cooptation integrate media-based and culture-based ecosystem entrepreneurship that emphasizes natural environments at local, national, and global scales.

Exercise:

Identify five stories from your organization.
What kinds of underlying simple rules are apparent in these stories?
Do they conflict or reinforce each other?
Consider each of the stories from multiple perspectives (self, others, ecosystem). Does that change the rules you perceive?
What is the sociomateriality perspective on the situation?
For each of the stories you just explored, draw pictures on the blank Venn diagram in Figure 4.5, depicting the social and material aspects of the situation and how they come together to form fractal operating processes through storytelling.

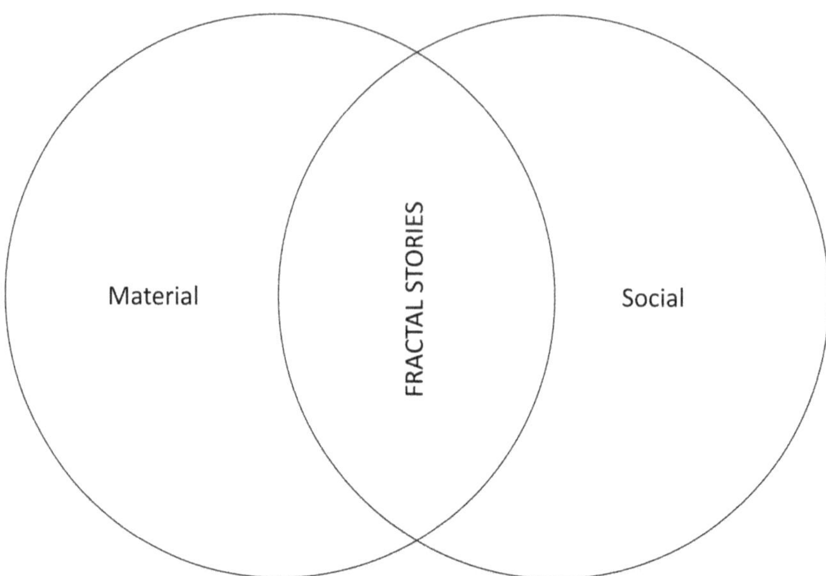

Figure 4.5 Fractal Stories Worksheet
Source: By Tonya L. Henderson. (Used by permission)

STORYTELLING AND TRANSFORMATIONS: GENERAL OVERVIEW

Storytelling theory and practice are grounded in poly-vocal discourse surrounding organizational dysfunction. Three kinds of stories are apparent in organizational discourse: rigid linear narrative, more dynamic living story webs, and future-focused antenarratives (Boje 2011b). Luhman and Boje (2001) tie narrative storytelling to complexity through laboratory manager and worker perspectives. Baskin and Boje (2005) consider storytelling an emergent phenomenon that "drives the human equivalent of attractors" (p. vi.). Such attractors are apparent in Shirky's (2008) descriptions of the emergence and dissipation of virtual organizations. For Boje and Baskin (2010a), storytelling is the substance in which self-organizing criticality emerges.

Third order cybernetic thought brings polyvocalism, as actors experience events differently (Baskin and Boje 2005, Krizanc and Boje 2006, Luhman and Boje, 2001). Boje (2008) ties complexity to control narratives, defining the third cybernetic turn (Boje 2008, 2011b, 2011d, 2011e). Bakhtinian dialogism supports third-order cybernetic polyphonic dialogue (Boje and Arkoubi 2005). Letiche (2000) Tamaraizes[3] the organization through phenomenal complexity theory. Storytelling is "the preferred sense making currency of organizational participants who live, work, and consume in a world of action" and is central to third order cybernetics (Boje 2011b, p. 13). "The most current of such transformations occurs in storytelling and generally in artistic trans positing of individual experiences" (Hannah Arendt 1958, 50). Consultants and change agents use storytelling to effect transformations.

EMBODIED RESTORYING PROCESS (ERP)

Embodied Restorying Process (ERP) is a matter of balancing the nested–fractal–attunements of past events with anticipated future ones. It is an embodied process of nested rhythms.

According to Vrobel (2011, p. 184), "Henri Lefebvre, the inventor of 'rhythmanalysis', recognized the coexistence of our social and biological rhythms and stressed that it is the human body which is the point of contact between those rhythms."

> Furthermore, this human body is the site and place of interaction between the biological, the physiological (nature) and the social (often called the cultural), where each of these levels, each of these dimensions, has its own specificity, therefore, its space-time: its rhythm. Whence the inevitable shocks (stresses), disruptions and disturbances in this ensemble whose stability is absolutely never guaranteed.
>
> (Lefebvre 2004, p. 81)

It is not in a linear sequence of past→present→future. Rather the future is arriving, and we are making that future Present, by the antenarrative bets we are placing. ERP is recontextualizing the events nested in the past, and events anticipated in a "moment of vision" of a potentiality-for-Being-a-whole-Self in the future (Heidegger, 1962). Future and past are reattuned into the Present, the Now of our Being-in-the-world. By acts of anticipatory resoluteness we can make choices of which potential futures we elect to act in the Present to bring into Being in spacetimemattering. Instead of the temporal perspective being in the past, or in the Now, ERP can mean a futural move away from stuck patterns of past and present. Becoming an authentic Self is an acquired skill.

In linear-thinking time is past→Present→future. In an existential ontology of time, temporality is cyclical, not linear. The Future→past→Present has the Future arriving "ahead-of-itself" in our BETS made on a possibility that is out of a multiplicity of possible futures. Being-futural means making sound "bets" based on acts of *deliberation, anticipation,* and *resolve.* To make "bets" more actualizing, ask the family about the contexts of involvement that brings about their potentiality-for-Being a whole-Authentic-Self.

For Heidegger, we get enslaved by the "they" that comes from socialization, education, military, corporations, advertising, and so on. In storytelling, the grand narratives of institutions and culture prescribe the "they" expectations to which we are expected to adapt, to enact as role and identity. In ERP we can challenge the received "they-self" by two radical temporal moves.

First, we can reclaim Little Wow Moments (LWMs) of exception to the grand narratives "they-self" prescriptions. This means instead of continuing to be enslaved by grand narrative roles and identities, we are able to move in-between the narrative sequence of events, and find those LWMs left out of the grand narrative.

Second, we can focus on the future, on our ownmost potentiality-for-Being, choosing a path among the multitude of future paths, then taking actions to make that path come into Being. This is fractal because we are not accepting the traditional clock time, or the calendar time as the *only* way time of events is happening. In the nested fractals, there are simultaneous, nonlinear, and future times arriving that can be attuned to our own actions, anticipations, and resolve.

GREAT STORYTELLERS?

According to Walter Benjamin (1936, p. 83),

> All great storytellers have in common the freedom with which they move up and down the rungs of their experience as on a ladder. A ladder extending downward to the interior of the earth and disappearing into the clouds is the image for a collective experience to which even the deepest shock of every individual experience, death, constitutes no impediment or barrier.

Restorying

One of our seminars includes methodologies for story research (deconstruction, theme analysis, grand narrative, plot analysis, etc.) and story intervention approaches such as *restorying* defined as collecting the dominant (oppressive) stories of the organization that set up its posture and power, and then intervening to constitute a new story that has liberatory potential (White & Epston, 1990). Here is how Mike Bonifer and David are developing the restorying intervention:

1. *Characterize* the dominant narrative as the problem, not the people as problem. Narrative empties out living stories, in-order-to focus on linear and cyclic-antenarrative recurrence.
2. *Externalize* the problem, viewed as separate character from any individual, as an external entity? Mr. Spiral is a strange character in

organizations, because we cannot see, hear, touch, taste, or smell spirals, and yet we can use tools and instruments to sense their shape and path-directions.

3. *Symphatize* what benefits does the organization derive from the problem? The benefits of spirals that cannot be accessed by sensemaking is that retrospective narrative is useless.
4. *Revise* disadvantages of the problem, benefits foregone, reasons to change. The negative consequences are that one relies on instruments and tools to observe a spiral, even though direct sensemaking cannot see, hear, touch, taste, or smell one.
5. *Strategize*: Find a "unique outcome" from the past, even a potential, which allowed the organization to defeat the problem in the past; those little wow moments, concealed by the dominant narrative. One little wow moment, for me, David, is that I have tactile sensing of spiral energy flows. Another is that I can see the instrument measuring spiraling energy currents. I have a storytelling awareness of spiraling even though my own five senses are not always picking up cues.
6. *Rehistoricize*: Make the "unique outcome" the rule (instead of the exception) in a "new" living story of freedom from the dominant-problem-narrative. There are times when I have spiral-awareness of updraft and downdraft environmental flows that cause the spiral to move or at least shudder.
7. *Publicize:* Enlist support for the new living story. Use letters, ceremony, etc. with friends to reinforce "new" living story web. What is the evidence of support and interest in the new Q-spiral-antenarrative and environmental-draft? I find some evidence in Heidegger (1971, p. 130) for drafts: "orbit of the whole draft" turns and "parting against the pure draft" (p. 125). This gets at what I call "inner ♥-space" of our Being-In-The-World ontological-existence, which in Heidegger (p. 130) is "the true interior of the heart's space." I find some evidence in Merleau-Ponty (1962, p. 244) for the "top and bottom, right and left, near and far" that is not from sensemaking by the five senses. I find some evidence from Deleuze (1994, p. 21) who says, "Spirals whose principle is a variable curve and the trajectory of which has dissymmetrical aspects as though it had a right and a left."

There are two kinds of dominant narratives in management practice: What David calls the "intellectualist" and the "empirical" narratives, after Merleau-Ponty (1962). Merleau-Ponty does not develop a narrative perspective. David has integrated some Heidegger (1962) framing of epistemic–ontic–ontological with it, but the classifications have differences. These are in antenarrative transformative relationship to the ontological "living story" (Boje, 2001, 2011b). An antenarrative is about what is "before" and the "bet of transformation" between our dominant narratives and living story ontology. For Merleau-Ponty and Heidegger, we call living story ontology consists of primordial, antecedes the subject-object duality of intellectualist/epistemic and empiricist/ontic.

We will be looking a materiality-narratives, and try to develop an epistemic-ontological understanding that Strand (2011, 2012) calls "material storytelling" something deeply rooted in Barad–Bohr–Boje–Bergson.

Equally popular are various cyclical-antenarratives transforming the relationship between intellectualist and empiricist narratives. Examples include product life cycle, organizational life cycle, market life cycle, leadership strategy cycle, etc. Each is a stage-by-stage sequence, and the antenarrative transformative connection is how the past is expected to recur in these exact same stages into the present and the future. The organizational life cycle for example begins with concepts like birth, then goes to growth, maturation, decline, revitalization, and back to (re)birth. The problem with

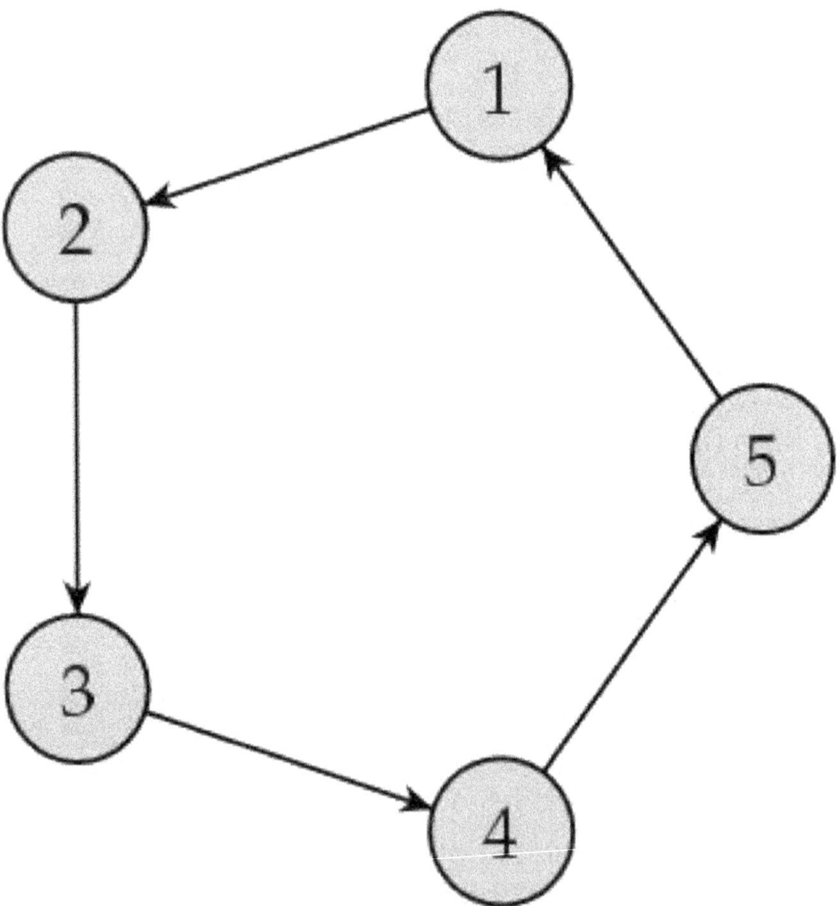

Figure 4.6 Cyclic-Antenarrative, Common in Management Practice
Source: By David Boje. Used by permission

cyclic-antenarratives that would bridge the intellectualist and empiricist narratives is that the subject-object split is not able to get beyond its duality to look at pre-subjective, and pro-objective living story ontology. They merely bridge the two dominant narratives (intellectualist and empiricist).

Two other antenarratives are increasingly popular in management practice, because the assumed cyclical rarely works out in management practice: cycles keep accumulating differences, becoming spirals, and the linear paths, keep accumulating multiplicities until they are more accurately recognized as rhizome-antenarrative.

Minahen's (1992) book provides the best definitions of spiral and vortex. The vortex is turbulence, and the spiral is more stable, and there is movement in between them. He defines spiral as "a continuous curve traced by a point moving round a fixed point in the same plane while steadily increasing (or diminishing its distance from this" (p. 149). There is an Archimedean spiral, such as a coil of rope, or whorl of a tomato plant, or threads on a bolt, where the distance interval between one whorl and the next is the same. There is a more logarithmic spiral where whorl to whorl differences accumulate (amplifying or contracting). Finally there are more irregular spirals, such as spiral galaxies (barred spirals with trailing arms). There are two-dimensional (flat) spirals, and three-dimensional spiral, such as the helix of increasing or decreasing circular movement between center and circumference (p. 156). The vortex is all about turbulence, defined "by one source as 'randomly distributed vorticity'" (p. 157). I am exploring the double vortices, with an upper centrifugal ascent and a lower centripetal descent, connecting this to Heidegger's drafts (see *Quantum Storytelling* film).

Rhizome comes from Deleuze and Guattari (1987) and is an interplay between two kinds of space (smooth and striated), and the lines of flight and transformation trajectories between them in practices of territorialization, deterritorialization, and reterritorialization (pp. 505–506). In particular, the spiral-antenarrative that bridges intellectual narrative and living story ontology, and the rhizomatic-antenarrative that bridges the empiricist narrative and living story ontology.

Exercise:

Oftentimes, the sinister side of the dominant narrative is hidden from public view, yet surfaces in the form of micro inequities (Haslett & Lippmann 1997). A micro inequity can be as subtle as a look, a gesture, or a seemingly innocuous word choice, even a tone of voice. Once example from our own lived experience came when Tonya was stationed overseas and often had lunch with a senior enlisted man from her unit. She is Caucasian, and her colleague was African American. They would eat at a military club on the base and he shared insights about the experience of being an African American man in a world where racism often takes the form of micro-inequities. One day he pointed out a specific occurrence that became a Little Wow Moment. When it was time to pay for lunch, he said "Watch what happens when we get our change. The clerk will touch your hand, but will not touch mine." They paid and that was exactly what happened. We believe this instance offers an excellent example of a micro inequity.

Another example is found on campus. Sometimes the constant offering of discounts and front-of-the-line privileges to military members can result in resentment from other students. Whereas few would argue that military members have sacrificed much and deserve our respect, some would argue that we have become a warrior culture, in which military personnel constitute a privileged class.

- How does granting a privilege to military members as a sign of gratitude relate to the concept of micro inequities?
- What simple rules might lie underneath the cashier's behavior? How about our perceptions of it?
- Consider racism and associated behaviors in terms of antenarrative. Which of the four types do you think applies? Why?
- What could be done to shift these patterns?

Prior to embarking on a path of restorying, it is important to gain a sense of awareness that generates a felt need for change. In yoga philosophy, it is said that avidya, ignorance of the world and of one's own true nature, is the primary source of human suffering. Awareness of one's ignorance is said to lead to the desire for education and embarking on a spiritual path. One cannot successfully engage in restorying while still operating in the nihilistic grasp of avidya. There must be an awakening that lifts the fog of distorted personal perceptions so that the person becomes receptive to growth and change. This situation is not unlike the requirement that a process consulting client experience a felt need prior to successfully engaging in an intervention. There must be a willingness to change prior to beginning the restorying process.

NOTES

1. Our reference to the *Between*, as such, relates to Anete Strand's (2012) work with material storytelling, wherein she explains the co-creative nature of the relationship between materiality and human activity and the lively nature of the things that happen at the edges of Barad's (2007) agential cuts. The notion of agential cuts suggests that the boundaries of any system are based on the choice of the observer, whether that choice is arbitrary or purposive.
2. Note: In citing Heidegger, # refers to the section number, since various translations have differing page numbers (e.g., #150 and #157) in Heidegger, 1962 are sections 150 and 157; *see searchable text*).
3. The Tamara play is performed as a set of concurrent exchanges among actors in different rooms ion, with audience members selecting characters to follow and comparing perspectives. (See Krizanc, J., & Boje, D. (2006). Tamara Journal Interview with John Krizanc (Vol. 5, pp. 70–77): TAMARA: *Journal of Critical Postmodern Organization Science,* ibid.]

REFERENCES

Ahmed, N.S.; Yasin, N.M. (2010). Inspiring a fractal approach in distributed healthcare information systems: A review. International Journal of Physical Sciences, 5 (11): 1626–1640, March.

Arendt, H. (1958). The Human Condition. Chicago: University of Chicago Press.

Bakhtin, M.M. (1981). The dialogic imagination: Four essays by MM Bakhtin (M. Holquist, Ed.; C. Emerson & M. Holquist, Trans.). Austin: University of Texas Press.

Barthes, Roland. (1974), "S/Z. 1970." Trans. Richard Miller. New York: Hill and Wang.

Baskin, Ken. (1995). "DNA for corporations: Organizations learn to adapt or die." *The Futurist* 29 (1):68–68.

Baskin, Ken. (2003). "Complexity and the Dilemma of the Two Worlds: The Dynamics of Navigating in Fantasyland." Emergence 5 (1):36–53.

Baskin, Ken. (2005). "Complexity, stories and knowing." Emergence: Complexity & Organization 7 (2):32–40.

Baskin, Ken. (2007a). "Ever the twain shall meet." Chinese Management Studies 1 (1):57–68. doi: 10.1108/17506140710735463.

Baskin, Ken. (2007b). "A Review of Complexity in World Politics: Concepts and Methods of a New Paradigm." Emergence: Complexity and Organization 9 (3): 112–113.

Baskin, Ken. (2008). "Storied Spaces: The Human Equivalent of Complex Adaptive Systems." Emergence: Complexity and Organization 10 (2):1–12.

Baskin, Ken. (2011). "How Chinese thought can lead the transformation in management practice." Chinese Management Studies 5 (4):354–367.

Baskin, Ken, and Boje, David. (2005). "Guest editors' introduction." Emergence: Complexity & Organization 7 (3/4):1.

Benjamin, W. (1936). Walter Benjamin Illuminations. Hannah Arendt (ed.). The essay "The Storyteller: Reflections on the Works of Nikolai Leskov" (pp. 83–109) was first published in 1936 (Orien Und Okzident); 1968 is the English translation. NY.

Bennett, Jane. (2010). Vibrant matter: a political ecology of things. Durham: Duke University Press.

Bodunkova, A.G., & Chernaya, I.P. (2012). Fractal Organization as Innovative Model for Entrepreneurial University Development. *World Applied Sciences Journal, 18*, 74–82.

Boje, D. (1995). Stories of the storytelling organization: a postmodern analysis of Disney as "Tamara-land" *Academy of Management Journal, 38*(4), 997–1035.

Boje, D. (2001). *Narrative Methods for Organizational & Communication Research.* London: SAGE.

Boje, David. (2008). *Storytelling Organizations.* Los Angeles: SAGE.

Boje, David. (2011a). "Quantum physics implications of storytelling for socioeconomic research methods: Experiences in small business consulting research form New Mexico State University." International Meeting of Research Methods Division of the Academy of Management, Lyon, France, 15 June, 2011.

Boje, David. (2011b). "Introduction to agential narratives that shape the future of organizations." In *Storytelling and the future of organizations: an antenarrative handbook*, edited by D. Boje, 1–15. New York, NY: Routledge.

Boje, D. (2011c). Ontological Storytelling Inquiry Methodology—For Dummies Las Cruces, NM.

Boje, D. (2014d). What is Living Story Web? Retrieved 15 May 2015, from http://peaceaware.com/Boje/What%20is%20Living%20Story.htm

Boje, D. (2014e). Six Dumb Cultural Habits of Storytelling about War, Veterans, Schooling, and Sustainability. Paper presented at the 13th IACCM Annual Conference BETWEEN CULTURES AND PARADIGMS: Intercultural Competence & Managerial Intelligence and 6th CEMS/IACCM Doctoral Workshop, Warwick, UK. http://peaceaware.com/Warwick/

Boje, D.M., ed. (in press, 2015 expected). *Change Solutions to the Chaos of Standards and Norms Overwhelming Organizations: Four Wings of Tetranormalizing*. London/NY: Routledge.

Boje, D., and Arkoubi, K. (2005). "Third Cybernetic Revolution: Beyond Open to Dialogic System Theories." *Tamara: Journal of Critical Postmodern Organization Science* 4 (1/2):138.

Boje, D., & Baskin, K. (2010a). When storytelling dances with complexity- the search for Morin's keys. In D. Boje & K. Baskin (Eds.), *Dance to the music of story: Understanding human behavior through the integration of storytelling and complexity thinking* (pp. 21–37). Litchfield Park, AZ: Emergent Publications.

Boje, D., & Baskin, K. (Eds.). (2010b). *Dance to the music of story*. Litchfield Park, AZ: Emergent Publications.

Boje, D., DuRant, I., Coppedge, K., Chambers, T., & Marcillo-Gomez, M. (2012). Social materiality: A new direction in change management and action research. In D.M. Boje, B. Burnes, & J. Hassard (Eds.), *The Routledge Companion to Organizational Change* (pp. 580–597). New York, NY: Routledge.

Boje, D., & Henderson, T. (Eds.). (2014). *Being quantum: Ontological storytelling in the age of antenarrative*. Newcastle upon Tyne, United Kingdom: Cambridge Scholars Publishing.

Boje, D. M., Jørgensen, K. M., & Strand, A. M. C. (2013). "Towards a postcolonialist Storytelling Theory of management and organization,". Journal of Management Philosophy, 12(1), 43–65.

Boje, David, and Wakefield, T. (2011). "Storytelling in Systemicity and Emergence: A Third Order Cybernetic." In The Routledge Companion to Organizational Change, edited by David Boje, Bernard Burnes and John Hassard.

Bygrave, W.D., & Hofer, C.W. (1991). Theorizing about entrepreneurship. Entrepreneurship theory and Practice, 16(2), 13–22.

Bygrave, W.D. (1993). Theory building in the entrepreneurship paradigm. Journal of business venturing, 8(3), 255–280.

Bygrave, W.D. (2007). The entrepreneurship paradigm (I) revisited. Handbook of qualitative research methods in entrepreneurship, 17–48.

Carayannis, E.G., & Campbell, D.F. (2009). 'Mode 3' and 'Quadruple Helix': toward a 21st century fractal innovation ecosystem. International Journal of Technology Management, 46(3), 201–234.

Carayannis, E.G., & Campbell, D.F. (2012). Mode 3 knowledge production in quadruple helix innovation systems (pp. 1–63). Springer New York.

Chia, R., & Chia, R. K. G. (1996). *Organizational analysis as deconstructive practice* (Vol. 77). New York: Walter de Gruyter.

Coppedge, Krisha. (2014). "The Preponderance of Evidentuality Enlightenment in Home Ownership." In Being Quantum: Ontological Storytelling in the Age of Antenarrative, edited by Boje David M and Tonya L. Henderson, 191–216. Newcastle Upon Tyne, UK: Cambridge Scholars.

Delany, S. R. (2011). *Silent Interviews: On Language, Race, Sex, Science Fiction, and Some Comics—A Collection of Written Interviews*. Hanover, NH: Wesleyan University Press.

Deleuze, G., & Guattari, F. (1987). A Thousand Plateaus: Capitalism and Schizophrenia (B. Massumi, Trans.). Minneapolis, MN: University of Minnesota Press.

Deleuze, G. (1994). *Difference and Repetition* (P. Patton, Trans. English translation ed.). New York, NY: Columbia University Press.

Duarte, G.A. (2014). Fractal Narrative: About the Relationship Between Geometries and Technology and Its Impact on Narrative Spaces (Vol. 12). Deutsche Nationalbibliotehek.

Etzkowitz, H., & Leydesdorff, L. (2000). The dynamics of innovation: from National Systems and "Mode 2" to a Triple Helix of university–industry–government relations. *Research Policy*, *29*(2), 109–123.

Gibson, W. (1995). *Neuromancer.* New York: Ace. Originally published 1984.

Haslett, B. B., & Lipman, S. (1997). Micro inequities: Up close and personal. In Nijole Vaicaitis Benokraitis (Ed.), *Subtle Sexism: Current Practice and Prospects for Change* (pp. 34–53). Thousand Oaks, CA, US: Sage Publications.

Heidegger, M. (1962). Being and time. Translated by Ralph Mahnheim. 7th ed. New York: Harper & Rowe Publishers. Original edition, 1926.

Heidegger, M. (1971). *Poetry, Language, Thought,* translated by A. Hofstadter. New York: Harper and Row.

Henderson, Tonya L., and Daphne Deporres. (2014). "Patterns of Perception Among Yoga Practitioners." International Conference of Management Cases, Greater Noida, India.

Kincheloe, Joe L. (2007). Postformalism and Critical Ontology—Part 1: Difference, Indigenous Knowledge, and Cognition. In Joe L. Kincheloe and Raymond A. Horn (Eds.), *The Praeger Handbook of Education and Psychology,* Vol. 1. (pp. 884–899) Greenwood Publishing Group. PDF] from academia.edu.

Krizanc, J., & Boje, D. (2006). Tamara Journal Interview with John Krizanc TAMARA. *Journal of Critical Postmodern Organization Science, 5:* 70–77.

Kuehnle, H. I. (2002). Guidelines for future manufacturing–necessity of a change of organizational structures in industry and ways to the "fractal company" [Электронный ресурс]. *WEB Journal, 12.*

Lefebvre, Henri. (2004). *RhythmAnalysis: Space, Time and Everyday Life.* Translated by Stuart Elden and Gerald Moore with an Introduction by Stuart Elden. London, New York: Continuum Press. Originally in French 1992.

Letiche, H. (2000). Phenomenal complexity theory as informed by Bergson. *Journal of Organizational Change Management, 13*(6): 545–557.

Letiche, Hugo, and David Boje. (2001). "Phenomenal Complexity Theory and the Politics of Organization." *Emergence 3* (4):5–31.

Luhman, John T., and David M. Boje. (2001). "What Is Complexity Science? A Possible Answer from Narrative Research." *Emergence 3* (1):158–168.

Mandelbrot, Benoit. (1983). The fractal geometry of nature. New York, NY: W.H. Freeman and Company. Original edition, 1977. Reprint, 1983.

Maturana, H.R., & Varela, F.J. (1987). *The tree of knowledge: The biological roots of human understanding.* New Science Library/Shambhala Publications.

McDonough, W. & Braungart, M. (2002). Cradle to cradle: Remaking the way we make things. San Francisco: North Point Press.

Merleau-Ponty, M. (1962). *Phenomenology.* Humanities Press.

Minahen, C.D. (1992). Vortex/t: the poetics of turbulence. University Park: Pennsylvania State University Press.

Noon, Jeff. (1993). Vurt. Great Britain: Ringpull Press. fiction.

Plate, Markus; Schiede, Christian; von Schlippe, Arist. (2010). Portfolio entrepreneurship in the context of family owned businesses. Pp. 96–122 in Nordqvist, T. and Zellweger, T, Transgenerational Entrepreneurship: Exploring Growth and Performance in Family Firms Across Generations. Edward Elgar Publishing.

Schindehutte, M., & Morris, M.H. (2009). Advancing strategic entrepreneurship research: the role of complexity science in shifting the paradigm. *Entrepreneurship Theory and Practice, 33*(1:, 241–276.

Sennett, R. (1998). *The spaces of democracy* (pp. 40–1). University of Michigan, College of Architecture + Urban Planning.

Shirky, C. (2008). *Here comes everybody: The power of organizing without organizations*. New York: The Penguin Press.

Sihn, W. (2002) Fractal businesses in an E-buisness world. In the 8th Internaitonal Conference on Concurrent Enterprising. Rome, Italy, pp. 17–19. June http://www.manubuild.net/projects/08/CE002/reforms/Business%20to%20Business/05_Sihn.pdf

Strand, Anete Mikkala Camille. (2011). Presentation on 'material storytelling' to 20th anniversary meeting of S'CMoi, meeting in Philadelphia, April.

Strand, A.M.C. (2012). *The between: on dis/continuous intra-active becoming of/through an apparatus of material storytelling*. (Doctoral Program in Human Centered Communication and Informatics (HCCI)), Aalborg University, Aaulborg, Denmark.

Vrobel, S. (2011). *Fractal Time: Why a Watched Kettle Never Boils*. New Jersey, London: World Scientific Publishing Company.

Wakefield, Tonya L. Henderson. (2012). "An ontology of storytelling systemicity: Management, fractals and the Waldo Canyon fire." Doctorate of Management Doctoral dissertation, Management, Colorado Technical University.

Warneke, H.J. (1993). The Fractal Company—production in the network. NY: Springer-Verlag.

Wenaus, A. (2011). Fractal narrative, paraspace, and strange loops: The paradox of escape in Jeff Noon's Vurt. *Science Fiction Studies*, *38*(1): 155–174.

White, M., & Epston, D. (1990). *Narrative means to therapeutic ends*. WW Norton & Company.

Part II

Exploring Fractal Organizing Processes in Situ

In this section of the book, we examine fractal organizing processes from lived experience. First we detail an ontological storytelling inquiry conducted under stressful conditions, examining the study, its findings, and how the sociomaterial unfolding of a fire burning uncontrolled within the city limits affected the data collection. This study was the genesis for this book and our current understanding of fractal organizing processes and how fractal storytelling methods can be used to tease out the simple rules affecting a particular social network's functioning. Next, we consider several cases from the experiences of others, using the examples as teaching tools accompanied by exercises designed to elicit reflection. These interviews were provided by experts in complexity, analytics, graphic design, and business consulting and draw from the subjects; extensive experience with major corporations. In each case, we take a view toward practicality, applying Fractal Change Management (FCM) theory in useful ways with implications in business settings.

5 From the Ashes

What We Can Learn From Nonprofit Leaders during a Crisis

It's the summer of 2012 and I have decided to go out for a jog. There are paved trails near my home and my dog, Spot, loves to go with me. There is a fire in the mountains to the west and the news reports that it has jumped the ridge and is threatening homes in Mountain Shadows, an upscale neighborhood nestled up against the front range amid the pine trees. Spot and I are doing a three and a half mile loop, around the park, and it is a beautiful, warm day. The jog is a welcome break from the work on my doctoral dissertation. We are on the second half of the round trip and the wind suddenly shifts. The sky becomes dark and cloudy. Ash falls from above and the air is so smoky it is as if I am leaning directly over a roaring campfire and breathing deeply. I cough a little and slow to a walk, still about a mile from home. Twice, strangers pull their cars over to offer us rides as the sky appears dusky in midday and my hair fills with ash. Clearly circumstances have changed. In the sociomaterial world of organizations, things can change rapidly too, calling for adaptation born of complexity.

This chapter describes a study done in Colorado Springs, Colorado, in 2012. It describes an ontological storytelling inquiry that explores the significance of fractal patterns manifested through storytelling. This study was the genesis of fractal change management theory. It examined the informal social network underpinning nonprofit work in the community. As an accident of fate, data were collected, whereas the community was facing a fire that burned 346 homes and caused the evacuation roughly 32,000 citizens. As such, the effects of turbulence were apparent in the stories told by participants. The study identified eight key themes, each of which was examined for self-similar scalability using four levels of analysis. Themes were developed into graphic models and presented to the participants in a focus group, where they indicated that the models offered a useful tool for expressing what it takes to succeed in their work environment.

For her doctoral dissertation, Tonya chose to look for the meaning of fractal patterns in human systems. She wanted to know what significance fractal patterns might have in the context of an informal social network supporting nonprofit work in her city. The Colorado Springs metropolitan area has a population of roughly 600,000. There are five military bases, numerous aerospace contractor facilities, and faith-based organizations. Prior studies conducted with local nonprofits suggested a plethora of rich, interpersonal relationships among leaders, volunteers, and civic groups (Joint initiatives for youth and families: An analysis of the collaborative network, 2011; Wakefield, 2011a; Wakefield, Robertson, & Wall, 2012). She found 11 nonprofit executive directors and communications professionals who were willing to participate in a three-part study to explore patterns in their experiences as members of the nonprofit community in their city.

The data collection process had three phases and was a variation of Boje's (2011) ontological storytelling inquiry methodology. The method was appropriate because it is designed to get at the underlying sense of Being in a given situation. An initial set of interviews was conducted, wherein each person described instances of perceived scalable, self-similar occurrences in the context of their work in the local nonprofit community. The same participants engaged in a second set of interviews, contextualizing their responses with those of their peers and reacting to the unexpected occurrence of a wildfire burning within the city limits. Finally, a focus group was held, wherein five participants attended and discussed the findings.

The Waldo Canyon wildfire began burning on Saturday, June 23, and was declared officially contained about two and half weeks later on Tuesday, July 10. When the smoke cleared, the fire had forced the evacuation of

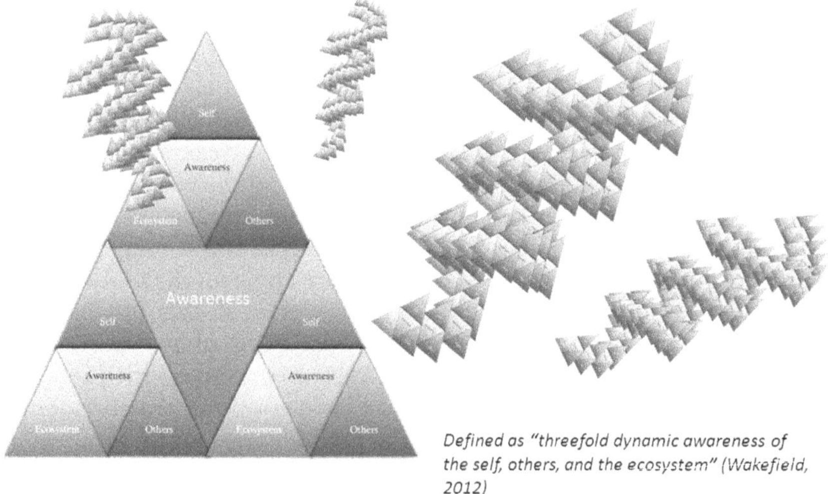
Relational Introspection
Awareness
Defined as "threefold dynamic awareness of the self, others, and the ecosystem" (Wakefield, 2012)

Figure 5.1 Relational Introspection
Source: By Tonya L. Henderson Wakefield. Used with permission.

more than 32,000 people, consumed 18,247 acres, destroyed 346 homes, left two people dead and was part of Colorado's worst wildfire season in a decade (2012). The eight themes identified were relational introspection, interconnectedness, agency, collaboration, materiality, communications, answerability, and perpetuating the system.

RELATIONAL INTROSPECTION

The concept that was most prevalent was that of relational introspection. Participants described a scalable awareness of self, others, and the ecosystem in their work. At an individual level, "relational introspection involves emotional reactions, interpersonal relationships, and the choices individuals make" (Wakefield 2012, p. 117). They seemed to maintain awareness of all three of these perspectives, at multiple levels of analysis as a mode of working. Figure 5.1 shows relational introspection as something that propagates and occurs in nested fractals at all levels of analysis. The drawing is inspired by the Sierpinski gasket and can be thought of as showing how such an awareness might exist at the individual, organizational, and cultural levels, extending through time to influence how we see the world and perceive patterns. This kind of awareness or attunement makes it possible to identify those patterns of human interaction that are scalable and self-similar, which has tremendous implications for strategic planning and risk management, as we discuss in Chapter 8, this volume.

Whereas relational introspection is not the only approach, it does offer a way for individuals to process multiple levels of systemicity and become attuned to patterns. Other approaches include the multilevel analysis technique used in Tonya's dissertation and in ontological systems mapping as described in Chapter 7 (Henderson and DePorres 2014, Wakefield 2012). For Glenda Eoyang, this kind of zooming in and out in social systems amounts to looking at systems as the micro, macro, and meso levels. She says,

> We talk about the whole, the part, and the greater whole partly because we work in so many different sizes of systems . . . Sometimes the whole is the group and then the part is the self and the greater whole is the ecosystem but in the work that we're doing in the field of conservation- the ecosystem is the whole, the part is the subsystems or the multiple systems, and the greater is the global stability. So, we- I think the three make a lot of sense. I think in the fractal systems we think of may be not an infinite . . . an indefinite number of layers and . . . But you can't think about them all at one time so you pick three, and I think that human systems have been in the habit of privileging the individual, at least in the West . . .
>
> —Glenda Eoyang (interview)

Examples of self-awareness were apparent at an individual level and in the aggregate. These included understanding one's own skills and limitations, personal history, and emotional state. Awareness of one's emotional state was exemplified by the research subjects' awareness of a wildfire burning within the city limits during the second phase of data collection. For example, one woman paused during an interview, and "joked that it was a 'fire zone' or mental health break, related to the stress of her evacuation" (Wakefield 2012, p. 120). There was a shared sense of vulnerability that permeated the discussions.

Consideration of others at the individual level of analysis is about recognizing similarities and differences in perspective. Examples included discussions of the variations in the amount of autonomy people have, and what brings joy to different people. For example a man who runs the food pantry suggested that the needy experience joy differently from the well fed, sometimes relishing in simple things like fresh cupcake, although he was careful not to make comparisons between validity of his own joy and those of the people he serves. The ecosystem discussion at this level of analysis centered on really paying attention and being present.

Zooming out to consider the space between individuals and organizations, self, others, and ecosystem are seen in a different light. Between individuals and organizations, discussions of self-awareness highlighted choosing among job offers, delivery of services to the needy, and discussions of bureaucracy. Others were discussed in terms of hiring veterans from social programs, soliciting and respecting feedback from clients even when it's not really helpful, feedback mechanisms, sharing vision, and how individuals identified with particular organization in terms of their sense of purpose. There was also a clear demonstration of organizational concern for individual emotions during that time. For example one Executive Director talked about addressing secondary trauma of her staff as they responded to news reports, and public displays of emotion not condoned under other circumstances were excepted and supported. Adaptations also discussed, included organizational adaptations to changes in the fundraising as donor dollars were directed primarily toward fire victims.

Self-awareness at the organizational level had to do with systemic strengths and weaknesses, mission based behaviors, principles and limitations tied to funding streams. There was evidence of an aggregate self-awareness tying to mission here. Additionally principle driven behaviors were important. Examples included the story of the former priest who houses people no one else would take without concerns for funding or safety. According to Wakefield (2012), "This man invites people that no one else will take, including sex offenders into his home to live among family members and grandchildren . . . Problems have been avoided because he is building a home, not running a program" (pp. 127–128). Founding stories, organizational culture, and alignment between organizational mission and fundraising activities for examples used to further illustrate this point. Mission was discussed in terms of knowing an organization's purpose and only using that organization for that purpose. This includes turning away grant money in some cases to ensure adherence to mission. Organizational strengths and weaknesses included discussion of financial model supporting independence, maintaining a level of services and not necessarily involving growth, only knowing what you're good at and focusing on that. Others at this level of analysis involved discussion of collaborative efforts and honesty regarding organizational limits like to sponsorship affiliation or funding sources. Collaboration agreements were stressed, along with Conversations about organizational limitations. This was especially important because mandates of one organization might cause it to stand in the way of collaborating organizations trying to do something. By understanding one's own organization, and others with whom he would collaborate, executive directors were able to maintain their organizational values and determine which collaborative arrangements are likely to be profitable. Ecosystem awareness at this level had to do with understanding the economic climate and sticking to one mission despite the temptation to chase dollars from unrelated sources because fundraising climate is very austere.

Awareness of others at the organizational level was demonstrated in many different ways. Healthy feedback mechanisms for organizations were one way of ensuring attunement to clients' needs, specifically including a respectful acceptance of feedback that is not particularly helpful. Organizational attunement to the general level of fear and stress throughout the city during the fire was apparent as well, with organizations allowing for the effects of secondary trauma among employees and directors of various organizations interfacing on professional and personal levels as they reacted to and anticipated community needs and comforted one another.

According to Quade and Holladay (2010), "In today's fast-paced turbulent, and highly diverse landscape, environmental scanning cannot be a once-a-year traditional exercise; it has to be an ongoing and well-supported search" (pp. 145–146).

Ecosystem awareness among organizations included both day to day matters and responses to the fire. Understanding seasonal trends at an organization supporting employment needs for women was important, as the number of clients fluctuated according to whether or not school was in session, because many of the women served could not afford daycare to attend training programs or work on their resumes when school was out. The need to tailor public speaking to a particular audience was addressed, as was the negative effect of starting new nonprofits without first surveying the field to be sure that one's new venture would not siphon donor funds away from other organizations engaged in the same work, at the same time dooming the new effort because of its redundancy. Some leaders took an active role in disaster relief efforts and actively brought that perspective back to the office, ensuring that their organizations were actively engaged. The presence or absence of key organizations in these efforts was noted. These examples of ecosystem awareness suggest attunement to the environment at an organizational level.

This scalable, threefold attunement was of central importance, as it gave support to all of the other themes, permeating the entire dataset.

INTERCONNECTEDNESS

The model, developed to show how interconnectedness featured in the story performances collected, suggests a generative tension between self-interest and teamwork wherein people find connection through conflict. Cross-disciplinary groups and a relational mode of working were described as central to functioning in the new generation of nonprofit leaders. There was a clear understanding that relationships are important and a sense that "nobody does it alone." Subjects took pride in interconnectedness and give and take among individuals and organizations, including their interactions with human services clients and the ways that individuals and organizations enjoy symbiotic relationships.

Organizations benefit from the social ties of individuals, particularly where donations and volunteerism are concerned, and individuals benefit from their associations with particular organizations, whether tangibly or through social affiliation. Compassion and building mutual understanding were emphasized, to include having leaders get to know each other so that they are less confrontational when engaging other organizations. This kind of camaraderie was especially strong among those who worked side by side in the disaster relief efforts. In teamwork, "trust, communication, and shared values are more important than the substance of what you are trying to accomplish" (Wakefield 2012, p. 151). Yet there was also a need to work through conflict when a particular organization's contributions were ignored in collaborative settings and when certain coalitions appeared to be a "boys club" of sorts. Working through conflict was important to the ability of organizations to jointly pursue grant money and execute the required work, something that often results in conflicting priorities and disagreements about how operations should proceed. Subjects took pride in serving as connectors and emphasized the need for relationships to support transparency and figuring out the right questions to ask. Interdisciplinary coalitions to help returning veterans and the idea of working with the whole family when delivering social services serve as examples of interconnectedness as well. It was also noted that turbulence in the shared ecosystem enhances mutual understanding, as was the case when nonprofits were struggling for limited donor funds in a down economy and when the community as a whole was united in fighting and coping with the effects of the fire. A particularly poignant illustration of working through conflict is found in one executive director's stories about a food pantry patron.

> . . . who believed that monsters were coming out of the sewers to get her. People at a local church call Margaret the Queen of England because she

> once told them that was her name (Phase two, Subject five, 1114–1116). She was allowed to come into the building and a staff member would sometimes transcribe her story, in the interest of extending hospitality, allowing her to feel attended to and "known by name" (Phase two, Subject five, 373–383). At some point in the past Margaret came into the soup kitchen with a baby and a vacant stare on her face, nothing resembling maternal instinct. He wondered aloud what happened to the baby and called Margaret one of the lost (Phase two, Subject five, 1130–1138). One year Margaret came to Thanksgiving dinner and seemed perfectly normal. She helped set the tables, then asked what the gamma ray forecast was. This shift from apparent normalcy to the outlandish was used to illustrate how quickly she could change and he said the staff worried about her. Yet they tried to accept her on her own terms, as part of their concept of hospitality (Phase two, Subject five, 1097–1109). These stories illustrate his organization's efforts to extend hospitality and care for an individual whose needs were substantial. They collectively entered into a relationship with her despite the difficulties inherent in doing so.
>
> (Wakefield 2012, pp. 156–157)

At an organizational level, there were varying perspectives about the need for intraorganizational collaboration, with some leaders emphasizing that the bulk of their particular missions could be executed independently. Yet teamwork was also emphasized, in that similar organizations often benefit from association as they collaborate to provide a service, share information, or obtain funding. Understanding what each organization brings to the table and engaging in team problem solving were stressed, to include a story of how two organizations with complementary missions developed a graphic depiction of their roles and interaction to help lessen donor confusion. This kind of collaboration even extends into private sector support to nonprofits as the interconnectedness of the organizations becomes apparent in various forums. There were also tales of failed collaboration attempts when organizations did not live up to the expectations of collaborators in providing services or when collaboration is time-consuming or detracts from one's mission. These kinds of concerns seemed to be lessened in terms of fire response efforts, as each organization brought its unique contributions forward and the desire to help trumped other concerns: "we normally seem to be a polarized town, with very vocal people on opposite sides of religious, cultural, and social issues, but in the crisis a surprising sense of community became apparent" (Wakefield 2012, p. 166).

Interconnectedness featured at all levels of analysis and was clearly supported by cultivating relational introspection. "Interconnectedness is manifested at multiple levels of analysis as a dynamic tension between self-interest and teamwork, with efforts to overcome conflict and build trust and mutual regard at the center" (Wakefield 2012, p. 168).

AGENCY

We define agency as "the ability to set emergent phenomena in motion or affect their outcomes" (Wakefield 2012). Agency in the study was developed as a simple, scalable process involving a moment of choice, the influence of past experiences and external influences, and ultimately an action that either differentiates from or repeats past behaviors. Leadership and influence were discussed at an individual level but were more prominent in the intraorganizational context, where organizations sometimes lead coalitions by establishing an agenda and asking what other organizations want to participate. Community leaders were widely praised for their response to the fire as well. Examples of past patterns of behavior included references to destructive tendencies among the generationally poor, as well as community-level tendencies to favor some constituencies at the expense of others. Discussions of the moment of choice included explorations of opportunity cost for individuals and organizations, the way that many in the city were opening up their homes to others during the fire, and a tendency among the needy to gravitate toward locales facing such disasters because of the outpouring of aid that becomes available. Difference in action was discussed in terms of readiness for change and growth, stories of redemption, and changes in behavior as a result of the fire. It was also noted that some organizations resist offering temporary services, even in crisis, as a matter of expectation management. The most poignant discussion of repetition was a story about how evacuated nuns continued their habit of caring for others even when displaced, themselves.

COLLABORATION

The model of collaboration developed was not a fractal one, but simply one of tension, as some forces supported collaboration and others acted to counter it. Personal efforts, good leadership and planning, supported collaboration. Detractors included unexpected work stoppages caused by the fire, conflicts of interest, board disengagement, and in-fighting among community leaders. Working through conflict in a group often requires getting "through that stormy, messy, muddy part, where the outcomes aren't clear; the reasons for being there aren't clear; the accusations back and forth are harsh," by keeping people at the table (Wakefield 2012, p. 189).

MATERIALITY

Materiality was manifest in discussions of the distribution of resources in light of the fire. With the median income of the affected neighborhood in the six figure range, there were some concerns that resources would be siphoned from the destitute in the short term and that the outpouring of support during the fire would adversely affect projected donations in the following months. "Competition for philanthropic dollars in light of the poor economic outlook and the tendency of donors to designate gifts specifically for natural disaster victims emerged as a major area of concern" (Wakefield 2012, p. 191). There were discussions about how hard the lives of needy people are and how they often lack the necessary cooking skills to prepare inexpensive, healthy meals. This discussion was less prevalent, however, than the resource discussions tied to the fire and displacement of the formerly wealthy, most of whom have resources to recover and were able to stay with friends.

There was concern for the financially vulnerable who had jobs in the affected area and lost days of work that they could ill afford, whereas living paycheck to paycheck, along with discussions of the difficulties inherent in dispensing the vast amount of resources that had suddenly become available. People in need of immediate assistance were sometimes unable to obtain assistance as red tape got in the way of dispensing aid. For the needy, obtaining services was made even worse by the closure of the human services center, which was located in the evacuated area. There were also discussions of funding at the organizational level, centering on the need to be selective in applying for grants, how grants are distributed, concerns about capital campaigns, and appreciation for consistent donors and stable cash flow where it is available. There were also discussions about the inequitable distribution of resources in the US and how there is likely enough to go around if this were remedied. There were also concerns that the wealthy persons displaced in the fire would drive rental prices up in the short term, as well as much discussion of how the familiarity between the affected persons and the door base likely resulted in greater support than might have been the case if a poorer area had burned.

COMMUNICATIONS

Communications were depicted using a very simple fractal model. Poor communications are sometimes simply the product of people being too busy to share critical information. Discussions included examples of how improving communications can affect organizational function, and how executive directors can craft messages for their boards of directors to request additional support. There was also some discussion of the need for sensitivity in discussing any concerns about the distribution of resources in the wake of the fire. Expectation management and crafting messages were discussed at length, to include the need for clear expression of what an organization's mission is so that people know what to expect. Thanking donors, crafting emotional appeals, and targeted messaging dominated the discussion of funding-related communications. Widespread use of social media during the fire was also noted. Stories of intraorganizational communications included discussions of a failed partnerships, deceptive metrics and statements, and a lack of information sharing that ultimately caused the death of a child. Communications related to the fire were largely considered successful by the research subjects. At a community level, these discussions centered on the use of social media, political discourse, and the selective broadcast of the story of the fire, in that many stories were never told, despite the widespread use of social media and more coordinated modes of communications.

ANSWERABILITY

Answerability ethics featured in the interviews as well. Grounded in Bakhtin's (1993) work, the idea of two-sided answerability was supported by the story performances. Answerability ethics suggest that vis-à-vis any action, one is answerable for the intent of the act as well as the act itself. In the study, this translated to the intersection of values and accountability. Values discussed included gratitude and when it is appropriate to compromise. The need for alignment between leaders' personal values and organizational values was discussed, along with stories about how those receiving stories can build or detract from their relationships with volunteers the same way. Organizational values and mission statements were emphasized as things that must be shared clearly with other organizations in collaborative scenarios and political activism was discussed as the stage for discussions of values at a cultural level. Discussions of accountability centered around personal accountability for agreements made with others and promises to oneself, along with lengthy discussions of faulty metrics applied to human services. The difficulty in choosing meaningful metrics and supporting data-based decision making was of concern, as were legislation and shared infrastructure to support nonprofits. "Answerability ethics are grounded in both morality and actual occurrence and constitute the missing link between considerations of values and the need for good metrics" (Wakefield 2012, p. 222).

PERPETUATING GENERATIVE SYSTEMICITY

The last theme discovered was the subjects' shared impressions about perpetuating the system in which they operate. Reflections about the health of the social system underpinning nonprofit work in the community suggested that the participants preferred to focus their efforts on long-term transformational change at a more global level, in contrast with quick, immediate fixes impacting one or two individuals. This preference is likely the product of the relative seniority of the participants, all of whom were either executive directors or communications specialists and had a reasonable amount of autonomy. A holistic view of human services was stressed, to include discussions of "wrap-around services" addressing a number of contributing factors using a team of professionals to address each case and support the affected party's entire family. The fire, however, did draw many into discussions of individual experiences and actions supporting friends whose homes were threatened, although these concerns were less apparent than discussions of the need for a systemic, holistic look at community problems.

We find this desire for a systemic look both refreshing and troubling. It is refreshing in that it honors the complexity and interconnectedness of myriad issues that tend to be examined one at a time as people start nonprofits and search for grant money. It is troubling because it is grounded in the idea of making an absolute agential cut when exploring a whole system, be it an organization or a community. We now expand on this idea and consider it in the context of generative systemicity, which we consider to be the promotion of patterns that support the sustainability and upliftment of all parties concerned to the extent possible.

Each of the eight themes was examined at multiple levels of analysis and developed into a visual model. These models then fit together to form a set of rules for operating in the nonprofit leadership sphere of the community, as confirmed during a focus group with some of the research subjects. Figure 9.2 shows how relational introspection supports and enhances all of the other concepts to perpetuate the social system that supports human services work in the community studied.

PRACTICAL APPLICATION

These themes and models were put together in a presentation titled "Eight Things Every Nonprofit Leader Needs To Know" and offered to the local nonprofit community. The feedback was very positive, but simply sharing and explaining the models seems inadequate. So we have provided two exercises below that support using these concepts to improve nonprofit leader performance.

RELATIONAL INTROSPECTION

Practice relational introspection in your home or office. Review figure 5.1 (triangle drawing above) before important meetings or put it on the refrigerator to cultivate awareness among family members. Why? When we improve our situational awareness and self-knowledge, we become more authentic in our interactions. We respond to others in more respectful and powerful ways and are easier for others to trust. Think through any interaction between your organization and others in this fashion as well, thinking in terms of your organization's mission, vision, and guiding principles; collaborators and competitors; and the competitive environment.

During periods of quiet reflection, ask yourself the following questions. Note how the answers change with each iteration of the exercise. Are you better able to spot patterns in group behaviors?

Self

- *Do I know myself well?*
- *What is my intention for this situation?*
- *How do I feel today?*
- *Am I in tune with my emotions?*
- *What am I projecting (voice, body language, word choice)?*

Others

- *Who are these people around me?*
- *What do they need?*
- *What do they expect of me?*
- *Are they truly present and focused on the task at hand?*
- *What can we accomplish together?*

Ecosystem

- *What's the context (business, social, family)?*
- *What's going on around us?*
- *Are things changing or is the situation stable?*
- *Is this a healthy environment? If not, what are my choices?* (Copyright 2014, Gly Solutions, LLC Used with permission.)

INTERCONNECTEDNESS

Take a sheet of paper and fold into thirds vertically. At the top of one side write "Self-Interest." At the top of the middle section write "Where The Good Stuff Happens." On the other side, write "Teamwork," as below. Now think of the next meeting or collaborative effort on your plate and examine it using this tool. First list all of the factors suggesting self-interest on your part, as well as your perceptions about what might drive others involved to act selfishly, whether as individuals or on behalf of a constituency. Now do the same for factors promoting teamwork, using the far-right column. Finally, consider those areas where collaboration might be possible, or where differences of opinion or opposing concerns might lead to the development of new ideas or opportunities.

Self-Interest	Where The Good Stuff Happens	Teamwork

REFERENCES

Bakhtin, Michel. (1993). *Toward a philosophy of the act. Translated by Vadim Liapunov.* Edited by Michael Holquist, University of Texas Press Slavic Series No. 10. Austin: University of Texas Press.

Boje, D. (2011). Ontological Storytelling Inquiry Methodology—For Dummies. Unpublished classroom material. Las Cruces, NM.

Boje, D., & Wakefield, T. (2011). Storytelling in Systemicity and Emergence: A Third Order Cybernetic. In D. Boje, B. Burnes, & J. Hassard (Eds.), The Routledge Companion to Organizational Change.

Henderson, T.L., & DePorres, D. (2014). Fractal based Ontological Storytelling: Finding Patterns of Perception among Western Yoga Practitioners. In G.D. Sardana & T. Thatchenkery (Eds.), *Leveraging Human Factors for Strategic.*

Joint initiatives for youth and families: An analysis of the collaborative network. (2011). In PARTNER: Program to analyze, record, and track networks to enhance relationships. Denver, Colorado: University of Colorado Denver.

Quade, Kristine, and Royce Holladay. (2010). Dynamical Leadership: Building Adaptive Capacity for Uncertain Times. Apache Junction, AZ: Gold Canyon Press.

Wakefield, T. H. (2011). *Client Report for the Women's Resource Agency of Colorado Springs.* Process consulting practicum report. Colorado Technical University. Colorado Springs, CO.

Wakefield, Tonya L. Henderson, Alfonso Robertson, and Kenneth Wall. (2012). "Nonprofit board service: a qualitative investigation using appreciative inquiry." Action research report International Conference on the Management Cases, Greater Noida (NCR), India, 29–30 November.

Wakefield, Tonya L. Henderson. (2012). "An ontology of storytelling systemicity: Management, fractals and the Waldo Canyon fire." Doctorate of Management Doctoral dissertation, Management, Colorado Technical University.

"Waldo Canyon Fire after action report suggests better training in the future." (2012). Huffington Post, 27 October. http://www.huffingtonpost.com/2012/10/23/waldo-canyon_n_2007447.html.

6 How Fractal Organizing Processes Unfold in Day-To-Day Business and Being

In this chapter, we offer a series of applications grounded in the lived experience of organizations. These practical examples are accompanied by exercises designed to bring the experiences into the classroom and beyond, as we encourage learning that supports practical application. It is our intention to provide the reader with tools for actively managing fractal organizing processes as they unfold in various settings.

A number of scholars and practitioners are engaged in groundbreaking work that involves managing fractal organizing processes in various settings. We were fortunate to interview scholars and practitioners who have been working with fractal patterns in organizations for many years, along with those who are looking at fractals in new and exciting ways. The stories that follow illustrate Fractal Change Management (FCM) and related theory using real world examples. After each, we offer a series of questions to guide reflection in individual and classroom settings. A list of the scenarios in the chapter follows.

- Dynamical Leaders and Fractal Awareness: How Leaders Can Shape Fractal Patterns in Organizational Behavior
- BIGstory: Practical Applications of Quantum and Fractal Storytelling
- Fractal-Branching of Departments in a College of Business: Emergent Organizational Structure
- Fractal Appeal in Marketing Design: the Gold Story
- Daniel Q. Boje's Entrepreneurship: Fractal-Spiral Story of the Trash Compactor
- Fractal Analytics: A Successful Multinational Consulting Company
- The Multifractal Network Case: Veta la Palma Fish Farm and Bird Sanctuary
- SPUD'S, And Horse And Restorying: Sociomateriality And Shifting Fractal Patterns With Veterans

Together, these cases offer examples of FCM in action, from a wide variety of industries, along with exercises and questions to elicit deeper reflection.

DYNAMICAL LEADERS AND FRACTAL AWARENESS: HOW LEADERS CAN SHAPE FRACTAL PATTERNS IN ORGANIZATIONAL BEHAVIOR

Dr. Kristine Quade has been working with complexity and fractals since she was first introduced to these concepts at the Human System Dynamics Institute in 2001. Her doctoral work centered on leadership and her book *Dynamical Leadership* is a practical guide for leading in a complex adaptive system (Quade 2011, Quade and Holladay 2010). We had an opportunity to interview Dr. Quade, who shared the following example.

> In the large-group work, their leaders would say, "Oh, we're just fabulous." And then, I would get in to a large group [to learn it was] totally messy.
>
> So, I would start to do work with a leadership team to make sure that they were really together . . . before moving into a large group. So, I would think of them as, you know, "Here is the seed that's gonna start this fractal." So, I want the change to occur in a large group. They'd better be together. So, that's where I really experienced it mostly with my client work.

She shared an example of how an organization's leader changed his behavior to positively influence patterns of behavior throughout the organization. In this scenario, a senior bank vice president was able to shift patterns in the organization by changing his leadership style after setting a negative tone in a meeting of over 900 bank employees.

> So, he comes in wearing a suit and we had told him, "No, this is business casual." So, he walked up and he started talking and somebody in the back of the room goes, "Take it off!" And he is like sort of, you know . . . pretty soon he goes, "Take it off. Take it off." And I leaned over and I said, "They want you to take the tie off." So, he is like, it's really pissy. He takes his tie off and continues and his voice changes and he starts to kinda bark, you know, and then I'm going, "hmm."
>
> So then, he goes, "Okay. Are there any questions?" Well, he missed that part of the instructions. So, I said, "Great idea Gerald. Umm, let's have the tables do some work about what do they fear, what are their reactions and what questions do they have?" So, while the tables are working, I again reinforced to them that they will go around the room in a random, not a random, but in a very organized way, but each table will ask their table question. And, so he if he can keep his answers fairly short and we can get a lot of meat. So, he answers a couple of them pretty spectacularly.

And then, somebody asked a question, and he goes, "I can't believe you'd ask such a stupid question, but I'll answer it anyway." I thought, "Oh my gosh."

You could have almost heard a pin drop. And then, he goes on in the next question of course the next person like timidly stands up and answered the question. Because, I mean, this is the, you know, the max mix of the whole organization. It's from the tower all the way up to the leadership team in the room. And, there's 900 in the room. It's not a small group. So, he answers a couple more of question and the next one comes up, "Oh, that's another dumb question." I leaned over [to] the logistics person and I said, "I don't care what status of the lunch is. Get it ready now."

So, I let him answer one more question, and we send them all of to lunch and I say, "Thanks a lot Gerald," and I sent them off to lunch. Well, I met with the design team over lunch and I said, "Okay. Now, here is the next piece coming up. . . . You know, we've been telling them that they are here to talk about how they are going to be empowered as, as employees to help the customers, and now they have just been abused. This is exactly the kind of behavior we're trying to change. So, what do we do?" They said, "We're going to continue." So, the next exercise in the afternoon was "What's working. What's not working?" Almost every table on the not working came up with Gerald even though the instructions were, "Please don't use names."

They, they would put Gerald. So then, we post the sheets around the room and everybody has dots and they're supposed to pick the top working and the top not working. Gerald overwhelmingly is in the not working and gets lots of dots. And then not to be finished with him, in the feedback for the day, highs and lows, lows was Gerald.

So, we get together with the design team to redesign the next day and we bring in the General Manager, and we said, "Okay. Look. We've got to deal with this now. It's gonna continue to mushroom. It's gonna totally derail the effort of this large group we have." He says, "I'll take care of everyone. Umm. Can you tell me what you have in mind? Let's get together in the morning." I go, "Well, what do we do?" He says, "Continue on with, with the design process and I'll come back with you in the morning." And I was like, "Okay."

So, the next morning, he came back and said, "Okay. I have handled it." Then, I go, "What do you mean?" "This is where Gerald is coming back." I go, "What do you mean?" "This is Gerald's coming back and We've talked." He said, "That was the toughest conversation I've ever had with my boss, ever. Trust me. It will work out." And I go, "I'm not sure I trust you on this, but we'll work with it."

So, as the morning starts; the design team member goes to the final stage and says, you know, "Highs for yesterday were . . . and comments about improvements for the day were . . . and so we have adjusted those and then, lows were Gerald." And so, Gerald is back. You kind of heard, I mean, dead silence in the room . . . Just "thud!" I mean, it was just like dropping a lead balloon, and it was like everybody was just dead silent.

So, Gerald comes up to the stage wearing a suit again, and I'm like, "Oh gosh. What am I gonna do here?" And, I'm getting really ready to do major damage control. He walks to the microphone. He takes off his tie. He takes off his jacket and puts it on the chair, and he goes to the microphone, and he says, "Yesterday, I behaved inappropriately. In front of you, I treated you in, in a way that was not respectful, definitely not consistent with the work you're doing. And, if my behavior has impacted the work that you're going to be doing, then I am truly sorry. I must apologize to you for my behavior. And, if my apology is not enough, then I'm going to lay down on the stage, and you can walk on me." And, he just flops down on the stage and he gets a standing ovation. So, at the end of that day the feedback on the highs was "Gerald."

[The] fractal continues because in the next event, the first-day evaluations are, "When is Gerald gonna come and talk to us?"

—Kristine Quade (interview)

When asked about what happened after that, she noted that she later worked with a group of top executives of which Gerald was a member and the conversation they wanted to have centered on how to change corporate culture.

Exercise:

In small groups, discuss the story of Gerald.

1. What kinds of patterns do you think were unfolding in the organization before Dr. Quade's workshop?
2. How was Gerald's behavior serving as a fractal generator?
3. What kinds of patterns might the "new and improved" Gerald inspire?
4. Explore Gerald's example through the lens of relational introspection. What do you think his relationship was with himself, others, and the larger organization? How about the external environment? How did that change, based on Dr. Quade's description?
5. What kinds of sociomaterial aspects can you see in this story? What was the impact of Gerald's suit and tie in the social context early in the story? How did that change over time?

Explore the following scenario. You are working with an organization where morale is poor. You meet with the core leadership team and discover that their attitudes are nothing short of toxic. Data collection within the organization suggests that morale is poor and that bad behaviors and negativity are present at all levels of the organization.

1. Drawing on Dr. Quade's example, how might you work with the client to encourage a Gerald-style change in attitude?
2. What kinds of behaviors are necessary for leaders whose patterns have previously had negative systemic effects in the past to demonstrate change in a way that is credible?
3. Are there ways that you as a consultant might interact with middle management and nonsupervisory employees to (a) determine if the fractal pattern of negativity still exists and monitor changes, and (b) help to reinforce the desired change?

BIGSTORY: PRACTICAL APPLICATIONS OF QUANTUM AND FRACTAL STORYTELLING

Mike Bonifer is the co-founder of GameChangers, LLC, and the author of *GameChangers—Improvisation for Business in the Networked World*. He has worked with several large companies including Disney, United Airlines, Allstate, Giant Eagle, the US Department of Energy, and Skype. We have been privileged to work with Mike for several years and he has been a long time participant in the Quantum Storytelling Conference (see http://quantum storytelling.org) held in Las Cruces, New Mexico. Here we highlight his current efforts to trademark a quantum and fractal inspired brand of consulting he calls Big Story. Mike's team is taking the notion of fractal patterns within quantum storytelling and using it to develop new ways for his clients to handle large data sets without losing the effects of context.

> Quantum storytelling is a field in organizational theory that explores how stories live in networks, communities, and organizations, and what the managers and leaders of those groups can do about it. Our commercial name for quantum storytelling is "Big Story." We describe it as a way of using story to make better sense of Big Data. A client of ours calls it "a theory of story." Which is cool. To that, we'll add, it is both Theory and Practice of story. And unless you're a Hopi shaman a quantum physicist or a trained improviser, the odds are it's unlike any theory or practice of story you've encountered. The theory of Big Story will give our clients more ways of seeing and expressing relationships between data and story.
>
> The practice of BigStory consistently improves the odds of a company or community's bets on the future. Welcome to our bet on the

future. Today, Big Story is what we do. We always have, really, we just never had the names to name it or the structure to define it. Today we do. Today, we own it, in order to share it with you.

You know, story was always at the center of everything and my work with improvisation was really an answer to a story problem in organizations, which is the quest for the dominant narrative or the competition for the dominant narrative, both internally within the organization and externally in the marketplace.

—Mike Bonifer (interview)

Here he offers us a candid look at how Game Changers became Big Story and what that means for the organizations they serve, sharing two additional examples of sociomateriality, quantum storytelling, and fractal storytelling as ways to hone in on effective ways to market a new product and to help a community organization to unify a group of voters.

BECOMING BIG STORY

So improvisation was my answer to that and that's why in 2007 I started Game Changers and I had discovered a way of generating stories that was not the linear way. I discovered it for myself. And um, so that led to quantum story-telling, you know, . . . so looking forward to the future, the vision to use the quantum story-telling model.

There's a way to do this where we fly solo together as a teacher of mine says . . .

I just intuitively knew that was a better way than these dominant narrative things which I had experienced and [which had] left a lot of people unhappy and were not a great way of managing an organization and not a great way of leading. So that was the vision. That was the future I saw. Oh okay I get the physics connection in the sense that we have to deal with flow . . . flow states and probabilities and nondeterminacy and all of that and that led me to David's work in quantum storytelling and the whole quantum storytelling network three and a half years ago or so, 2011.

And so um, then I had to understand quantum storytelling sufficiently for myself so that I would know what was going on with it and I had some catching up to do and David is a challenging first-read. You know, that's not the easy way in. You're jumping into the hundred foot deep water right there at the start and swimming like crazy and there's waves it's getting deeper all the time and you know, it was crazy that I have to try to read that or to want to try to read it and I couldn't even believe that I was trying to read it at a certain points. I was just go to . . . I would go, wow this is, you know, really like my brain is like, you know, jacked and yet . . . but I knew there was something there like it was real to me.

I stayed away from story from quite a while because I wanted to think about improvisation in game and spontaneity and serendipity and a lot of things and once you go into story . . . I feel like I have fought such a hard fight to be under to make story understood as not just comedy that I didn't want to jump right back into story because I knew that another battle loomed where story was concerned and that I would have this to explain story as not the phenomenon you necessarily think it is and just abuse yourself like I would always do with improvisation. It's not just "Whose line is it anyway?" It's not just comedy. Here's why . . .

—Mike Bonifer (interview)

SOCIOMATERIALITY IN A NEW PRODUCT LAUNCH—CREATING A NEW COMMUNICATIONS FRACTAL FOR THE DEVELOPERS OF A HIGH-TECH SLEEPING MASK

So I think, you know, bought myself a little time [avoiding storytelling work] but I knew that that would come so it came in 2014 and with these guys and they go, "We only know how to talk to tech media." That was their fractal, that was their pattern and everybody we know when we talk to tech media and all the start ups in Silicon Valley and that we know of at the Stanford based startups, they only know how to talk to tech media and tech media is the make it or break it.

It wasn't the usual start up thing. So they said, "How do we talk to people other than technology media?" and I said, "That sounds like a job for quantum storytelling." And so, we started looking at the materiality, I would call it, of sleep and napping. What are the environments? Who's doing it? Why are they doing it? What is the sandbox that people are sleeping in? And then how do you participate? What role might the product play in that? If all of this is the materiality, so I will give you one example is airline pilots and people on airplanes generally. So we would go, "Well, people sleep on airplanes. Great." And then we would examine the materiality of the airplane experience including the pilot sleeping which is where it gets interesting because if they are going to come out bootstrapped which they did, which they are, then they had to be very selective in how they see it at the market.

And that said, either you have to figure out a way to get first class passengers wearing these or maybe pilots and we were talking about that. We were playing with the material. And Neo, one of the sampler guy says, "You know, it is interesting the U.S. Airline Pilot Association is the only one in the world that does not allow its pilots to nap on long haul flights." And I said, "Hmm, where there's an anomaly, there's a game, as we say in the improvisation world. So that's an anomaly, let's figure out a game for that." And so they got involved, they made a small bet which was to support an existing petition to allow airline pilots, U.S. Airline pilots to sleep on long haul flights. So they took something that was already there in terms of the materiality and they decided to play with it and support it and make a small bet on that action, that petition.

And we probably figured out fifty or sixty bets like that . . . they put their engineering minds to work and we got into sizing the bets and calculating the odds for the bets and we got into—and they had a scoring system for how they were going to calculate the odds, you know, we did high, medium, low. . . . We just basically had fun creating a way of sizing these bets, determining what the expected pay off might be and that sort of thing and then also how to define the bets themselves . . . We call the game E-R-G-O Environment Rules Guidelines Objectives and so that is the mechanism that we use to define in these bets.

Whoever was involved and is necessary to carry out that petition and who decides the Federal Aviation, the FAA, so they are the ones that have the provision right now. So that mechanism really, that idea of using game as mechanism, in a way it's just a structuring, you know, a way to think about structure and then guidelines or the trickiest part, you know, you've got to figure out how much budget, how much time you're going to spend on it, you know, what kinds of outputs you're committing to with this mechanism.

So they got their Kickstarter oversubscribed, raised something like fifty thousand dollars on Kickstarter and we're going to be visiting it in the first quarter about, okay, now that you've got your first prototypes and you're paying off the [loans], what does this look like now? We'll go back to the spreadsheet I'm sure and try to connect the Kickstarter idea, like, who's using these and, you know. Who buys them the first round and how do you get them out there and—I think we'll go back right to that idea, how do you generate stories with these in the non-tech media?

MERGING THE MULTIFRACTAL STORYTELLING OF PEOPLE WITH A COMMON INTEREST

[There was a] Latino environmental group . . . so they want to unite the narratives . . . [of] people in the united states with Latino roots and their older national narratives are different and in conflict with one another in some way and that national pride gets in the way of delivering what could be a powerful block of voters or customers—55 million people . . . You start talking real numbers with politicians and policy makers and brands but not if they're fractured . . . and so what he saw was the one thing that unites them all is the earth, is care for the land and let's do that and if they're thinking more in terms of politics . . . I'm keeping one eye on the branding piece, but they wanted to affect climate policy and so we're working with them and using quantum storytelling to find themes that both address the environmental concerns and unify these fractured narratives.

So the fractals there are these national fractals, and somehow through the care, the heart of care for the planets and the earth and the closeness to the earth, we wanna get at the inflection points that ease those divisions and create immunity and you know, political will for jobs creation . . .

Exercise:

Consider the following questions regarding Big Story.

1. How does Bonifer bring the sociomaterial aspects of FCM to his clients?
2. What patterns of behavior among air passengers, pilots, legislators, and society must shift for the sleeping mask to come into common usage? Consider the rules, both formally stated ones and the unwritten rules, as they exist today and as they might change to make the product take off.
3. How is changing the game similar to the idea of shifting a fractal organizing process to create a new pattern?
4. What are some ways he might approach the conflicting patterns of perception in the Latino community in order to help the organization generate a fractal pattern intentionally, the way that Quade and Eoyang suggest in their examples?

FRACTAL APPEAL IN MARKETING DESIGN: THE GOLD STORY

We recently spoke with Heidi Meredith and Renée Walker, founding partners of GOLD, a graphic arts consulting firm. They invented something they call the "Wikia Fractal Story" as part of a branding effort on behalf of an Internet company that supports the organic development of web-based content. Renée Walker spoke with us at length about the project.

Wikia faced the problem of how to tell their story as a pioneer in a new media landscape. GOLD developed the metaphor of the fractal as a storytelling device to describe Wikia as a living organism, constantly changing, morphing, growing as pages are created and the Wikia community participates.

The fractal story, tells about the changing, morphing, and growing of Wikia community in a visual graphic display. Renee and Heidi worked with marketing people from Wikia for 18 months to come up with this visual graphic, to brand a Wikia fractal story. This is just one of many drawings.

"Gold worked with *Wikia* to create a series of infographics that would reveal patterns in Internet usage among Generation Z users. The fractal metaphor describes a living organism, constantly changing, morphing, growing as pages are created and the *Wikia* community participates" (Meredith, & Walker, n.d.).

Let's zoom in to see the branching-fractal depicted in Figures 6.1 and 6.2 and its scale of self-similarity at a high magnification.

Fractals that are self-similar show visual structures at all zoom-scales (observed/measured at different spatial resolutions). Here we see that beginning with Scriptoriums and then Guttenberg's printing press, there is a branching into TV and Radio mediums. TV branches into Internet, which splits into branching of Blogging, Social Media, etc. Radio branches into video and many other unspecified mediums.

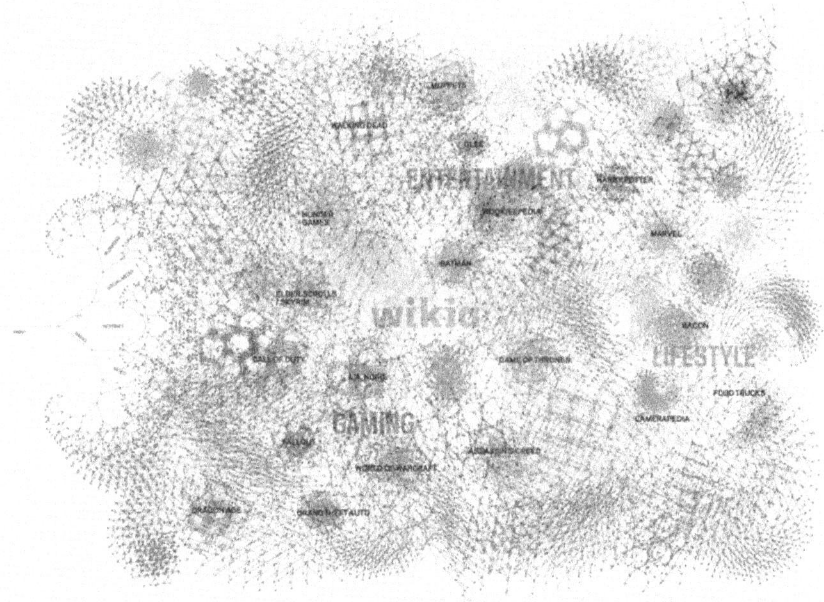

Figure 6.1 Wikia Fractal Story
Source: Used by permission of Gold Jan 2015

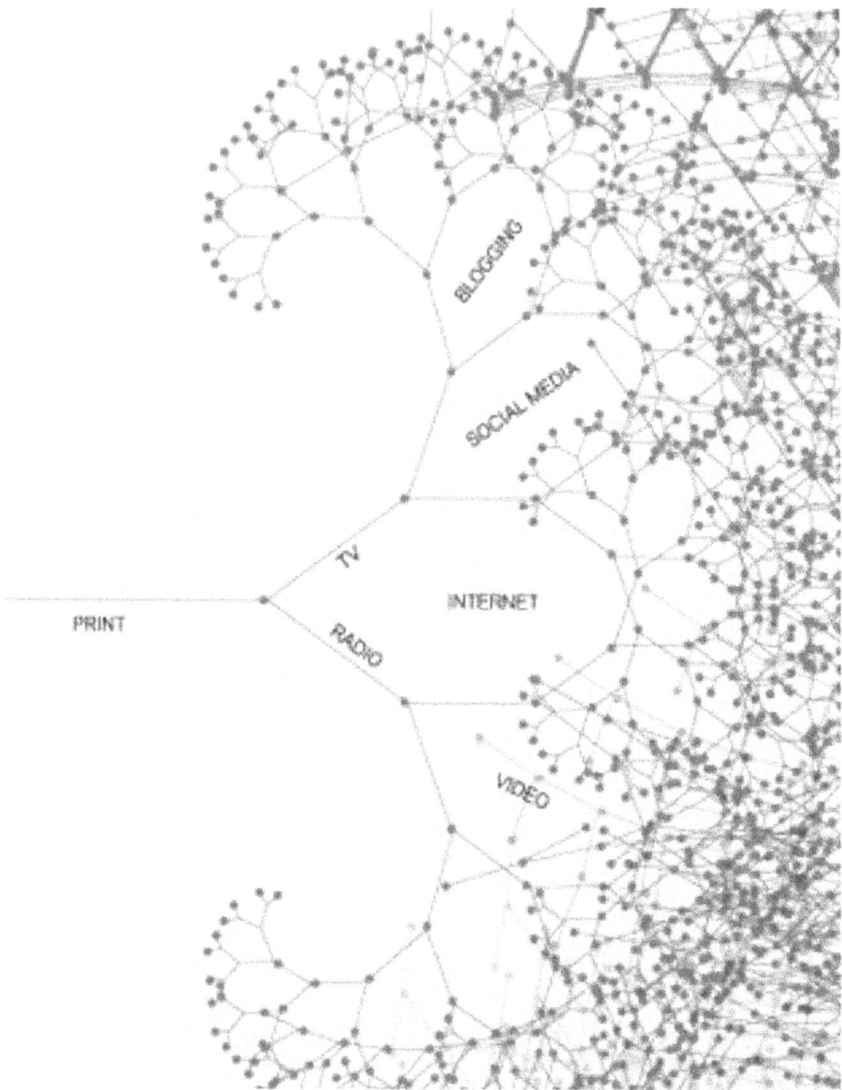

Figure 6.2 Zooming In on the Fractal-Story Pattern

What we want to point out here is that the branching-fractal is transformed in the visual graphic to a Fibonacci fractal-spiral. In turn, moving from left to right, the fractal-spiraling transformed into a rhizome (clusters of interactivity, moving every which way, without a central axis). Before we get into rhizomes, let's talk more about spirals.

Italian mathematician Leonardo Fibonacci (c. 1170–c. 1250) introduced the Fibonacci number sequence, where each next number is the sum of the previous two: 1 + 1 = 2; 1 + 2 = 3; 2 + 3 = 5; 3 + 5 = 8; 5 + 8 = 13; 8 + 13 = 21; 21 + 13 = 34, etc. creating the Fibonacci Spiral, a pattern we see in Snail shells, the Sunflowers, and so on.

The Fibonacci fractal-spiral shown in Figures 6.3 and 6.4 is a visual graphic representation. In the next example, we show how this applies to depicting entrepreneurship as a fractal-spiral story.

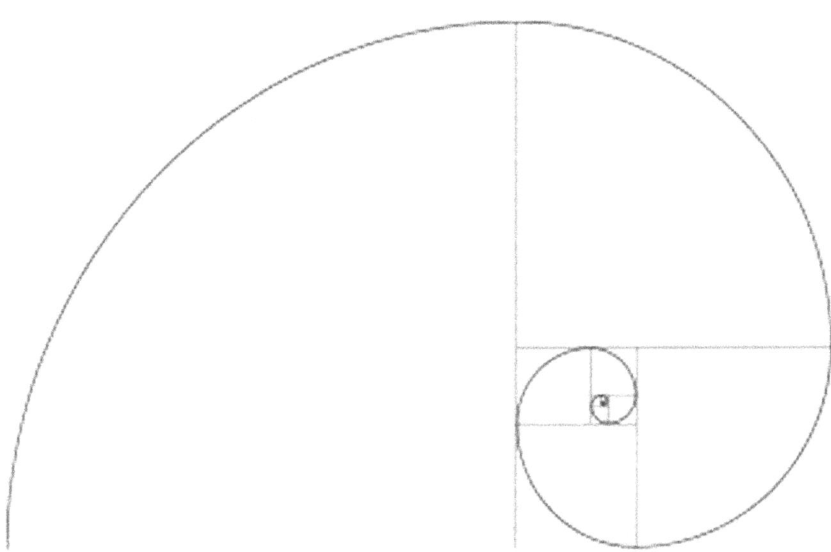

Figure 6.3 Fibonacci Fractal-Spiral
Source: (Icey, 2006, no permission needed)

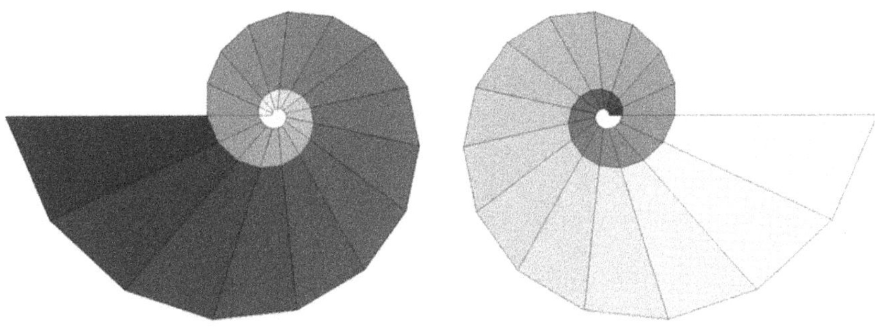

Figure 6.4 Fractal Nautilus
Source: https://commons.wikimedia.org/wiki/File:Fractilus.pdf

Table 6.1 An Exercise in Branching Fractals

Node level (first, second, third—progressing from the first line and expanding out)	Total number of branches coming out of the nodes this distance from the starting point in your diagram	Next number in the Fibonnaci sequence
1		2
2		3
3		5
4		8
5		21

Exercise:

Consider the branching exercise above. Starting at the first node or branching point, count the number of new branches at each level of the diagram and fill in Table 6.1 above.

Does your diagram's expansion follow the Fibonnaci sequence? Should it? Why may it deviate?

DANIEL Q. BOJE'S ENTREPRENEURSHIP, FRACTAL-SPIRAL STORY OF THE TRASH COMPACTOR

This is from a Quantum Storytelling conference proceedings paper (Boje, 2014). I will trace the intertextuality of 52 patents incorporating or extending Daniel Boje's patents, from the 1960s to the present day (see Appendix A for listing). Figure 6.5 is the original patent drawing my dad sketched out and submitted.

When I (David) was getting out of high school in June 1966, my dad filed his first patent October 20, 1966, August 9, 1967, and again May 2, and May 21, 1968, for his "waste compacting device" (United States Patent O 3,384,007 WASTE COMPACTING DEVICE Daniel Q. Boje, Fairfield, NJ, and Samuel Taylor Permutt, Jamaica Estates, and Sol Kestin, Bronx, NY).

He had just filled his initial patent for a Trash Compactor, and the partners to his (ad) venture. It was, at the time, a mechanical device, with gears driving a plunger, into a funnel-shaped cylinder. Sol sold his jewelry business for the cash to get the Trash Compactor manufactured, and his brother-in-law Samuel (Sam) got legislation passed in New York and New Jersey to require the Trash Compactor in apartment buildings with over 10 units, as an alternative to the Smoke Scrubber, that was a more expensive solution.

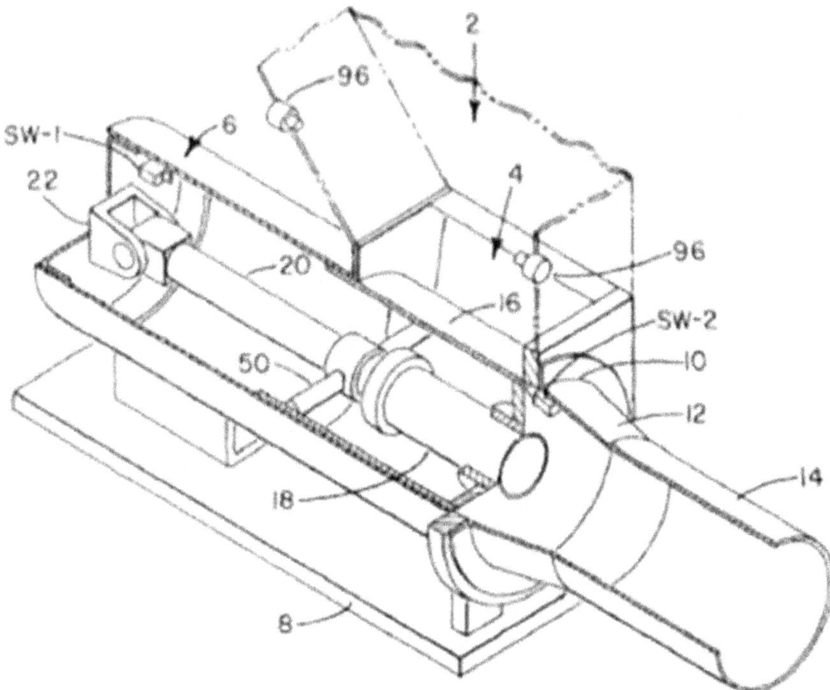

Figure 6.5 Daniel Q Boje US Pat NO. 3,384,007 issued May 21, 1968 Patented April 9, 1974 (approved)

Dan, Sol, and Sam were assignors to Compactor Corporation, a corporation of New York Continuation–impart of application Ser. No. 588,050, Oct. 20, 1966. When you calculate the 52 patents filed by other corporations, referencing my dad's 1966 patents, you get a pattern of intertext referencing like this one.

In this figure, you can see a "Fractal Story" depiction of patent-intertextuality that looks much like a Fibonacci spiral. Patent-intertextuality is defined as the patents that follow on, referencing the original patent. The Commercial Trash Compactor entrepreneurial sociomateriality exhibits the regular, recurring, fractal-spiral of self-sameness approximating a Fibonacci series (1 + 1 = 2; 1 + 2 = 3; 2 + 3 = 5; 3 + 5 = 8; and so on).

I have a project in mind: to trace out the patents referencing other prior patents, of all 52 patents now citing my dad's patents. As they branch into all kinds of industries, I predict it will look something like the Wikia fractal-spiral story we examined, with all kinds of Fibonacci fractal-spiral offshoots.

My dad's time is over. As he told me time and again, the age of the independent entrepreneur is done, and now corporations have taken over the patent game. It's a game played with a strategy of surround and capture.

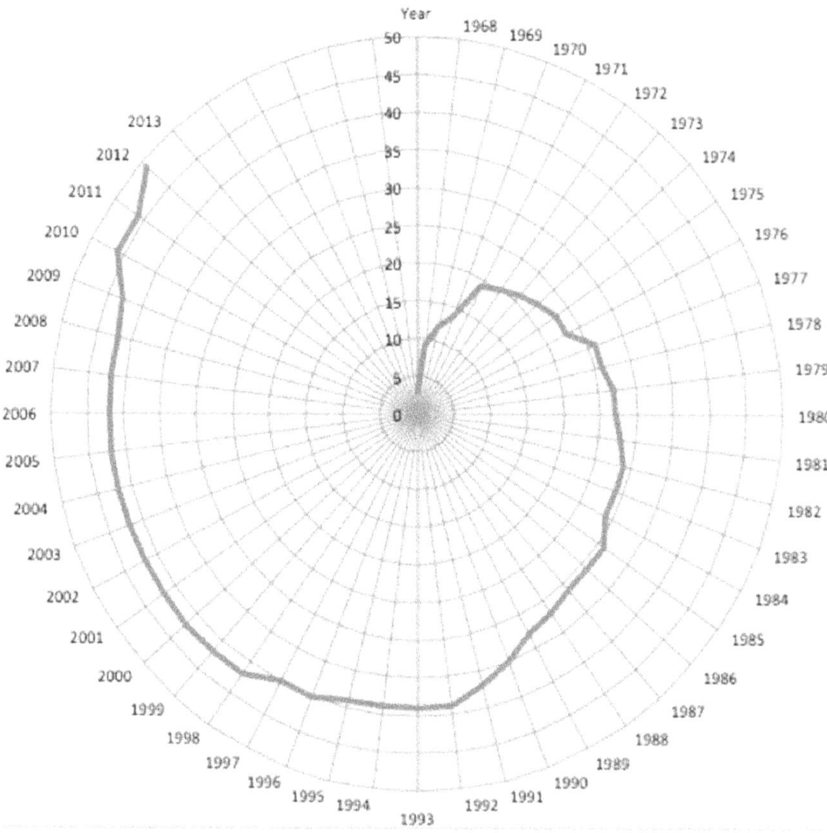

Figure 6.6 Cumulative Number of Patents Referencing Daniel Boje's Patent in Their Own

As Gavin Clarkson (2004, p. 75) describes it, there is a "patent thicket": "When organizations in technology industries attempt to advance their innovative activities, they almost always must be cognizant of the intellectual property rights of others. When further innovation is thwarted, however, the situation can be described as a patent thicket." A patent thicket is defined by Clarkson and DeKorte (2006: 180) as "unintentionally dense webs of overlapping intellectual property rights owned by different companies that can retard progress." In this case, the patent thicket barrier was breeched and a fractal-spiral emerged.

Exercise:

1. Have you ever had a great idea that seemed innovative? Did you see it through? Apply the lens of relational introspection to consider the situation in terms of your idea's appeal to yourself, others, and the larger ecosystem in which it might have been marketed.

2. What were the sociomaterial aspects of the concept? How did the right materials and ideas come together at the right time? If they didn't, why not?
3. Was your role in the situation consistent with the other patterns you see in your worklife? Why or why not? What might you do differently?

FRACTAL ANALYTICS CONSULTING COMPANY: THEY WERE DOING BIG DATA BEFORE IT WAS COOL

What is Big Data? It can be thought of as the wealth of information ranging from customers' locations and preferences to geopolitical activity that is available to companies today. The amount of information we share through our activities on the World Wide Web, social media, GPS receivers, and a plethora of other electronic devices has created a new problem in business. Instead of digging for information, today's analysts are inundated to the point where the real challenge is to make sense of it all. That's the environment where the team at Fractal Analytics thrives.

Some fractals cannot be visualized. They come out of a discipline called Fractal Analytics. There is a consulting company by this same name, Fractal Analytics. It was founded in 2000, has 13 offices and established a *Fractal Science Lab* for developing tailored analytics and tools that include reusable model components. They are doing Big Data and *fractal analytics,* analyzing large data sets to support efforts in areas ranging from visualization to marketing and machine learning. They work to develop an "understanding of consumers and earn customer loyalty, and make better data-informed decisions. Leading global companies partner with Fractal Analytics to build breakthrough analytics solutions, set up analytical centers of excellence, and institutionalize data-driven decisioning" (TA Associates, 2013).

The incumbent cofounders of Data Analytics are Srikanth Velamakanni (Chief Executive Officer) and Pranay Agrawal (President, Client Services). In 2000, when they realized how their skills could impact the way businesses engage with consumers, vendors, partners, and employees, they launched Fractal Analytics. Today they have offices in Mumbai, Delhi, Singapore, London, Dubai, New York, and San Francisco (now their corporate headquarters), and most recently expanded into Guangzho, Geneva, and Rome. They currently work with clients in 150 countries, leveraging Big Data to create predictive and descriptive analytics for their clients. They consult using a wide range of fractal analytics, from visual graphics to forecasting programs. They offer analytics in the form of consumer insights, optimized decisions, business support simulators, business performance, and visual storytelling for more accurate and faster decisions.

1. First, you need to transform your Big Data into meaningful information elements that feed into business intelligence and predictive analytics.
2. Next you need the kind of insights and predictions to fuel the decisions your business users need, including a deep understanding of your customers, your business, and interactions within your market and competitive landscape.
3. And last, analytics need to be delivered to business users in a visual way so they can quickly and easily absorb, diagnose, and solve problems to meet their objectives.

(Fractal Analytics: Overview, 2015)

We had an opportunity to talk with Fractal Analytics' Cofounder Srikanth Velamakanni about his company and how they got started. While working in the financial services industry, he and cofounder Pranay Agrawal discovered that companies needed to use better math to support decision making about issues like consumer debt default trends, etc. Most analytical tools available were backward looking, for example using historical data to make decisions about downgrading financial securities, etc. They knew that math could be applied to the expansive data that was becoming available make a bigger difference in the world.

The name, Fractal Analytics, was chosen because it represented the idea of finding underlying order amid chaos, which seemed a propos to what they hoped to accomplish with analytics. In the early years, before people had any conception of what Big Data was or would become, the idea of analytics was a hard one to sell. So they had to communicate it to clients in terms of return on investment, the idea that using math to support their decision making in this way could lead client companies to make or save money. Because the field was so new, there was also a struggle to define themselves as an analytics firm at the outset, to include hiring the right people without a clearly defined career path in the industry.

Because the principals were all engineers and MBAs, they had an advantage in communicating complicated concepts to the business world. It was very important to sell the business side, not just the analytics and their ability to speak both languages, as it were, was a real advantage because they could simplify things for business users and consumers. He likened it to the experience of driving a car, wherein most people don't want to know exactly how the engine works; they just want to drive the car. The acquisition of Mobius from another Fractal Analytics cofounder, Nirmal Palaparthi, will help the company to deliver a more tailored customer experience (Fractal Analytics Buys, 2015). Mobius makes use of a plethora of data including geo-location, purchasing habits, etc. to provide helpful suggestions to customers using mobile devices, something he feels is the future of marketing.

The company also uses something called visual storytelling to help business users grasp complex analytics and sophisticated models by allowing them to understand what is driving business performance through visual interpretations of data. CEO decisions tend to be driven by simple visual stories. So the consumption layer of their products is streamlined to be simple, visual, and easily consumable, with the intent of supporting real-time decision making. With their combination of mathematical acumen, business and communications savvy, and global reach, Fractal Analytics is making its mark in the world of Big Data.

Exercise:

1. Have you ever been in a situation where you had to really look hard to find supporting data for a decision you needed to make? How about the opposite extreme? What is it like to have an overwhelming amount of information and no way to process it all?
2. Consider the idea of having complex analytical methods finding patterns in consumer data and the marketplace as a whole. How does Fractal Analytics' approach to the consumer experience capitalize on existing patterns of behavior and shape those patterns?
3. How does visual storytelling as described herein relate to our earlier discussions of narrative?

THE MULTIFRACTAL NETWORK CASE: VETA LA PALMA FISH FARM AND BIRD SANCTUARY

The next case was inspired by Taylor Burgett's presentation and lesson plan, January 27, 2015, and adapted by David M. Boje (January 28, 2015). It explores sociomaterial fractal organizing processes in agribusiness.

Veta la Palma is a vast farming estate covering more than 27,000 acres situated in the heart of the Marshlands of Spain's Guadalquivir River and is an example of the world's first Sustainability Plus fish farm.

> Once a natural wetland that was drained to raise cattle, a sophisticated reverse pumping and channeling system was developed to re-establish a marshland habitat on the Estate lands by drawing water in from the Atlantic via the nearby river. This new ecosystem benefits from a natural filtration process of aquatic vegetation that results in the natural cleansing of the water, which leaves the farm cleaner than it comes in. This natural enhancement to the environmental quality of the entire area has created a habitat for raising fish species such as Sea Bass, Grey Mullet, and Meagre in natural, pristine conditions. It has simultaneously becoming one of the largest bird refuges in Europe, attracting almost 250 species of birds to the Estate annually. Those fish lost to birds are simply viewed as a sign that the entire ecosystem is balanced and thriving.
>
> (Brown Trading Company 2015)

What fractals form a multifractal in Veta la Palma's fish farm? How is it different from the usual old and unsustainable agribusiness fish farm business model? The usual agribusiness fractal is called a "mono-fractal" defined here as a single design rule that is monological and mono-focused in ways that erode and diminish its own ecological capital resources (fertile soil, fresh water, abundant vegetation, vibrant microbiology, etc.). The Veta la Palma fish farm, by contrast, is a multi-fractal, defined here as a variety of different kinds of fractals, interacting to form a balanced ecosystem.

Chef Dan Barber's (2010) Ted Talk ("How I fell in Love with Fish" https://www.youtube.com/watch?v=4EUAMe2ixCI) is an amazing storytelling event, where in our terms, he presents a case in Fractal FCM. The marshlands habitat (ecosystem) of the Guadalquivir River were drained to raise cattle using the old agribusiness model. The result was both the fish and the bird species as well as aquatic vegetation species, went into a downward fractal-spiral, in order for the ranchers to "farm" only one kind of species, cattle. The old agribusiness model was "high on capital, chemistry, and machines, and it's never really produced anything good to eat" and the result was a down-spiral (Barber, 2010). It was a world unto itself, intensive, a system of agribusiness closed off from its ecology, in order to maximize cattle production.

Veta la Palma is an ecosystem multifractal-network. Dan Barber does not only a storytelling about a multifractal, but his presentation style is that of a "fractal narrative" (Duarte, 2014). Durarte makes the point that since Mandelbrot's fractal geometry in the 1970s, many social and physical science fields have been inspired to use fractals as a metaphor: films, novels, visual graphics. Barber uses a storytelling rhythm of speech acts, an iteration of tellings, and of Ted Talk visuals, that is itself fractal, a fractal narrative alternating between facts and humor. For example, Dan Barber says, the pink flamingos (one of 250 bird species) feed on the fish (consuming 20%), the fish feed on the aquatic vegetation in an *extensive* farming. "Isn't a thriving bird population the last thing you want on a fish farm?" (Barber, 2010, Ted Talk). The biologist Miguel Meialdea, replied, "No, we farm extensively, not *intensively*, this is an ecological network" (as cited by Barber, 2010). The flamingos eat the shrimp, the shrimp eat the phytoplankton, and so on, so the pinker the belly of the flamingos, the healthier the system, because the water has no impurities, despite flowing from the Guadalquivir River that has the usual industrial and urban pollutants, and somehow this results in an extensive ecological network. Every morning, the pink flamingos fly 150 miles to the fish farm, from their nesting grounds. Every evening they fly 150 miles back, following the broken white line of Highway A92 "No kidding!" (Barber, 2010).

> "It is rare for a farmer to appreciate the predators that eat the animals he raises. But Miguel Medialdea is hardly an ordinary farmer. Looking

> out on to the carpet of flamingos that covers one of the lagoons that make up Veta la Palma, the fish farm in southern Spain where he is biologist, Medialdea shrugs. 'They take about 20% of our annual yield,' he says, pointing at a blush-colored bird as it scoops up a sea bass. "But that just shows the whole system is working."
>
> (Abend, 2009)

How do biologists, like Medialdea, in what we will call the multifractal-network, measure success? As Dan Barber puts it, "So the pinker the belly [of the Pink Flamingos] the better the system!" "So Let's review. A farm that doesn't feed its animals, and a farm that measures its success on the health of its predators—a fish farm, but also a bird sanctuary. . . ." (Abend, 2009).

In the Ph.D. Seminar in Storytelling for Change Management, we have been focusing on FCM storytelling. Taylor Burgett, majoring in computer science and engineering, was facilitating the class. He teaches young students, something called computational thinking. It is like "critical thinking" but its more about "iteration." Iteration that is fractal is the recurring pattern of self-sameness of scale that comes from implementing a design rule. The agribusiness model of fish farming (and cattle farming) follows a fractal-iteration rule of *intensive* agriculture with massive amounts of capital, chemicals, and machines. The *extensive* agriculture fractal-iteration rule of Veta la Palma fish farm is the *multifractal* (defined as fractals of different types such as the pink flamingo feeding and nesting journey, in daily iterations, 150 miles each way, combining with the algae cycle, the water purification of the river cycle, and so on).

What Burgett stresses is just how much more efficient the Veta la Palma ecological network is, the multifractal design rule of iteration is than the old agribusiness model of intensive factory farming. Instead of a down-spiral fractal, the result is an up-spiral of FCM. In the old agribusiness model, one billion people will go hungry today because the fractal rule focuses human attention on intensive, rather than extensive system practices. Instead of seeing what Henderson and Boje (in press) call higher magnification scales, the old model is focused intensively on a very narrow spectrum of the ecosystem, what we call here the mono-fractal.

The mono-fractal is monological (single logic), mono-voices (one-voice), hierarchical (top-down). The multifractal is polylogical (many logics), polyphonic (many voices), and heterarchy (lateral, upward, downward, and latticed) ways of leading. It's what Rosile, Boje, and Nez (in review) call "ensemble leadership." Heterarchy is a system of organizing that Deleuze and Guattari (1987, Chapter 14) call the rhizome-fractal, where parts are self-organizing, reterritorializing and deterritorializing lines of flight, generating nonhierarchical fractal patterns of multiplicity. They give the example of Benoit Mandelbrot's fractal geometry in the section on smooth and striated spatial dynamics.

Table 6.2 Contrasts of Old and New Agribusiness Fish Farm Models

Contrasts:	Old Agribusiness Mono-Fractal Fish Farm	Reclaimed Multifractal Fish Farm
1. Design Rule	Iterations of one kind of fish by feeding them chicken bits	Iterations of many kinds of species, and fish not fed anything
2. Measurement	Maximization of number of one kind of fish	The pinkness of the pink flamingo's belly
3. Focus	Intensive agriculture	Extensive agriculture
4. Control	Hierarchy	Heterarchy
5. Thinking	(Un)Critical Thinking	Computational Thinking
6. Logic	Monologic	Polylogical
7. Dialogue	Polyphonic	Dialogic
8. Storytelling	Mono-fractal narrative	Living story fractal-web

The monomyth fractal (Palumbo, 2002) retells the Joseph Campbell (*The Hero with a Thousand Faces*) in a reductionist formula plot for science-fiction and fantasy films and novels. The hero who, refuses then accepts the call, is challenged, fails and finally attains the boon, spiritual transcendence, returns to his or her community. This is repeated in Asimov Foundation series, as well as *The Matrix, Avatar, Star Wars, Dune,* and most other Hollywood films.

We can summarize the FCM model as follows:

By noticing and gathering local living stories, we get at the *who, what, where,* and *when* of how the fractal patterns are happing as depicted in Figure 6.7. It allows us to understand the fractal design rules in use, and to implement fractal change interventions. By reterritorializing from hierarchy to Heterarchy, as Figure 6.8 suggests, we can implement and sustain changes that are multifractal instead of the old monofractal, monomyth of Hollywood movies.

Finally Taylor Burgett makes a strong closing point. If we can move to a fractality understanding, we change the level of our fractal-awareness from monofractal and monomythic to the multifractal.

Most of the work in operationalizing fractals in change management uses the branching-fractal, usually, kind of two-dimensional display. Above the dimensions are time, power, and efficacy. Both examples are hierarchical progressions of command and control over time, by iterations of subbranching.

An alternative is the nonlinear fractal and multifractal models such as spiraling.

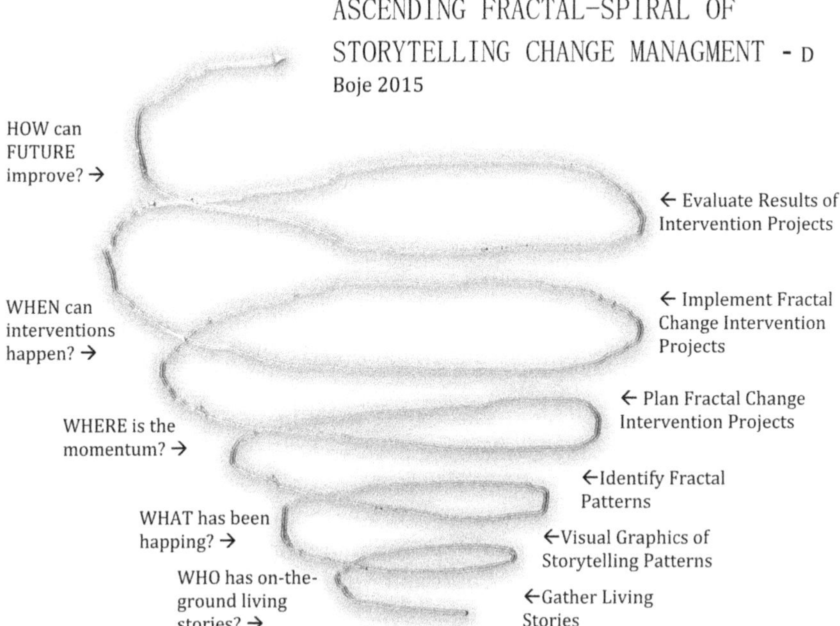

Figure 6.7 Fractal Change Management Model

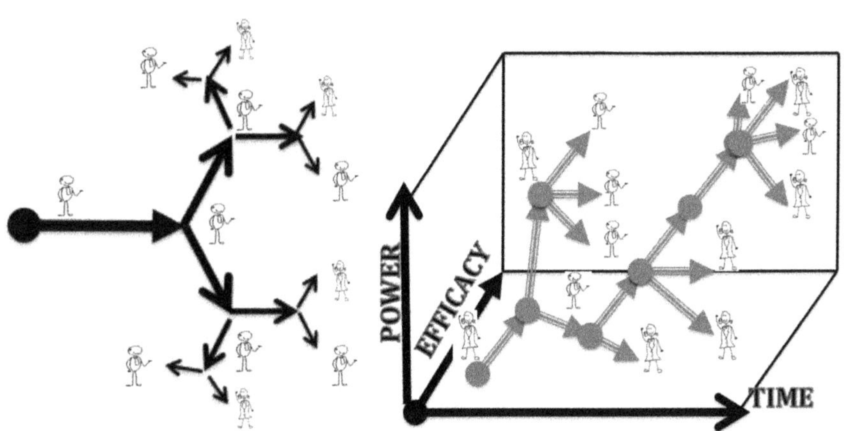

Figure 6.8 Moving from Two-Dimensional to Three-Dimensional Branching Fractal Depictions of FCM

Source: Drawings by Boje. Used by Permission.

SPUD'S, AND HORSES AND RESTORYING

This case was written by David M. Boje January 29, 2015 and is used with permission (www.peaceaware.com/SPUDS).

We veterans run our lives by the fractal rules we learn in the military. A fractal rule is way your storytelling patterns your life in material ways. I am godfather to the "Material Storytelling" Lab founded by Anete Strand in Denmark (Strand, 2012). We use sand trays and let people pick material objects (action figures, toy animals, military ware, vehicles, etc.) to nonverbally tell stories.

We also use a big sand tray, an arena with live humans and horse, interacting with each other and with material objects such as rails, cones, hula hoops, barrels, and so on. At some point we ask veterans and their family members to set up the objects to depict their life story before and after deployment, and then the challenging part, walk the horses through it.

The "We" is Kenneth Hacker and Jeanne Flora (Arts & Science College, Communication Studies Department); Elizabeth England-Kennedy and Wanda Whittlesey-Jerome (Health & Social Services College, Social Work Department); Kourtney Vaillancourt and Merranda Marin (College of Agriculture Consumer & Environmental Sciences, Family and Consumer Sciences Department; and Grace Ann Rosile, Meghan Downes, and David Boje (College of Business, Management Department).

SPUD'S (SHIFTS–PATTERNS–UNIQUE–DISCREPANCIES–SELF-AWARENESS)

> Our research team (professors from four colleges) is adapting the SPUD'S observation protocol we use in Equine-Assisted Psychotherapy (Mandrell, 2014) in our "embodied restorying" work with veterans and their family members, some of whom have PTSD and TBI, and others just work on improving family relationships after deployment (Boje, DuRant, Coppedge, Chambers, & Marcillo-Gomez, 2012) We can use SPUD'S in both the sand tray and the arena work:
>
> - **Shifts** (S) in the behaviors, encounters between people, and between people and horses, and with other materials (cones, railings, chairs, ropes, etc. in the arena), in the encounters of sociomateriality of organizing, and including actual physical placement of horses and humans, the moving, changing relationships, for good or bad.
> - **Patterns** (P), the times a pattern forms, such as horses running in circles around the arena, clients interacting with horses, and horses interacting with each other, and when we as trainers bring up these patterns to for the participants to comment on.

- **Unique** (U), moments in a session where as an observer/facilitator, you think, "Wow, I've never seen anything quite like that before" (EAGALA Manual, 2012, p. 58).
- **Discrepancy** (D), people's verbal communications against the backdrop of no-verbal messages between people, between people and horses. Observing such moments of communication indicates possibilities for change, such as when there are types of incongruences between what they are telling, and what they are doing.
- **Self-Awareness** ('S), or "My Stuff," the countertransference, we ourselves are making with our research agenda, our habits of practices, our assumptions that can be possible counterproductive enabling ways of interacting with people and horses.

SPUD'S is the Equine-Assisted Growth & Assisted Learning Association (EAGALA) approach to training facilitators to do learning and unlearning sessions of counseling and therapy that is being increasingly used with organization clients, as well as with veterans and their families, to facilitate change through a process of self-examination, reflection, and self- and other-observation in a situation of cross-species communication. Patti Mandrell (2014) says it is a method for "reconstructing the family story" and "transforming experience into story" using s "system's perspective" to family psychotherapy (pp. 29–30). Grace Ann Rosile and I were trained by Patti and her husband Randy to use SPUD'S observation and facilitation methods, and we become certified by EAGALA in doing "Veteran and Family Deployment Support" as an EAGALA Military Services Provider on October 1, 2014.

The purpose of SPUD'S is to maximize the number of alternative stories and unique little wow moments (LWMs) outcomes that are generative in the encounters between humans, horses, and facilitators. Each EAGALA facilitator teams up with a licensed counselor, psychologist, or psychoanalyst, who used the SPUD'S to react to what is going on in the arena, and decide what, if anything to do as intervention, such as designing a challenging problem for people and horses to solve. Mandrell refers to White and Epston's (1990) classic work on 'restorying.' It was originally a way to intervene in family systems, using a text-based approach. However, in its current use, we take our own 'embodied' approach to avoid the pitfalls of 'textualizing' others. The role of the EAGALA horse person (such as myself) and the counselor is to be a team that focuses attention and awareness on the systems behavior, while giving freedom to the family memes to narrate in their own ways, without our interruptions or expert over-narratives getting in their way. The advantages of horses are that they don't lie, and they react to humans' emotions and behaviors. Horses are "honest teachers" (Mandrell, 2014: 35). Horses give honest feedback to people about emotions, stress, and react in by moving away from stress-filled people, or moving closer to sad ones. Further the horses are herd animals, and when several are loose in an arena, they form patterns with each other and with the humans. And this gives people a way to understand their own patterns.

The SPUD'S method can easily be adapted to studying and changing the standards-fractals using Tetranormalizing 'researcher interventions.' The first-order change is to enter the daily life of people in organizations to observe without interruption the Shifts-Patterns-Unique-Discrepancies (SPUD) and our own Apostrophe-S (Self-Awareness, 'S) of our own over-narrating that interrupts others' living stories. The second-order change is to act as a "Systems' therapist" (Mandrell, 2014: 32) to intervene by taking people to a different place, opening up "new vistas" that were before, quite invisible and to teach them how to see those SPUD'S for themselves.

SPUD'S gives invitation to people to share their stories, and system-facilitators to use observational statements (by monitoring their own 'S, self-awareness and self-reflexivity). There is question asking of people and reflective listening using clarification statements, and awareness of the metaphors in use. In SPUD'S you notice the blaming, the attributions, the assessments, and the judgments about people and other beings. Making observational statements is a learned skill in the EAGALA training. The question asking avoid 'could', 'should', and 'would' by the systems-intervener in order to give the client space to make their own attributions. Once the client labels an organization pattern as 'bureaucratic,' 'mechanistic', 'political', 'heartless', or 'organic'—then the systems-intervener begins to use that same metaphor and ask questions that unpack it. At times it is helpful to invite people to name the organization, to give it a metaphor. Once in use, the questions can begin: Who or what are doing 'bureaucratic' acts? The metaphors (labels) can change over the course of the systems research interventions.

Agent-Based Fractal Modeling: Agent-based-modeling is being combined with something we are calling 'fractal rules' for living one's life. Fractal material storytelling is an assemblage of rules that create behavioral interaction cycles (or loops). Here are examples of military fractal rules that generate recurring patterns in a veteran's life story.

1. Be strong, always!
2. Never show weakness!
3. Man Up! Suck it up! Get back to work!
4. Never ever tell the 'man' you have PTSD!
5. Telling a PTSD story in the military means you return from deployment to PTSD confinement!
6. Telling a PTSD story means you will never get promoted!
7. Telling a PTSD story means you will be discharged!
8. Telling a PTSD story leads to Social Stereotyping!
9. Telling a PTSD story leads to permanent Pathologizing!
10. Here's a fractal rule: Just take your meds and keep quiet!

The fractal rules a veteran enacts select the cycles of events they live out with others (humans and in our arena work, horses). The fractal assembly rules determine the cycles of restorying and the cycles of social withdrawal increase reliving the past traumas, which can decrease future storying, so the options for life get fewer and fewer. The interaction of the two loops (self-efficacy-embodied restorying) with the (social withdrawal-reliving past traumas and on future storying), works out the suicide-prevention or suicide-enactment double fractal loop pattern.

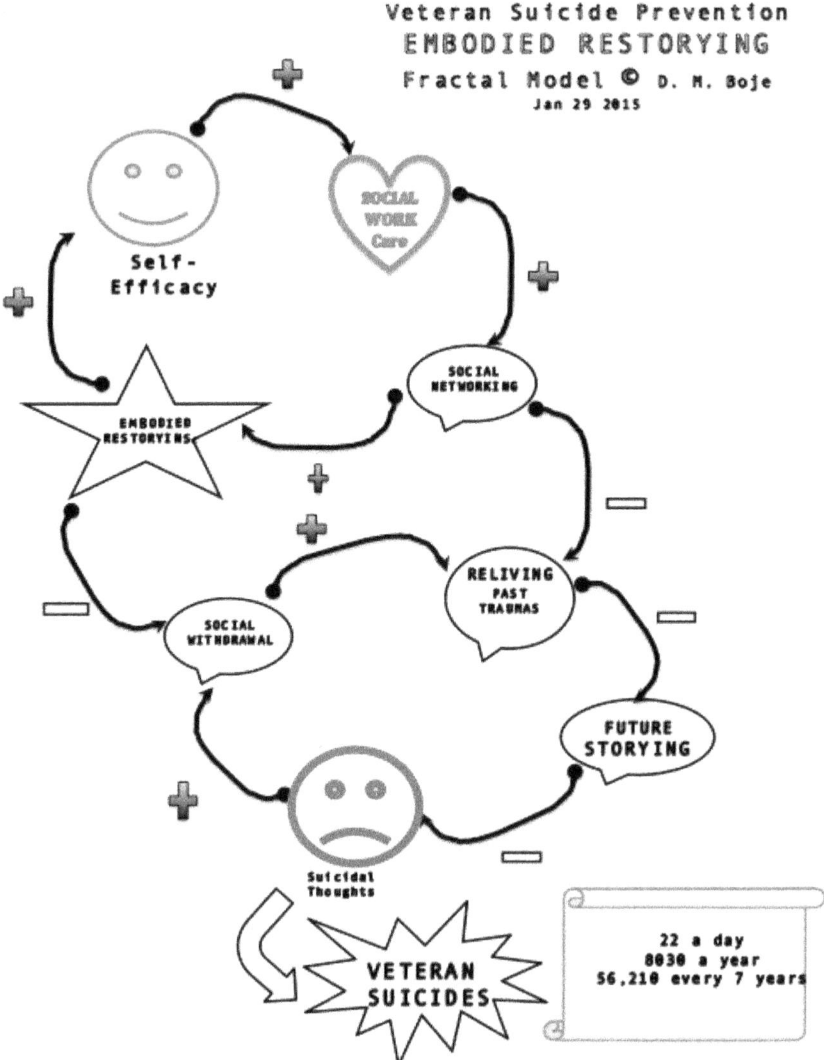

Figure 6.9 SPUDS and Shifting Veterans' Fractal Patterns in Generative Ways
Source: By David Boje. Used by Permission.

> A simple example, is a the fractal rules about not telling PTSD story leads to social withdrawal, reliving past traumas, getting stuck in the past, again and again, until there is no future storying, no possibilities to escape the endless loop.
>
> Our research project is to collect the veteran's and family member's 'fractal rules.' There are different types of fractal rules. A 'frequency fractal rule' such as 'reliving past traumas' by itself merely assembles all those past combat (and non-combat) traumas over the course of one's life history, and attracts similar fractal rules: "I freak out when I go outside my house!" And the result, the veteran does 'social withdrawal' with greater frequency, spends inordinate time in dark room, in front of TV or lost in video games.
>
> (Boje 2015)

Exercise:

1. Consider the stories of the veterans going in. What were the simple rules under which they operated? Apply the relational introspection concept to consider how these rules may have been applied and perceived in the context of combat military experience and in the new context of civilian life after discharge.
2. How does an embodied practice like the one described above help people to identify fractal patterns in their lives an experiences that may be unproductive?
3. How does restorying with the help of materiality help to make alternate paths and outcomes tangible for the veterans?
4. Using some objects or tools and a sandbox, tell your own material story. Think about the simple rules that may be perpetuating successful or unsuccessful outcomes. If desirable, reposition the objects and restory as in the above example.

REFERENCES

Abend, L. (2009, June 15). 'Sustainable Aquaculture: Net Profits,' Time, Retrieved 8 March, 2015, from http://content.time.com/time/magazine/article/0,9171,1902751,00.html

Barber, D. (Producer). (2010, 8 March 2015). How I Fell in Love with a Fish. [TED Talk] Retrieved 8 March, 2015, from https://www.youtube.com/watch?v=4EUAMe2ixCI

Boje, D. (2014). Fractal Story and Fractal Ethnography of Entrepreneurial Sustainability: Daniel Q. Boje's Trash Compactor Patents and Enterprise. Paper presented at the Quantum Storytelling Conference, Las Cruces, NM.

Boje, D. (2015). The Multifractal Network Case: Veta la Palma Fish Farm and Bird Sanctuary (inspired by Taylor Burgett's presentation and lesson plan, Jan 27 2015) by David M. Boje (January 28, 2015). Case study. New Mexico State University.

Bonifer, M. (2008). *Gamechangers: Improvisation for Business in the Networked World*. Gamechangers.

Browne Trading Company: Veta La Palma Seafood. (2015). Retrieved 8 March, 2015, from http://www.brownetrading.com/products/fresh-fish/veta-la-palma-seafood/

Clarkson, G. (2004). Objective identification of patent thickets: A network analytic approach. *Harvard Business School Doctoral Thesis.*

Clarkson, G., & DeKorte, D. (2006). The problem of patent thickets in convergent technologies. *Annals of the New York Academy of Sciences,* 1093(1), 180–200.

Deleuze, G., & Guattari, F. (1987). *A Thousand Plateaus: Capitalism and Schizophrenia* (B. Massumi, Trans.). Minneapolis, MN: University of Minnesota Press.

Duarte, G. A. (2014). *Fractal Narrative: About the Relationship Between Geometries and Technology and its Impact on Narrative Spaces.* Wetzlar, Germany: Majuskel Medienproduktion.

EAGALA (2012). *Fundamentals of EAGALA Model Practice Training Manual.* 7th edition. Retrieved from http://eagala.org

Fractal Analytics: Overview. (2015). Retrieved 1 February, 2015, from http://www.fractalanalytics.com/products-and-solutions/overview

Fractal Analytics Buys Mobile-Based Context-Aware Big Data startup Mobius Innovations (2015, 15 January). Retrieved 15 May, 2015, from http://www.fractalanalytics.com/news/fractal-analytics-buys-mobile-based-context-aware-big-data-startup-mobius-innovations

Icey (2006). A fibonacci sequence of quarter-circles inside squares, estimating the Golden Spiral. Wikimedia Commons. Retrieved 15 May, 2015, from http://en.wikipedia.org/wiki/File:Fibonacci_spiral.svg

Mandrell, Patti. (2014). *Introduction to Equine-Assisted Psychotherapy: A Comprehensive Overview.* Second Edition. ISBY 978-0-9916291-0-7 United States: Author.

Meredith, H., & Walker, R. (n.d.). Wikia Fractal Story. *Information Design.* Retrieved 8 March, 2015, from http://www.gold-collective.com/wikia-fractal-story/

Palumbo, D. (2002). *Chaos theory, Asimov's Foundations and Robots, and Herbert's Dune: the Fractal Aesthetic of Epic Science Fiction* (No. 100). Westport, CT: Greenwood Press.

Quade, Kristine. (2011). "Simple rules leaders use to guide their organizations during times of rapid change." Ed.D. Doctoral Dissertation, Graduate School of Education and Psychology, Pepperdine University.

Quade, Kristine, and Royce Holladay. (2010). *Dynamical Leadership: Building Adaptive Capacity for Uncertain Times.* Apache Junction, AZ: Gold Canyon Press.

TA Associates Announces Investment in Fractal Analytics. (2013, June 24). TA Associates: TA News. Retrieved 13 May, 2015, from http://www.ta.com/News/Fractal-Press-Release.aspx

United States Patent O 3,384,007 WASTE COMPACTING DEVICE Daniel Q. Boje, Fairfield, NJ, and Samuel Taylor Permutt, Jamaica Estates, and Sol Kestin, Bronx, NY.

White, M., & Epston, D. (1990). *Narrative Means to Therapeutic Ends.* New York: WW Norton & Company.

Part III

The Fractal Manager's Toolkit

In this section, we explore practical tools for using Fractal Change Management (FCM) in organizations. The first is the fractal action research model (FARM), derived from Tonya's doctoral dissertation. The model makes use of ontological storytelling inquiry and antenarrative concepts to affect change in organizations. The second, we suggest an FCM-derived approach to strategic change in organizations. This model is nonsequential and includes ontologically derived steps in addition to sociomaterially tangible considerations. Third, we examine what we call *ontological systems mapping* that describes how ontological storytelling inquiries using a content-agnostic fractal-based protocol can elicit deep reflections from research subjects. This approach is especially useful in that it gets past the proclamation of espoused values to reveal the simple rules behind aggregate behavior in social networks, including hidden rules and behaviors that people are not particularly proud of. Collectively, these chapters offer the reader a reasonably robust set of tools for working with fractal organizing processes.

7 The Fractal Action Research Method (FARM)

One outcome of the study described in Chapter 5 was the development of a fractal-based model for action research. It is "grounded in the ontic recognition of patterns, consideration of their ontological meanings, and the calculated use of agency" (Wakefield 2012, p. 255). Figure 7.1 depicts the model, which was conceived of as a way to use fractal-based insights as a tool for organizational development. We will walk through the model, illustrating each step of the process with a case where possible.

Fractal change management theory and its attendant Fractal Action Research Model (FARM) suggest a brand of action research and strategic planning specifically geared toward modern organizations facing turbulent environments. It replaces traditional approaches with an ontologically based method of looking for self-similar, scalable patterns in storytelling and gauging their future implications. Patterns are identified thematically and explored for self-similarity and scalability, then explored using David Boje's antenarrative typology. Alignment with organizational aims and values is then considered, opening the door to risk management and decision-making processes based on observed patterns in lieu of linear projections.

First Principles of the FARM

- Groups of people self-organize as a matter of course
- The patterns of self-organization are scalable and self-similar with people as elsewhere in nature
- Patterns that occur repeatedly on multiple scales offer clues to the nature of any organization and are likely to continue occurring, even if circumstances change
- Storytelling is one place where these patterns appear as groups of individuals engage in aggregate sense-making
- Inherent in sense-making is the construction of antenarratives

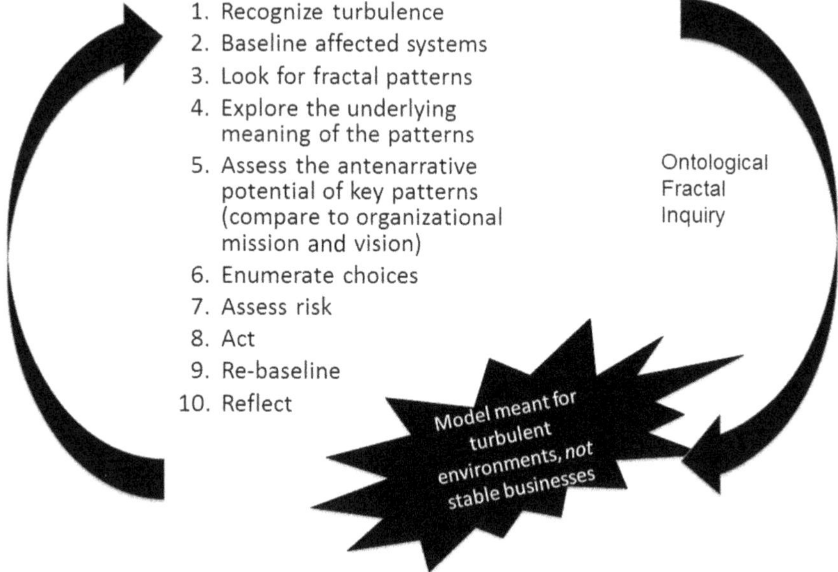

Fractal Action Research Model (FARM)
1. Recognize turbulence
2. Baseline affected systems
3. Look for fractal patterns
4. Explore the underlying meaning of the patterns
5. Assess the antenarrative potential of key patterns (compare to organizational mission and vision)
6. Enumerate choices
7. Assess risk
8. Act
9. Re-baseline
10. Reflect
Ontological Fractal Inquiry
Model meant for turbulent environments, not stable businesses

Figure 7.1 FARM Process Ontological Inquiry Steps
Source: Tonya Henderson Wakefield, 2012. Used by permission.

Antenarrative is

> defined as the double move: a bet (ante) on the future and the before (ante) of our living story on its way to grand narrative coherence—which is part of his triadic theory of storytelling (in which antenarrative connects the living stories to the grand narratives).
>
> (Boje 2014)

STEP 1: RECOGNIZE TURBULENCE

The first step in this process is to determine if the model is suitable for the situation at hand. It was designed for organizations facing turbulence. The following questions may be of help.

1. Is the organization operating in a competitive and/or changing environment? If the industry and customer base are stable, the FARM may not be a good fit.
2. Have there been any organizational upheaval and/or social problems that impact accomplishment of work? If there are no apparent issues (i.e., there have been no reorganizations, changes of leadership, or apparent disgruntlement), then the FARM may not be a good fit.

If the answers to the above questions are yes in either case, proceed to the next step. Otherwise, we recommend a simpler approach grounded in more traditional organization development methods.

STEP 2: BASELINE THE AFFECTED SYSTEMICITY

Next it becomes important for the consultant to engage in some informal and formal data collection, taking special care to avoid choosing the wrong metrics based on what is easy or readily available. We recommend several days of observation, to include reading official reports that describe the dominant narrative of the organization, followed by an ontological storytelling inquiry such as the one described in Chapter 5. It is necessary to select a group of individuals whose stories are likely to interconnect and whose proximity to the issue at hand suggests that they have their eyes on the unfolding process of the organization's unfolding over time. A word of caution, though. Be careful not to select a homogenous group, whose stories are likely to parrot the dominant narrative. Instead, consider the informal power structure as well as the formal one and try to include perspectives from all levels of the organization if appropriate. This method can help the consultant to identify themes and develop an ontological map of the systemicity studied, as described in Chapter 9. Chapter 9 also contains a sample interview protocol that can be adapted for use in any organization, association, or social network. At the end of this step the consultant should have identified key themes from the data and be ready to explore their deeper meaning.

STEP 3: LOOK FOR FRACTAL PATTERNS

Having collected and analyzed participants' perspectives about where scalable, self-similar patterns occur in their network's behavior, the consultant should be prepared to revisit the data set at multiple levels of analysis. Although the levels of analysis may vary according to the situation, in a typical organization it is simplest to begin with the following categories: *individual, group/work-center, organizational, and community level behaviors*. Whereas there are many approaches possible, we like to pick an individual theme and go through the associated story performances, further sorting them according to the level of analysis at which they appear to occur. When this step is finished, we can turn our attention to those patterns that appear to exhibit fractal scalability and self-similarity, based on the expectation that these patterns are significant indicators of the organization's typical behaviors.

STEP 4: EXPLORE THE UNDERLYING MEANING OF THE PATTERNS

This step involves revisiting those interviewed in step two and sharing the themes identified. They should then be afforded the opportunity to discuss their perceptions of what the themes mean in the context of their lived experiences as well as how their responses may have been congruent with or different from those of the other respondents. Collect and analyze their ideas about what this means in terms of the organization's present state and its future.

STEP 5: ASSESS THE ANTENARRATIVE POTENTIAL OF KEY PATTERNS

Drawing on Boje's taxonomy of antenarrative types, categorize the most important patterns identified and consider the likelihood of each one continuing to perpetuate through the network, to include the likely effects if it occurs on a very large scale and/or at an unexpected or inconvenient time. Now consider the patterns in combination and their effects on one another and the organization itself. Use the organization's mission, vision, and guiding principles to consider the alignment between these patterns and what the organization is trying to accomplish. Next consider the potential influences on the broader spectrum of stakeholders, to include the environment and future generations.

STEP 6: ENUMERATE CHOICES

Decide which patterns merit attention, whether through active reinforcement of healthy patterns, trying to change destructive ones, riding out the storm, or even being bold and attempting to generate entirely new patterns.[1] For each pattern identified and explored above, create a worksheet with the following headings.

- Pattern Name:
- Description:
- Scalable? (Y/N)
- Self-similar repetition? (Y/N)
- Context:
- Type of antenarrative potential:
- Alignment to the organization's mission, vision, and guiding principles:
- Likely effects of its perpetuation or dissipation (as observed, on a large scale, and/or at unpredictable times):
- Other patterns it may interact with:
- Our options:

It is important that these worksheets not be filled out in a vacuum. They should be explored with the help of as many stakeholders as possible, within the bounds of time and budget constraints.

STEP 7: ASSESS RISK

Based on the above analysis, consider the risk to the organization's aims and long-term sustainability for the patterns described individually and in tandem, considering every combination possible as well as other potential effects that could occur in the environment. We approach this from a rhizomatic perspective. The assessment of risks, drawing from socioeconomic management (SEAM), is tied to coherence between organizational principles and behaviors. When sociomaterial factors are not in alignment with the simple rules governing the organization's espoused values and mission, the conditions are ripe for unseen factors to emerge, not unlike unchecked weeds that spring up in unexpected places in a garden (Savall, Zardet, Bonnet, p. 33). In complex adaptive systems, unseen connections are especially important because of the high susceptibility to butterfly effects. Risk management in this frame necessitates the consideration of patterns seen in small contexts with a view toward exploring the potential outcomes of their propagation and appearance at unexpected times, in additional contexts and reverberation throughout the system.

STEP 8: ACT

This part of the process involves not only taking action, but the choice to act with purpose, using a pattern-based perspective. To use this model, we begin by examining the patterns using the following questions. These questions are recommended to be used in conjunction with the model of action suggested in Chapter 8.

1. Given what we know of the pattern we are concerned with, what do we normally do in this situation?
2. What other influences from leadership, new knowledge, etc. has bearing on the problem?
3. Are there worries, misconceptions, etc. that prevent us from focusing on the task at hand? Are all those involved in decision making for this issue truly present and engaged?
4. Examining the choices enumerated in Step 6 above, which ones are consistent with our past actions and which ones constitute a different approach? Is once course of action preferable or can we consider them in combination?

Choice and Pattern Shifting

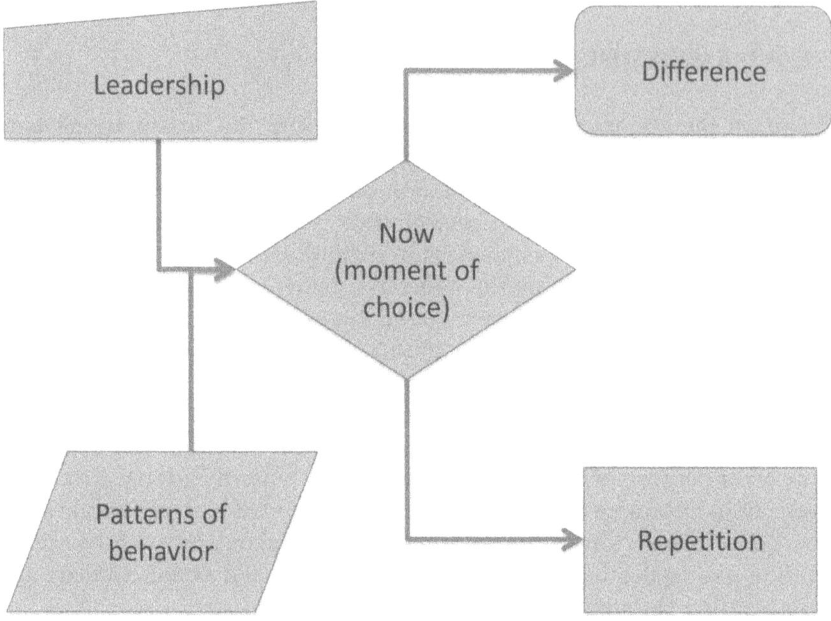

Figure 7.2 Simple Model of Choice
Source: Tonya Henderson Wakefield 2012. Used by permission.

It is important to note that efforts to deviate from the course of action that an organization would typically take under a set of circumstances can be tricky. Change is uncomfortable for most people, even when the change is clearly appropriate. Add to that the confusing nature of complex environments where there are no guarantees. "If you do X, then Y will occur." There is no guaranteed return on investment—the panacea of the small time entrepreneur. When we find ourselves in unanticipated white water, it is only natural to cling to the sides of the boat we are in, eyes firmly closed as we hang on and head toward the falls. So it behooves the fractal manager to be patient with others to the extent possible as we are often asking leopards to consider changing their spots.

Once a course of action is taken, consider the timing and likely outcomes vis-à-vis all stakeholders, both internal to the organization and external to it. If the risks are acceptable, execute the course of action, paying careful attention to timing. (See Chapter 8 for more on timing.)

STEP 9: REBASELINE

Revisit the people whose inputs were received in Step 2. This should be accomplished a reasonable time after the course of action has had a chance to take effect. How long that is will depend on the type of action taken, how interconnected the people and processes are, and the context as a whole. It is not necessary to repeat Step 2 in its entirety, unless time and resources permit this level of thoroughness. A simple focus group will suffice. The following questions are provided as a guide for data collection at this stage.

1. What has happened in the time since we engaged with you all the first time?
2. What, if anything, has changed as a result?
3. What are your thoughts concerning the key patterns as they exist today?
4. What choices do we have now? (Revisit the worksheets from Step 6.)
5. Does it make sense to repeat the cycle completely, conduct an abbreviated cycle (Steps 5–10), or leave things alone?

STEP 10: REFLECT

Leaders and other stakeholders should be encouraged to engage in quiet reflection upon completion of Step 9. A minimum of three days after completion of the focus group, an open space inspired meeting should be held (Owen 2008). In this meeting, stakeholders are invited to participate in a forum wherein people self-select to form small groups centered around the processes that interest or concern them. A time for unstructured group discussion is allowed, after which the small groups report back to the whole room to share their findings. During this meeting, a facilitator should follow open space ground rules, take notes, and employ the rationalization of conflict model suggested by Emery and Purser (1996).

Rationalization of conflict involves the facilitator making a visible note about areas of conflict, ensuring that the topic is not forgotten, but allowing the group to move forward rather than get bogged down or sidetracked. Emery and Purser (1996) use the method in the context of search conferences. It is very important to properly document the outcomes so that future cycles can build upon what was done. The process should become part of the institutional memory so that processes and unintentional patterns are understood and monitored for changes as a matter of course. Philosophically, one must be willing to allow the organization to adapt its form and modes of operation around core principles, accepting that as it unfolds, things may look much different than what leaders originally envisioned.

Entrepreneurs fill in the free moments and free spaces of fractal-sociomateriality, whereas others are not aware of these free niches because they are focused and habituated to ordinary fractal-sociomateriality practices of their work organization and/or consumption practices. Once embedded and habituated into a fractal-sociomateriality, it is difficult to see through an alternative observational apparatus to some other fractal-sociomateriality horizon of *spacetimemattering*. In Schumpeter's terms, the entrepreneur is creatively producing new fractal-sociomateriality awareness horizon, whereas creative-destructing the old fractal-sociomateriality habitude of their era. For example, what Internet, cell phone, iPads, iPhones, and so on did to redefine fractal-sociomateriality to some new horizon of awareness. Entrepreneurship occurs in a socioeconomic context, in the situation of a waveform of business cycles (with amplitude and frequency that is measurable). However to measure it, requires we look at an appropriate "observational apparatus." It is not something we can see with our eyes alone. The observational apparatus I have in mind is called fractals. Schumpeter takes the "long wave" view and does not want to interfere with the amplitudes of the wave, betting that the entrepreneurs will flourish in both creative production and creative destruction (boom and bust cycles of the waveform).

Fractal-sociomateriality is present in multiplicity of fractal-observation-apparatuses, that we choose to be absorbed in, rather than alternative ones.

NOTE

1. See Boje and Wakefield (2011) for a discussion of options in the face of emergent phenomena.

REFERENCES

Boje, David M. (2014). Meet Our Faculty: Dr. David M. Boje, Management. In NM State Business Outlook, edited by Wenkai Zhou. Las Cruces, New Mexico.

Boje, D., & Wakefield, T. (2011). Storytelling in Systemicity and Emergence: A Third Order Cybernetic. In D. Boje, B. Burnes, & J. Hassard (Eds.), *The Routledge Companion to Organizational Change* (pp. 171–181). New York: Routledge.

Emery, Merrelyn, and Ronald E. Purser. (1996). The search conference. 1st ed. San Francisco, CA: Jossey-Bass, Inc.

Owen, Harrison (2008). *Open Space Technology: A User's Guide*. 3rd ed. Berrett-Koehler.

Savall, H., Zardet, V., & Bonnet, M. (2008). Realizing the potential of enterprises through socio-economic management (English Edition ed.). Geneva, Lyon: International Labour Office Bureau for Employers' Activities Socio-economic Institute of Firms and Organizations Research Institute Associated with the University of Jean Moulin.

Wakefield, Tonya L. Henderson. (2012). "An ontology of storytelling systemicity: Management, fractals and the Waldo Canyon fire." Doctorate of Management Doctoral dissertation, Management, Colorado Technical University.

8 A Fractal-Based Strategic Change Model

In many organizations, strategic planning is something we do with a board of directors periodically—sometimes quite effectively. We gather in the board room or at an offsite retreat to discuss our mission, vision, and guiding principles and tie them into goals for the coming year. Sometimes such gatherings bring about strategic changes in the form of restructuring, changing emphasis in markets, the launches of new products . . . revolutionary stuff. This approach has worked well in many settings and withstood the test of time. Yet it has its limitations. We limit our understanding to the knowledge available in the room at the time, to board members' experiences, the institutional memory, and whatever preparation has been done. Frequently we miss patterns of behavior that appear among staff members and clients, collaborators, and in the organization's interaction with the external environment. We make the link between an ontological and principled mode of existence and the actions of the organization by checking the alignment of actions with the strategic guidance in positive generative ways as well. There is much good in the old ways.

Yet in a complex adaptive system operating in a turbulent environment, things can change very quickly. To react quickly requires the kind of adaptability attributed to Eoyang's (2009) and Quade's (2011, 2010) descriptions of simple rules.

> The principle in that one is that a spider, if you put a pin in its brain, it stops functioning. Period. [With a] starfish, you cut off one of the arms; it will grow another one. So, you look at the Taliban structure, they are like a starfish . . . You cut up one of the arms; they grow 15 more. You know . . . They just know how to reemerge, end we are the spider, Democracy. Quote end quote,[1] democracy is a spider because we go at it with very strong judgment and a lot of righteousness.
>
> —Kristine Quade (interview)

To that end, we propose a model for strategic change that can be used not only in the boardroom, but in the day to day Being of leaders at all levels of the organization, to include the community, societal, and global levels as well. Change management is not a periodic occurrence that is undertaken in response to major events or leaders' initiatives. Instead it becomes and organizational way of Being, wherein change is accepted as a daily thing, be it large scale of smaller scale changes that happen every day. The amount of communication and coordination associated with the response will vary according to the scale and circumstances, but the following aspects apply at all levels.

THE FIVE *AS* OF FRACTAL CHANGE MANAGEMENT

We propose a change management theory and practice, based on attunement to fractal patterns. This Fractal Change Management (FCM) approach offers scalable rules of design and growth that can be used in self-similar ways in organization change and development practices. Building on the fractal action research model (FARM) described in Chapter 7, we now suggest a model for strategic change rooted in the awareness of intra-active, cocreative fractal patterns. Here we focus on *awareness, attunement, alignment, action, and antenarrative* processes that are, as Barad (2003, 2007) puts it, in dynamic "intra-activity."[2] The steps are described sequentially, but can be taken out of order and revisited as appropriate, creating an iterative, flexible architecture for change management processes. For example, in the early stages of working with this model, one may elect to focus on awareness to a great extent, but over time this step may require less attention, being revisited only periodically in the interest of gaining new education and insights.

Whereas relational introspection is discussed primarily under the heading of awareness, it is important to consider each step in terms of its implications at multiple levels of analysis, including consideration of the self, others, and the ecosystem. The depiction of each of the steps as central to a relational introspection triangle is a reminder of the need for such considerations across the board, as FCM becomes a mode of Being in strategy, instead of periodically "doing strategy."

The following questions provide a starting point for reflection as you undertake this mode of operation using relational introspection.

Self (Organization)

- What does our strategic guidance (mission, vision, guiding principles, goals) say? Is it an accurate reflection of where we are?
- What do we hope to achieve with this interaction? Why?
- Are we all behind this project? What do we disagree about internally.
- What is our morale like?
- What are we collectively projecting (voice, body language, dress code, word choice)?

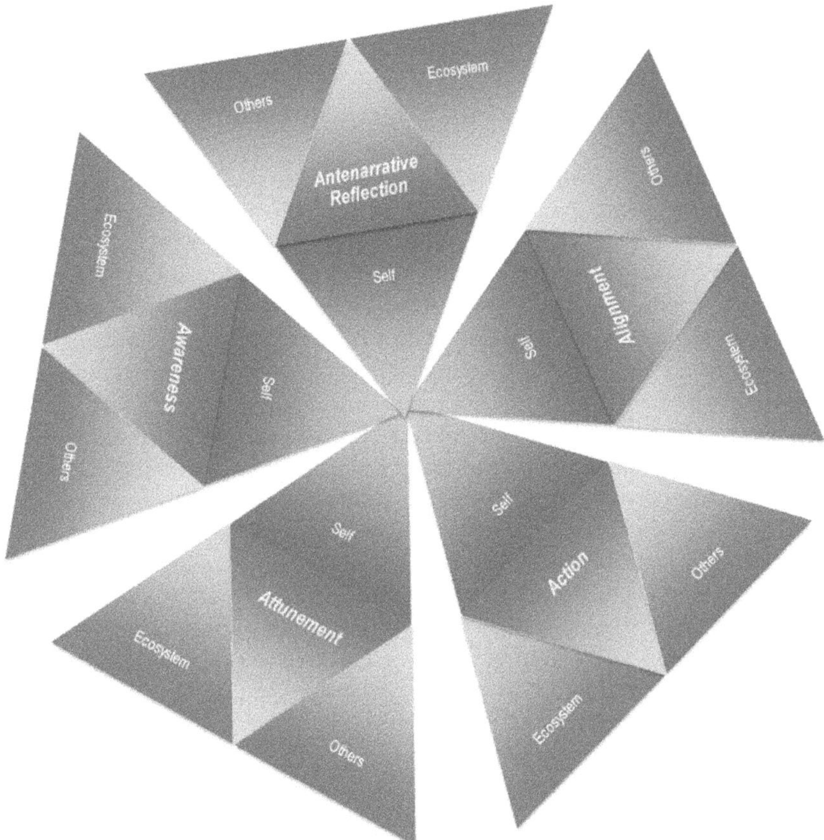

Figure 8.1 Five *A*s of Fractal Change Management: The Pinwheel Approach to Organizational Change

Source: By Tonya L. Henderson. Used with permission.

Others (Collaborators/Competitors)

- What are their missions?
- What kinds of work do they typically engage in and with whom?
- What do they need?
- What do they expect of us?
- Are they truly present and focused on the task at hand?
- What can we accomplish together?

Ecosystem (Competitive Environment)

- What's the context?
- What's going on around us?
- Are things changing or is the situation stable?

- Have we seen these kinds of situations before? Where?
- What are our choices?

We now turn to the five *A*s of FCM, considering their practical application in more detail.

1. *Awareness:* To improve our patterns or those of our organizations, we first have to be aware that there are most likely self-similar, scalable patterns of behavior occurring right under our noses.

Understanding the fractals has diagnostic use and points to the underlying systemic values and principles that serve as generators. What matters is where shifts occur, whether organically, or under the influence of purposive choice enacted by individuals acting as part of a greater system. If we own our own efficacy in the context of a complex adaptive system, then we recognize the ability to purposively shift patterns in ourselves (for example by practicing yoga's spiritual and physical components), in our organizations, and in the larger ecosystem, Step 1 is relational introspection as a higher form of awareness. Scale Transformations: How are scale transformations happening in organizations? We assume that people in organizations become scale dependent, and therefore attuned to different fractal-resolution patterns. The classic view is those at the top of the hierarchy of an organization have a wider field of vision, but are not sensitive to the finer structures, as are those in the technological core, or on the ground, in the bottom of the hierarchy. Managers, then, are in-between, making out both the wider and narrow resolutions of fractal structures.

Our approach to building awareness is grounded in relational introspection, a concept that became apparent during the study described in Chapter 5. The situation with a fire burning inside the city limits left everyone keenly aware of the sociomaterial processes unfolding as the fire left some formerly wealthy families homeless, cost those in the service industries much in lost wages, and created scalable self-similar unfoldings of generosity, concern, and caring for fellow citizens. In organizations, we can apply this kind of awareness strategically, cultivating a consistent openness to the sociomaterial processes that are unfolding around us. We consider each situation we encounter in terms of ourselves and our organizations, our competitors/collaborators, and the larger operating environment. It is important that, in defining the latter, we not limit ourselves to consideration of a bounded, closed system—for example just one product area or geographic sales region. We must understand that there may be other sociomaterial patterns unfolding in other areas that can affect us, that boundaries are a matter of choice. Whereas an organization might be constrained in terms of its product line or sales area, adaptation requires consideration that the goings on outside of those limitations are at least of some interest.

2. *Attunement:* Get used to spotting these patterns. What kinds of things happen seasonally in your business? What kinds of things do you see in terms of behaviors, especially those things that appear in individual and

group settings? Identify patterns in your work so you can decide if they deserve to be part of documented processes, need to change, don't matter, or simply bear watching.

In attunement, we become accustomed to pattern spotting and engage in modes of operation that reflect this understanding. We must not simply say "Look! A fractal!" Instead, we must get used to seeing the organization as a combination of unfolding and dissipating processes whose cocreative interaction constitutes the nature of the systemicity itself. We begin to accept that unproductive patterns may dissipate as quickly as they emerged, allowing for fewer knee-jerk reactions. We look for those patterns with large and small scale instantiations, paying attention to the various contexts they appear in, their duration, leading and lagging indicators, and apparent effects.

One way to address attunement is to consider what Boje (2015, in press) calls moods. Figure 8.2 offers some areas for consideration. These circles do not represent emotions, but rather ways of Being in attunement to fractal organizing processes as they unfold.

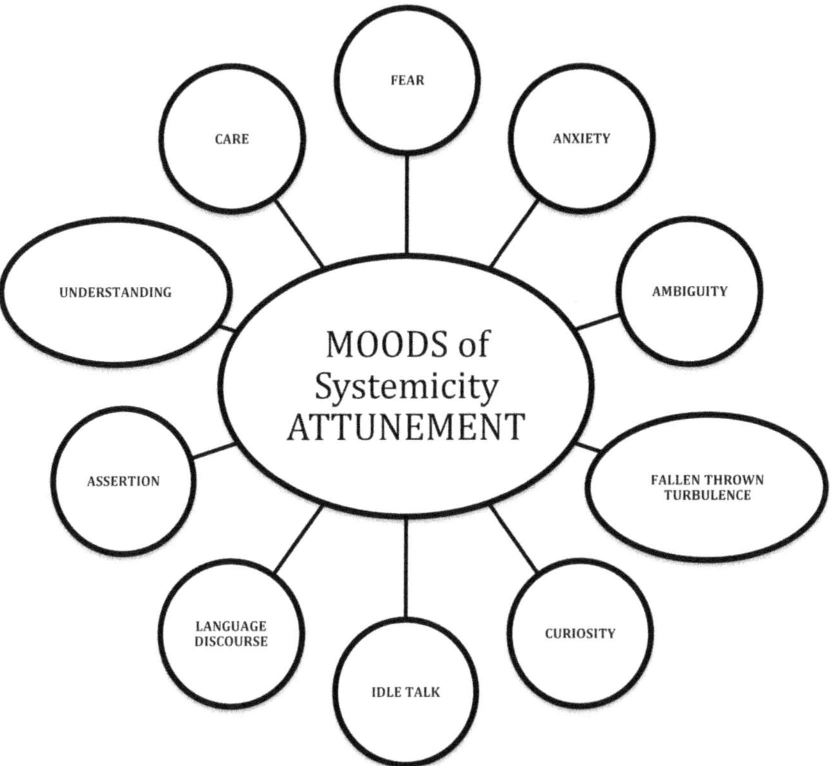

Figure 8.2 Moods of Systemicity Attunement
Created by David Boje. Used by permission (*source:* Boje, 2014)

We may be attuned to any one of these factors, or to multiple factors at once as we take our awareness of patterns to the next level desevering ourselves from the situations. For leaders at all levels of organizations, the concept of self-as-instrument applies (Seashore, Shawver, Thompson, and Mattare 2004). We pay attention to moods in response to the situation at hand, cocreatively interacting with the sociomaterial processes unfolding in and around our organizations.

3. *Alignment:* This step is consistent with the use of the term in business strategy (Grant 2010). We suggest that organizations consider the sociomaterial processes observed in terms of their congruence with or opposition to the organization's strategic guidance along with the other patterns considered generative in a particular industry. For example, if an emergent trend is observed in the clothing industry, a clothing design firm might consider how the trend looks vis-à-vis their own company's aims using the following questions:

- How does the pattern I am seeing align with my organization's strategic guidance?
- Is this pattern good for business?
- Is it sustainable?
- What if it happens on a larger scale or at an unexpected time and place?
- What does it look like in concert with the other patterns I am seeing? (Henderson 2014)

When we consider alignment vis-à-vis fractal organizing processes, we make assessments about the fit of the unfolding pattern of sociomateriality when it comes to the organization's strategy as it exists at the time. Once we have learned to consider self, others, and ecosystem in our interactions, we can begin to adjust our gaze and see scalable self-similarity in our organizational processes, both internal (employee behaviors, etc.) and external (market forces and the like).

During this phase, it is important to identify key processes that are essential to the organization's mission, as many other methods suggest. Where we differ from some other approaches in this regard is that we suggest exploration of not only formal processes, but also the kinds of patterns we see unfolding in associated social networks and informal power structures as well. Once we accept these kinds of patterns, it becomes easier to be a productive actor in the organization's unfolding. For example, the famous model of group dynamics suggests that newly formed teams first go through a period of newness termed *forming*. Then comes jockeying for position and general discontent termed *storming*. Next, group norms are established as people accept their own roles and things begin to solidify: *norming*. Finally, people have settled into their roles and group interaction enough to begin *performing*. Some versions of the model also add a phase wherein the group disbands upon completion of its tasks (Tuckman 1965). This model has been taught to facilitators, executives, and military officers for decades because it is a known pattern that has been demonstrated in all sorts of environments, on large and small scale projects in various contexts. This pattern is a likely candidate for continued scalable, self-similar repetition. There are myriad patterns like this unfolding and dissipating within any group of people at any given time. Sometimes they reinforce each other. Other times they clash, with one pattern overwhelming the effects of another.

As an organization becomes attuned to these kinds of patterns and their effects, individually and collectively, a process-centered view can emerge that allows for a different kind of decision making. When the members of an organization recognize an emergent phenomenon, there are choices available to all concerned. The first is the choice to accept or reject what appears to be happening. One may simply refuse to accept the indicators and elect to "weather the storm," making no changes and hoping for the best. If the pattern that appears to be forming is accepted, then an organization may collectively elect to "ride the wave," adapting the organization, its products, or methods according to the trend. The other option available is to attempt to shape the phenomenon. This last choice is the riskiest and, arguably, the bravest (Boje and Wakefield 2011).

We find examples of this kind of risk in marketing. In turbulent markets, actions taken to try and shape consumer desires may backfire. Spam email adds and targeted advertising on social media are prime examples. In both cases, the advertiser seeks to put content in front of a specific audience that is likely to purchase a particular service or product. Yet errors in identifying the demographics of a particular customer can ensure that the prospect will never buy from that company even if circumstances change. When consumers are targeted for products in the wake of a family tragedy or based on what appears to be an inappropriate amount of knowledge concerning their preferences, they may feel offended or as if their privacy has been invaded. For example, there is a fractal pattern in real estate tied to the circumstances under which people tend to sell their primary residences. When someone dies or gets divorced, selling the house can often be part of that process. As a result, some unscrupulous real estate companies bombard grieving families and the newly single with offers to purchase their homes for pennies on the dollar, leaving some families offended and convinced not to ever do business with the companies that have invaded their time of grief. The salesmen are reacting to a pattern, but the exact outcome is unpredictable because they cannot begin to know the vast array of other factors at work—factors that have their own fractal patterns, which may reinforce the observed trend, counter it, or deflect it into an entirely unexpected direction.

As part of a strategic planning and risk management process one must consider the alignment of personal, organizational, and/or community values and missions with patterns that are expected to recur. The following questions are suggested as a starting point for such an analysis. The following questions can be used to improve attunement to patterns in the work situation.

Self (Primary Pattern of Interest)

- Why is this particular pattern sticking out in our minds?
- Where have we seen it before? How did that go?
- Who has experience with this kind of pattern?
- If it follows the patterns of similar occurrences we have seen, what is likely to happen next?
- How does this possibility align with our organizational aims as stated in our strategic guidance?

Others (Other Relevant Patterns)

- What other patterns do we see?
- How might these reinforce or counteract this one?
- Have we seen these kinds of patterns combine before? Where?
- Have we considered what the pattern looks like from the perspectives of other stakeholders, both internal and external?
- Who has experience with the other relevant patterns we see?
- If the primary pattern of interest runs counter to our organizational aims, can we expect it to dissipate or strengthen in light of these other patterns and their influence?

Ecosystem (Context)

- How complex is the environment this is happening in?
- Is it like a pond, where effects may ripple out or is it like a section of rapids on a river where there is so much going on that dropping a pebble makes little difference? Maybe it is like a drum, stretched so tight that the smallest impact at one end is felt immediately and keenly throughout.
- Can this pattern or collection of patterns unfold and dissipate in a vacuum, or are there other situations and systems it will likely affect?
- What are the likely effects of our various potential courses of action in light of the environment where this is unfolding? What are the other patterns we might see as a result of each course of action?
- What patterns would we like to see?

4. *Action:* When we see patterns of behavior clearly, whether in ourselves or in our organizations, we may wish to react in several different ways. Maybe you notice a pattern, but it is of little consequence. You may decide not to react. On the other hand, you may witness something disturbing that requires some action on your part to prevent its recurrence, perhaps letting go of an

employee who has been dishonest or promoting someone who exhibits positive leadership traits consistently. You may try replacing a negative behavior pattern with a more helpful one. You may choose to help add fuel to the fire of an emergent trend in the marketplace by blogging or advertising your products. Options will vary according to the situation (Henderson 2014).

Once this analysis is completed, we can begin to consider deciding on a course of action, bearing in mind that choosing not to act is an option and that waiting until it is too late for any hope of affecting outcomes is also a potent choice. Choice is an interesting topic, both in the individual realm and that of organizational development. Covey (1989) famously discussed the space between stimulus and reaction as people interact with one another. Edie Seashore was notorious for reminding us that the things we do in the workplace are a matter of choice, and asking "How's that working out for you?" (Seashore, Seashore, and Livingston 2010). When we get away from our preprogrammed responses and reflect individually and in groups, the door is open to minimize conflict and make more generative choices, choices that align with our chosen life paths and organizational aims.

We see most choices in the organizational context as a matter of difference or repetition, drawing from Deleuze's (1994) famous work. In each moment of choice, we have to consider the echoes of our past patterns, how we handled similar situations in the past, along with the influences of others,

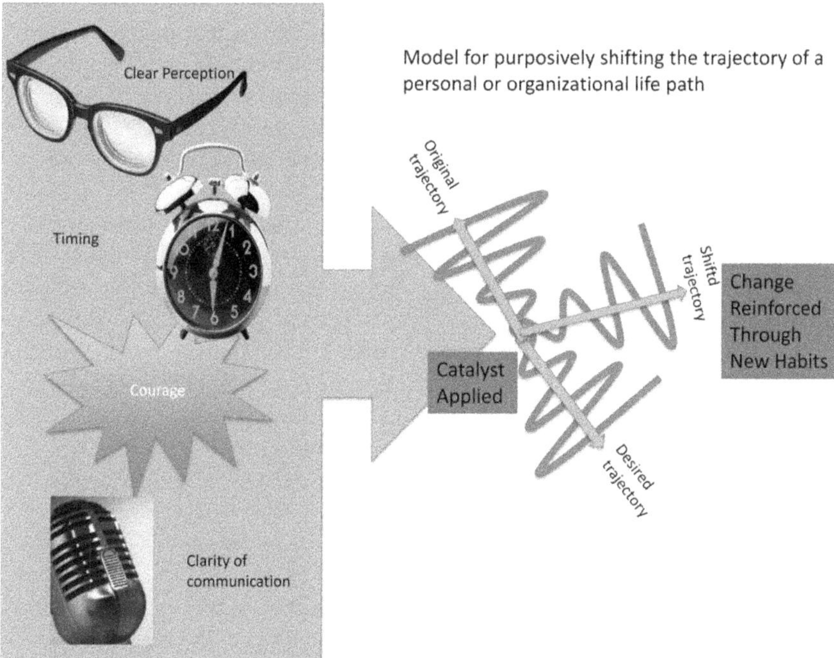

Figure 8.3 Changing the Trajectory of an Organization
Source: Created by Tonya Henderson. Used by permission.

be it in person, through the written word, media, etc. . . . At that choice point, as sentient beings possessed of agency, we choose to repeat prior patterns or to differentiate by trying something new (Wakefield, 2012). Figure 7.3 in the previous chapter provides a simple depiction.

Accepting this model as a simple way to think about choices and efforts to shift our own patterns and those of organizations, there are certainly conditions that influence our efficacy in shifting our own patterns and influencing patterns at a systemic level. The four elements that we consider central to taking action in a complex system are clarity of perception, Kairotic time, courage, and clarity of expression, shown in Figure 8.3.

CLEAR PERCEPTION

Clear perception has to do with recognizing our own biases and roles in cocreating the situations we experience and respond to. Yoga practitioners cultivate this type of clarity through the practice of nonjudgment. Kairotic time comes from the work of Gerri McCulloh (2014), who describes the Greek god of opportune time in the context of nonlinear time constructs and perception. Given the fast-paced, interconnected nature of today's business world, timing is very important. Launch a product too early and it might not make sense to the consumer. Wait too late, and your competitors may have already cornered the market. Courage to act comes from a variety of sources, ranging from a sense of urgency that can be fear based to a sense of moral conviction or simple desire to make a change. Clarity of expression has to do with communication to others. All of these conditions, if attended to, can increase the likelihood of success in our efforts to affect the trajectory of an organization or some aspect of our own workplace behaviors and outcomes.

Clarity of perception is always an ideal, something one can approach asymptotically over the course of a lifetime, but never really achieve. As humans we are bound by the blessing and curse of our own power to shape what we see and experience, so much so that to turn off the lens of perception and claim objectivity is necessarily dishonest. Even the most objective scientist is bound to see the world through the scientific lens, thereby missing those aspects of truth that do not bend to the scientific method, opting to reveal their nature in spontaneous and wily ways.

Yet we find it useful to strive for clarity to the extent possible, approaching understanding through a postmodern approach to relational introspection. Each person considers the situation in terms of self, others, and ecosystem, zooming in and out among levels of analysis to spot patterns amid the unfolding story around him. When we come together as a group, trying to engage in aggregate sensemaking, we begin to see the ways in which the various patterns reinforce or cancel one another out, just as with diffraction among electromagnetic signals.

In many ways, how we perceive the reality of our organizations mimics the way that an FM radio receiver works. At any given time, the airwaves are full of competing signals, not just in the radio wave part of the spectrum, but at all different frequencies. Yet our radios only play the stations we tune our receivers to. All other signals are filtered out. While choosing to listen to only one frequency allows us to receive clear information, making it comprehensible through the elimination of noise, we lose the ability to understand what the airwaves as a whole might be telling us—the bigger picture of the environment at that time.

According to Quade and Holladay (2010), "Patterns ebb and flow from view as other pressing issues surface for the leader to confront. Being ignorant of the pattern does not mean the pattern is not in operation" (p. 98).

If I use my radio or television to get my sense of the world, or even limit myself to a particular brand of scholarship, I neglect lived experience and exploration; I choose to only hear one viewpoint at a time. If I like this viewpoint I may never even change the channel, instead staying in my comfort zone through force of habit. I see the world one way. It is either my way or an other . . . either/or . . . yes or no . . . right or left . . . I tune in to one frequency at a time, discarding the rest, and rejoice in the clarity of the signal. Sometimes, I might disengage with external stimulus entirely tuning into my own perception of how things are, or distort the information I receive from the outside so that nobody else would recognize any material basis for my reality. This is how we often see situations in the workplace, if we only listen to the yes men, congregate only with like minds, or allow ourselves to obsess over perceived situations. We create artificial barriers against the flow of information, knowledge, creativity.

Yet there are many different perspectives to be had and our one favored view may not suffice if it is to be the basis for decision making that has far reaching effects. It is important to understand that for one's actions to have far-reaching effects, especially in the context of a tightly coupled system, one need not be in a position of authority. For example, in the restaurant industry, workers earning minimum wage routinely take charge of restaurant cleanliness, prepare food and serve customers. Even though these individuals are not high in the power structures of their respective organizations, their choices in terms of hygiene, food preparation, etc. can make or break a restaurant's image. Lea Thompson's (n.d.) Dateline report about fast food restaurant cleanliness and similar reports paint an abysmal picture that undoubtedly impacts sales for several major chains. Restaurant managers would do well to understand that the actions of those who have little institutional power can have tremendous effects. The reality of their lived experience can give them voice on a global scale in the modern age, where everyone's a journalist/blogger and sensationalist stories spread globally overnight via the internet. The power of the pen is not so easily limited to those with publishing credibility in the digital age.

Even when we approach our quest for clarity from a postmodern perspective, there is the question of what it is that we seek. It is not the objective, external, untouched "truth" but rather a cocreated, relational perspective deriving its validity from acceptance of multiple inputs. One might call the postmodern, process-oriented variant of truth, "truthicity." This is a truth of aggregate lived experience in which subjective discourse is part of the unfolding story. It is the quickly shifting truth of the living story web, which changes faster than one can write it down, thereby eschewing an over role in the dominant narratives men might impose.

KAIROTIC TIME

Following the work of Gerri McCulloh (2014), we wish to expand on the notion of opportune time. She views "kairos as a time, force, energy, or wave frequency that allows emergent phenomena to be noticed" (p. 54). This is very important in the context of managing fractal organizing processes, as not all processes and/or multifractal emergences are visible at a given time, necessitating iterative reflection as noted above. As circumstances change, different elements come together in assemblage to make others visible or generate new emergences in their confluence. Karen Barad's (2007) discussion of the coming together of an underpaid researcher whose subpar cigar smoke interfered with an experiment to make an interesting phenomenon visible is such a case. In each case, there is a confluence of time–space–mattering that makes a particular emergence possible and/or visible. To illustrate the point, we will share a story of poor timing, wherein a confluence of *spacetimemattering* could have been affected positively, had the timing of an act been different.

At age 39, Tonya had an opportunity to participate in a sprint triathlon, as part of a team with her coworker. She had been swimming at a local pool, felt confident that the 750 meter swim was something she could achieve, and signed up. She had been told that the lake where the race was to occur would be cold, but did not feel the need to rent a wetsuit. A few days before the race, she had second thoughts and went to a local sporting goods store, where she purchased a wet suit, unaware that the kind of wetsuit one wears for triathlon is much different in design from the ones they sell for waterskiing and riding jet skis. Confident that the short wetsuit would remain in her bag, unused, she considered it a mere precaution and did not pay attention to the details. Race day came and, prior to her start time, Tonya decided to go test the water temperature. She gingerly stepped into the lake. "Brrrrr!" She returned to the starting area and took out the wet suit. She put it on but folded the top half around her waist while waiting because it was warm out, and she saw others doing the same. Finally, it was time to line up for her wave to enter the water for the swim. Confident that all was well, she waited nervously with over 100 other women for the starting gun, pulling up her wetsuit and zipping it at the last minute, taking her cues from the more experienced athletes. One of the race organizers tapped her on the shoulder and asked, "Who helped you with your wetsuit?" She replied, "No one. Why?" The woman told her it was on backwards just as the starting gun went off, making it too late to change anything. Tonya ended up side-stroking the entire swim, with only about one-third of the needed range of motion for her arms and the collar feeling tight around her throat. After exiting the water and passing the timing chip to her teammate, Tonya wished she had been given that information at a more appropriate time.

The timing of any intervention in any complex adaptive system is crucial. In this example, kairotic time was not in effect. The convergence of factors that made it possible for the backward wet suit to become apparent to anyone, including its wearer, simply did not occur in time to change the outcome. The business world is rife with such examples, often linked to sequencing. Bringing forward information about a flaw in product design is best accomplished prior to production. Advertising for a play or event must happen early enough that people can plan to attend, but not so early as to be set aside and forgotten. Realizing that a person is a poor fit for the organization is best done early in the hiring process. For each set of circumstances in business and in life, timing is a key component of effectiveness. Yet it is important to note that the interconnected nature of time, space, and matter may be such that the circumstances aren't supportive of the desired sequence of events, as in the wetsuit story, or they may not be right for a particular intervention to occur at all. The following questions may be helpful in assessing the timing of a course of action designed to affect or react to unfolding fractal processes.

- What might have happened if we had done this at some earlier date?
- What are the present circumstances?
- What would be the ideal circumstances for taking this kind of action?
- When, where, and how might those circumstances occur?
- Is the opportunity perishable/time-sensitive?
- What happens if we wait?

COURAGE

Without the courage to act, and the wisdom to avoid hasty interventions as well, clarity of perception and observation of proper timing mean little. For example, for many years Tonya worked as a defense contractor, doing work that was meaningful and technically interesting. There were many people in the community she worked with whom she respected and considered friends, even mentors. Yet there were an inordinate amount of frustrations as well. With one source of income, as an employee dependent on a fickle agency funding line, she and her colleagues spent a lot of time explaining why the mission was important, continually justifying the work at the expense of doing it. Efforts to make progress toward systems integration were often slowed by rice bowl guarding, where a person's primary aim is the preservation of his own job at the expense of collaboration. She knew that she needed a change of career, but it was not until her mother's death that she went back to school to learn a new skill set that would enable her to find the courage to leave a job that she found dissatisfying in her role at the time. Once we know the action we wish to take, it can take courage to change old patterns. Fear kicks in. "This is all I know. What if I fail?" The same kinds of concerns happen when groups of people try to change their collective patterns of behavior. The group that challenges every new idea may have difficulty implementing new approaches without an inordinate amount of scrutiny and allowing sufficient time for the naysayers to develop trust in new technologies and those who propose them. It seems to be a central part of the aggregate human condition. We feel the need to establish some sense of order and control as we begin cooperating for mutual gain.

Think about the patterns of group behavior that we see in organizations, households, and even on an individual level. Ruby Payne's (2001) work *Bridges Out of Poverty* demonstrates these sorts of patterned behavior in the context of the generationally poor.

5. *Antenarrative Reflection:* Consideration of the antenarrative aspects of each fractal organizing processes is an important step toward understanding and interacting with unfolding organizational patterns. Taking the prior discussions of antenarrative into account, we are called to engage in reflective sense making at regular intervals. Of the patterns observed, we must consider their unfolding and how they might continue or change before taking action and afterwards, at a minimum. Considering how the patterns we perceive have unfolded over time, their current states, and the likelihood of continued propagation in ways that are consistent with linear (beginning–middle–end), cyclical, rhizomatic, spiral, or a hybrid combination of these types allows us to consider their implications and behave more ethically.

In this chapter, we have provided a model for fractal change management that is both ontologically based and grounded in tangible sociomaterial realities. We propose that strategic planning is not a periodic event to be conducted in a boardroom, but that leaders at all levels of the organization should be thinking strategically as a matter of course. The five *A*s of fractal change management offer a meaningful way to consider organizational change as an ongoing, unfolding sociomaterial process.

NOTES

1. Dr. Quade cites Brafman and Beckstrom (2006).
2. These steps are adapted from what Tonya first expressed as the four *A*s of fractal management theory (Henderson 2014).

REFERENCES

Barad, Karen. (2003). Posthumanist Performativity: Toward an Understanding of. *Signs: Journal of Women in Culture and Society*, *28*(3).

Barad, Karen. (2007). Meeting the universe halfway: Quantum physics and the entanglement of matter and meaning. Durham, NC: Duke University Press.

Boje, D. M. (2014, 23 August). Study Guide for answering Questions about the Grander Narratives of General Systems Theory, Open Systems Theory, and Quantum Systemicity Model. Retrieved 8 March, 2015, from http://business.nmsu.edu/~dboje/655/study_guide_grandnarratives.htm.

Boje, D. M. (Ed., in press, 2015 expected) Change Solutions to the Chaos of Standards and Norms Overwhelming Organizations: Four Wings of Tetranormalizing. London/NY: Routledge.

Boje, David, and Tonya Wakefield. (2011). "Storytelling in Systemicity and Emergence: A Third Order Cybernetic." In David Boje, Bernard Burnes, and John Hassard (eds.), *The Routledge Companion to Organizational Change*. New York: Routledge.

Brafman, Ori, and Rod A. Beckstrom (2006). *The Starfish and the Spider: The Unstoppable Power of Leaderless Organizations*. New York: Penguin.

Covey, Steven R. (1989). Seven habits of highly effective people: Simon & Schuster.

Deleuze, G. (1994). *Difference and Repetition* (P. Patton, Trans. English translation ed.). New York, NY: Columbia University Press. Original edition 1968.

Eoyang, Glenda. (2009). *Coping with Chaos*. Edited by Human Systems Dynamics Institute. Circle Pines, MN: Lagumo.

Grant, Robert M. (2010). *Contemporary Strategy Analysis* (7th ed). West Sussex, UK: John Wiley & Sons.

Henderson, Tonya L. (2014). "Are Your Patterns on Purpose? The Four A's of Fractal Management." 21 October. http://www.glysolutions.com/—!Are-your-patterns-on-purpose-The-Four-As-of-Fractal-Management/c1q8z/A5C4A23C-3564-4C7E-B6BC-A91359694E9E.

McCulloh, Gerri Elise. (2014). "Summoning Kairos: Atavistic Processes in Quantum Adaptive Rhetoric." In *Being Quantum: Ontological Storytelling in the Age of Antenarrative,* edited by Gavid M. Boje and Tonya L. Henderson, 51–89. Newcastle upon Tyne, NE6 2XX, UK: Cambridge Scholars Publishing.

Payne, Ruby K. (2001). *Bridges out of Poverty*. Highlands, TX: aha! Process, Inc.

Quade, Kristine. (2011). "Simple rules leaders use to guide their organizations during times of rapid change." Ed.D. Doctoral Dissertation, Graduate School of Education and Psychology, Pepperdine University.

Quade, Kristine, and Royce Holladay. 2010. *Dynamical Leadership: Building Adaptive Capacity for Uncertain Times*. Apache Junction, AZ: Gold Canyon Press.

Seashore, E., Seashore, C., & Livingston, R. (2010). Workshop on intentional use of self. Workshop materials. Colorado Technical University. Colorado Springs, Colorado.

Seashore, Charles, Mary Nash Shawver, Greg Thompson, and Marty Mattare. (2004). "Doing good by knowing who you are: the instrumental self as an agent of change." OD Practitioner 36 (3): 42–46.

Thompson, Lea. (n.d.). Dirty Dining? 'Dateline' hidden cameras investigate cleanlines of America's top 10 fast food chain. In Consumer Alert on Dateline.

Tuckman, Bruce. (1965). "Bruce Tuckman's 1965 Forming Storming Norming Performing team-development model." [Web Page] Accessed 14 January, 2010. http://www.businessballs.com/tuckmanformingstormingnormingperforming.htm.

Wakefield, Tonya L. Henderson. (2012). "An ontology of storytelling systemicity: Management, fractals and the Waldo Canyon fire." Doctorate of Management Doctoral dissertation, Management, Colorado Technical University.

9 Ontological Systems Mapping

A Tool for Ethical Engagement

When a manager changes observation devices, then the scale of fractal resolution, that is an observational apparatus move, changes what is seen in the organization-and-environment systemicity of spacetime. This apparatus move amounts to a sort of "zooming in and out" to look for scalable self-similarity in the patterns of behaviors that characterize the situation and the organization itself. So, what is the apparatus? We contend that storytelling is the best apparatus for viewing the emergence and dissipation of fractal organizing processes in the aggregate human frame. Just as the living story web breathes and shifts with the organization's unfolding over time, the stories of individual system members change, shift, dissipate, and emerge in new ways. If we pay attention to the stories told by members of the system over time we can begin to see the repeated patterns that characterize not only those individuals, but the system as a whole.

However, longitudinal studies are expensive and time consuming. Organizations and managers want rapid data collection to support decision making in the near-term. To that end, a more rapid means of identifying these patterns is called for. We suggest an ontological storytelling inquiry using a fractal-based protocol as a means to identify an organization's ontological footprint. Just as doctors often observe the symptoms in a patient in order to make a diagnosis, so we observe the patterns in a system's behavior in order to understand the principles at work, the fractal generators.

Koch's snowflake is generated through a simple, iterative act. When we look at Figure 2.7, the signature of the repeated act, adding an inverted triangle,[1] is apparent if we look closely at a small section of the shape, then zoom out to look at more of it, eventually zooming out as far as we can practically accomplish. It is important to know that we may never be able to see the "whole system" because it will continue to change and grow, perhaps even mutating, faster than we can explore its nature. Upon zooming in and out, we might ask ourselves, "What kinds of acts contributed to the development of this pattern I see? What is its nature? What can it tell me about the system I am looking at?" Just as one might discover the way to draw Koch's curve, one can also discover the principles governing social systems.

The true nature and shape of a social system becomes apparent through the iterative embodiment of its underlying principles through actions and perceptions best captured through storytelling.

When Glenda Eoyang works with organizations to identify their simple rules, she insists that they be stated in positive language, not inconsistent with the positive psychology approach used in Appreciative Inquiry (Cooperrider 1986, Cooperrider and Whitney 2005). In appreciative inquiry, the power of positive psychology is used to unite parties that may otherwise disagree. Eoyang helps groups of people to identify the rules they live by in their organizations themselves, noting that sometimes the values and traditions that members of an organization hold most dear sometimes have negative consequences.

> I was working with a group of people who had case studies in a lot of interviews from an African nation, trying to figure out what were the simple rules for corruption and what they realized was if they weren't just rules for people who are corrupt, they were social rules that generated a pattern of corruption. One was, take care of your family and yourself, well, of course you take care of your family and yourself, but, when you're given power in a political or legal framework and you take care of your family and yourself that equals a pattern of corruption. So it's not that the rule is negative, it's the rule as it plays out over time . . . with negative consequences
>
> —Glenda Eoyang (interview)

David's work with veterans suffering from posttraumatic stress disorder (PTSD) drives the point home. Military values lead those on active duty to adopt a consistent attitude of strength and confidence, protecting others. This arguably noble and enabling set of values and beliefs can be so entrenched as to prevent persons who have been traumatized from seeking psychiatric help. Tonya has witnessed a similar dynamic among active duty personnel and defense contractors whose jobs place them under a great deal of scrutiny. Fearing the loss of a job if they show what may be considered signs of mental instability, many deal with trauma, addiction, and other debilitating problems without seeking counseling of any kind.

The rules we adopt in one context, combat and training for combat, may not serve us well in other contexts such as family life or a return to the civilian workforce. It then becomes incumbent upon the individual to find rules that work for the new context, increasing adaptability by considering new options. We think of this shift as following Ashby's (1958) law of requisite variety. When we move into a new environment, becoming attuned to that new set of circumstances, it becomes necessary to find a new set of rules for success by opening ourselves to new possibilities for ways of Being. Forcing oneself to consider abandoning engrained values, beliefs, and associated practices can be very difficult. For personal growth and adaptation to occur, we as individuals we have to accept the death of certainty and embrace the tension inherent in change.

In organizations, it can look like this. To build adaptation, it is necessary to accept a certain amount of tension and disagreement in order to foster adaptation:

> A group that I was working with this week came up with a simple rule that was stand in conflict. Stay in conflict, stay in conflict—because they wanted, as a creative force, to hold tension in a community to set the context for a generative coherence.
>
> —Glenda Eoyang (interview)

The need for organizations to keep people at the table during tense discussions was also apparent in Tonya's doctoral study, where one research subject talked about her work with political opponents around the same table.

> Collaboration isn't always an instant success. Working through conflict in a group often requires getting "through that stormy, messy, muddy part, where the outcomes aren't clear; the reasons for being there aren't clear; the accusations back and forth are harsh," by keeping people at the table (Phase two, Subject one, 244–275).
>
> (Wakefield 2012, p. 189)

In each case, the ability to move to a new pattern as a group was heavily dependent on the ability to come together as a system that includes multiple perspectives and allow for disagreement. We conceptualize this as changing the agential cuts made in forging organizations. Karen Barad (2007) explains that in any inquiry, we are deciding what to look at, bounding systems that are naturally part of a much larger system and choosing an apparatus for viewing them, which then must be considered part of the observed phenomenon itself. As Hoverstadt (2011) acknowledges, how we form organizational boundaries is central to the development of a group identity. The rules change.

Bruno Latour has an excellent discussion of boundaries in his book *Pandora's Hope* (Latour 1999). The reader is treated to a vivid and thought-provoking description of a scientific expedition meant to discover whether the forest is encroaching on the savannah or the other way around. Analysis of soil samples and vegetation showed that there was not a clear cut boundary. One could not draw a line on the ground and say, "The forest ends and the savannah begins here," or vice versa. It is the same with social systems when they are brought together.

Tonya had a recent experience with someone she holds dear. Over an omelet, they discussed their very different views on politics. Her friend, a political conservative, was worried that her liberal perspectives would be a source of conflict. Yet the more they allowed for respectful tension and listened to each other, the more points of agreement they found. Instead of being divisive, the discussion revealed that neither was particularly judgmental and that their different approaches to politics were grounded in common values and desires for a vibrant, tolerant society. The convergence of their individual patterns of behavior and associated values and beliefs yielded a constructive dialogue forging a new pattern of mutual respect. Both were surprised by the areas of agreement, echoing Bakhtin's (1993) suggestion that surprise is the hallmark of generative lived experience. Two very different perspectives nonetheless overlapped in surprising ways.

FRACTAL BASED ONTOLOGICAL STORYTELLING INQUIRY: AN APPARATUS FOR ONTOLOGICAL SYSTEMS MAPPING

The process is simple. As depicted in figure 9.1 below, there are six steps that can lead one to observe some of the key organizational values and beliefs

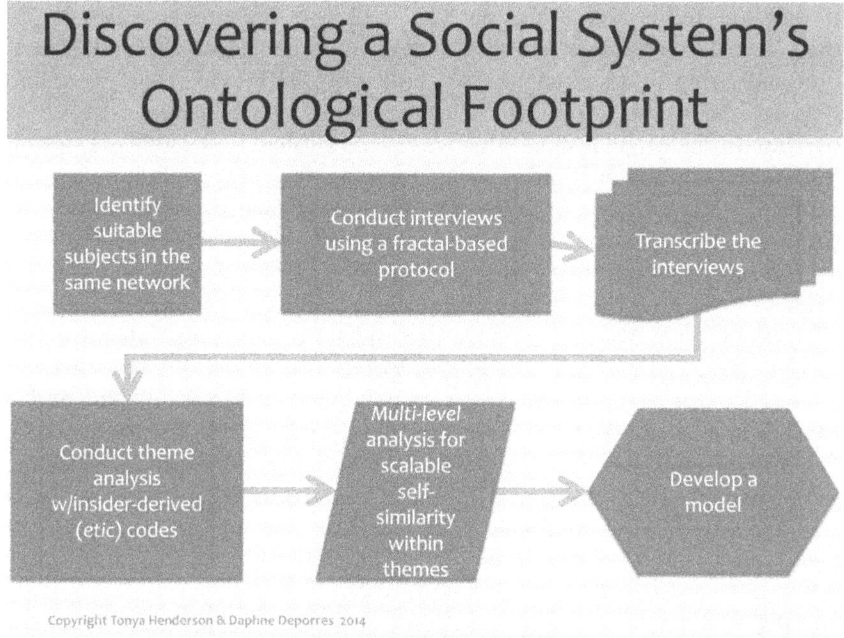

Figure 9.1 Ontological Systems Mapping Process
Source: By Tonya L. Henderson and Daphne DePorres (2014). Used by permission.

driving iterative, scalable patterns of behavior in a social system. Values and beliefs may be thought of as fractal generators, given their propensity to affect action that is self-similar and scalable (Henderson and Deporres 2014; Wakefield, Boje, and Lane 2013). Thus, we explore the patterns of a social system in order to find the iterative processes and governing rules that produce the patterns we see. This approach takes us beyond overtly stated espoused values and can reveal unflattering systemic truths as well as those people want to acknowledge publicly. Only then can we begin to get at the true nature of the system. This knowledge is very useful in terms of predicting the types of patterns that are likely to persist over time, and to begin exploring how difficult it might be to change these patterns.

STEP 1

First we identify suitable subjects. Whom do we select? Whereas it would be nice to interview all of the members of a system, that can be hard to do when we consider the artificial nature of boundaries. We might interview everyone on the payroll, for example, and still miss the perspectives of key stakeholders or disenfranchised persons. Traditional random sampling is also unsuitable for this method, as we are looking to capture localized effects. Purposively selected samples of people whose experiences are likely to overlap are best, as they allow one to capture the emergent patterns in their shared living story web, thus uncovering their shared modes of operation and Being in a shared context. Following Wakefield (Henderson and Deporres 2014), we recommend selecting subjects whose stories are likely to overlap. In the original work, this was accomplished by selecting nonprofit leaders and communications personnel serving "in a civic, volunteer or nonprofit role affecting one or more organizations engaged in work supporting Colorado Springs' social or economic viability" (Wakefield, 2012), p. 79.

The optimum number varies according to the circumstance, but prior studies of this kind have been accomplished with between 5 and 11 subjects (Wakefield 2012). Whereas we have also used the fractal-based interview protocol to elicit rich, reflective responses from a restaurant manager, the data captured was nonetheless based on a single perspective yielding something more akin to a case study (Henderson and Deporres 2014, Wakefield 2012). Because the analysis phase is intensive, we do not recommend interviewing more than 15–20 people unless multiple researchers are available to assist with the analysis and funding is available to support a larger scale effort.

STEP 2

Next we conduct interviews. The first iteration of this method involved a simple explanation of what a fractal pattern is, followed by open-ended questions about where the subjects saw scalable, self-similar repetition in their work and peer group. Subsequent iterations have refined the protocol such that a detailed explanation is not provided and technical jargon is avoided (Wakefield, Boje, and Lane 2013). A variation of the protocol from our recent study of perceptions among yoga practitioners follows.

- When you think about your involvement in the yoga community in Colorado Springs, recall an observation or experience where you saw repeating dynamics, interactions, patterns of behaviors. What did you observe or experience?
- For your recollection to indicate a pattern, it was something you saw repeated multiple times, and even at multiple levels of the yoga community. (Examples of interaction *roles*: interactions between you and other practitioners; interactions between practitioners and teachers; interactions between teachers and teachers; interactions between studios.) Where do you think these patterns come from?
- Do you see any scalability in these patterns, (Example: the patterns you see in practitioner–practitioner interactions where you are involved, you also see "scaled" at the level of the community.)
- How do you see these patterns influencing the future of the yoga community in this city? (Henderson and Deporres 2014, Wakefield, Boje, and Lane 2013)

STEP 3

Transcribing the interviews is a simple, albeit time-consuming, process. Following standard procedures or outsourcing this effort makes little difference. However, having the researcher transcribe them himself does yield a mush deeper understanding of the data and allows sufficient attention to bring out subtleties that might otherwise be missed. Terse tellings, pauses, changes in the speaker's pitch and tenor . . . these nuances can point the way to significant points that might otherwise be overlooked. In the interest of validity, member checking, and/or having an objective third party check the transcripts may be advisable, particularly in the case of doctoral dissertations.

STEP 4

Theme analysis is a simple, iterative process and can be conducted using a variety of software applications, or a simple excel spreadsheet. Boje (Henderson and Deporres 2014, p. 142) provides detailed instructions for thematic analysis using insider-derived codes. It is important to use codes derived exclusively from the data itself, called *etic* codes, in order to avoid any preconceived notions about the nature of the social system you are looking at. This approach differs from the *emic* approach, wherein a researcher begins with a list of categories derived from the literature or another source and assigns story performances to those categories. Whereas the latter approach is valid from a research perspective, it is not well suited to an ontological storytelling inquiry because we are trying to get at the very nature of a particular social system, which may be quite different than similar systems in other contexts or even the same system if examined at a different point in time.

STEP 5

Multilevel analysis adds an additional layer to the analysis process. Whereas many studies stop with a set of relevant themes, this kind of study requires one to look for scalable self-similarity of the story performances associated with each code. In some cases, there are clear fractal patterns of behavior or perceptions. In other cases, themes appear but do not reflect scalable concepts. This level of attention, exploring the data at the level of individual, group, and interorganizational interactions draws our attention to those patterns that are clearly fractal. While we do not advocate discarding relevant themes that are not scalable, we want to emphasize those that are. Just as the patterns that tell a botanist what kind of plant he is looking at, or an avalanche expert the sort of activity and snowpack he is considering, the fractal patterns in a social network's living story web tell the organizational development researcher the character of the organization studied.

STEP 6

Developing a model or a series of models that characterize a particular system is often the simplest part of the process. After conducting this type of analysis, relationships among themes and emphasis of specific concepts as drivers of unfolding organizational behaviors often appear obvious to researchers. Figures 9.2 and 9.3 are examples of models derived in this manner.

The model in Figure 9.2 was validated using a focus group. Participants in the study were invited to take part in a discussion and were presented with this over arching model and eight others. Those who attended provided valuable insights that resulted in the revision of two of the eight submodels originally developed. Sharing the models not only improved the study's validity, but gave participants a graphic depiction of the rules by which they operate, something they were pleased to have.

The process of ontological systems mapping provides a complexity-derived method for examining perceived fractal patterns within a social network. The analytical process involves a simple thematic analysis, followed

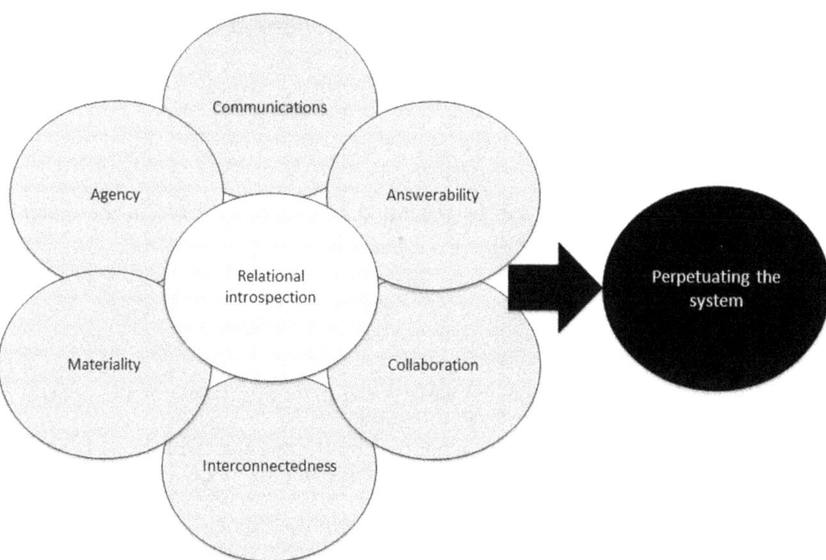

Figure 9.2 Ontological Systems Model of a City's Nonprofit Community
Source: Wakefield 2012. Used by permission.

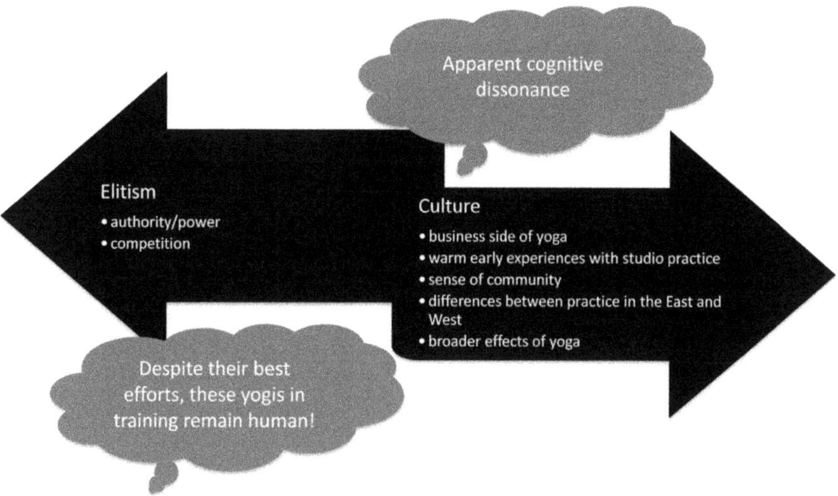

Figure 9.3 Ontological Systems Map of a Community of Western Yoga Practitioners
Source: By Tonya L. Henderson and Daphne DePorres (2014). Used by permission.

by an additional step that looks for scalable self-similarity in the patterns identified through storytelling. It can be used to explore potential fractal generators in a human frame in ways that get beyond espoused beliefs in a content-agnostic way.

NOTE

1. Alternately, this fractal can be generated by inserting a bend in the center of each line segment iteratively.

REFERENCES

Ashby, W. Ross. (1958). "Requisite variety and its implications for the control of complex systems." *Cybernetica* 1 (2):83–99.

Bakhtin, Michel. (1993). Toward a philosophy of the act. Translated by Vadim Liapunov. Edited by Michael Holquist, University of Texas Press Slavic Series No. 10. Austin: University of Texas Press.

Barad, Karen. (2007). *Meeting the Universe Halfway: Quantum Physics and the Entanglement of Matter and Meaning*. Durham, NC: Duke University Press.

Boje, D. (2001). *Narrative Methods for Organizational & Communication Research*. London SAGE.

Boje, D. (2011c). Ontological Storytelling Inquiry Methodology—For Dummies Las Cruces, NM.

Cooperrider, David L. (1986). "Appreciative inquiry: Toward a methodology for understanding and enhancing organizational innovation." Ph.D., Department of Organizational Behavior, Case Western Reserve (8611485).

Cooperrider, David L., and Diana Whitney. (2005). Appreciative inquiry: A positive revolution in change. San Francisco, CA: Berrett-Koehler Publishers.

Henderson, Tonya L., and Daphne Deporres. (2014). "Patterns of Perception Among Yoga Practitioners." International Conference of Management Cases, Greater Noida, India.

Hoverstadt, Patrick. (2011). *The Fractal Organization: Creating Sustainable Organizations with the Viable System Model*. Hoboken, NJ: John Wiley & Sons.

Latour, Bruno. (1999). *Pandora's Hope: Essays on the Reality of science Studies*. Cambridge, MA: Harvard University Press.

Wakefield, Tonya L. Henderson. (2012). "An ontology of storytelling systemicity: Management, fractals and the Waldo Canyon fire." Doctorate of Management Doctoral dissertation, Management, Colorado Technical University.

Wakefield, Tonya L. Henderson, David Boje, and Michael Lane. (2013). "Fractals and Food." Standing Conference for Management and Organization Inquiry (SCMOI), Alexandria, VA.

Commencement

In this book, we have built upon the foundations of complexity theory as it is applied in human systems, blending it with concepts from storytelling and other fields to consider organizational change as a sociomaterial, fractal emergence that occurs over time in order to define Fractal Change Management (FCM). We have provided the reader with theoretical underpinnings, practical examples and exercises, and proposed tools and methods for working with fractal organizing processes. Throughout much of the book we have used the lens of relational introspection to encourage an ethically answerable approach to understanding fractal organizing processes that is grounded in care and understanding.

Yet to actually *do* FCM and fractal action research model (FARM) we need to get better at scaling our understandings. One approach is to use the technique of tetranormalizing as they are defined in Boje (2015, in press). Tetranormalizing allows us to take the levels of analysis from relational introspection and apply this zooming in and out to organizations on a global scale, while considering specific contexts in a way that draws on the socio-economic model of management (Boje 2010b; Savall, Zardet, and Bonnet 2008). This ties to the application of fractal ethics as described above, promoting answerability in four different areas in particular, although we need not be limited to four in the long term. We will provide a brief summary herein and suggest further reading for a fuller explanation and applications.

TETRANORMALIZING

Savall, Zardet, and Bonnet (2008) developed the theory, method, and practice of socioeconomic management (SEAM). Their pioneering efforts to demonstrate the relationships between social factors in the workplace and lost productivity and profit ushered in a new mode of thought in organization development as social and technical systems were merged into a common understanding.

There is a connection to be made between micro- and macro-fractal organizing processes. There is scalability, but at the macro level, there are regional, national, international, and global levels of the sociomaterial and socioeconomic. There are interaction effects between microfractals of very small organizations and macrofractals of generative patterns that are global in scope, but with global–local (glocal) interactions. Double, triple, and quadruple helix models are explained in Boje (2015, in press). The triple helix is exemplified by the triple helix bottom line.

For example, instead of people or profits, someone woke up to the ecological crisis, and there is all this fuss about the Triple Bottom Line (profits–people–planet), and on to the cradle-to-cradle Fractal Triad (or fractal triangle) (McDonough and Braungart, 2002) that inspired the design of eco-effective products (Schindehutte and Morris 2009, p. 264). Carayannis and Campbell (2009, 2012) apply Etzkowitz and Leydesdorff (2000) theory of university–industry–government, in a fractal approach to entrepreneurship at a scale of analysis beyond the individual entrepreneur, and beyond the single entrepreneur organization, to interorganization network of communication. And these triadic fractals have gone Tetra (four wings instead of three). The Triple Helix Fractal (university–industry–government) scalability of relationship patterns has now morphed to a fourth partner, the ecosystem (Carayannis and Campbell, 2009), making it a Quadruple Helix Fractal: university–industry–government–ecology. For our book purposes, we are Quadruple, the Four Fractal Wings of Tetra are Social/Cultural, Ecology/Quality, Economy/Accounting and Trade of Tetranormalizing (Boje 2015, in press).

Tetra means four, and normalization is seen as an alternative to standards, one that allows a bottom up response to the imposition of excessive regulations that in many cases amount to the imposition of a dominant control narrative, as opposed to the notion of regulation in the name of safety and generative efforts to encourage interoperability. Standards are, in many cases, a tool of hiearchical-disengagement. Norms are a tool of ethical engagement. Social norms are embodied in sociomateriality. Standards try to shape and enforce ethics from a regulatory body, such as AACSB, ISO, World Bank, or World Trade Organization. It is important to keep this distinction between norms and standards in mind. The distinction becomes crucial now that we have transitioned to a flexible capitalism of global marketplace from the days when the corporate bureaucracy reigned supreme. The four kinds of tetra-norms are social norms, trade norms, economy/accounting norms and ecology/quality norms.

Norms and Global Tetranormalizing. Susie Vrobel (2011) assumes that "each tribe lives under the influence of a single norm, common to all individuals" (p. 202). In economic exchange, the assumption of a single and simple norm is assumed in e-trade (reputation-bases cooperation) by individuals loosely connected and geographically dispersed (p. 201). The common norm contributes to overall cohesiveness and identity of a tribe (p. 204). When different tribes are "'under the influence' of different norms" the overall fitness of a tribe will vary, and intertribe conflicts (war, etc.) are assumed (p. 204).

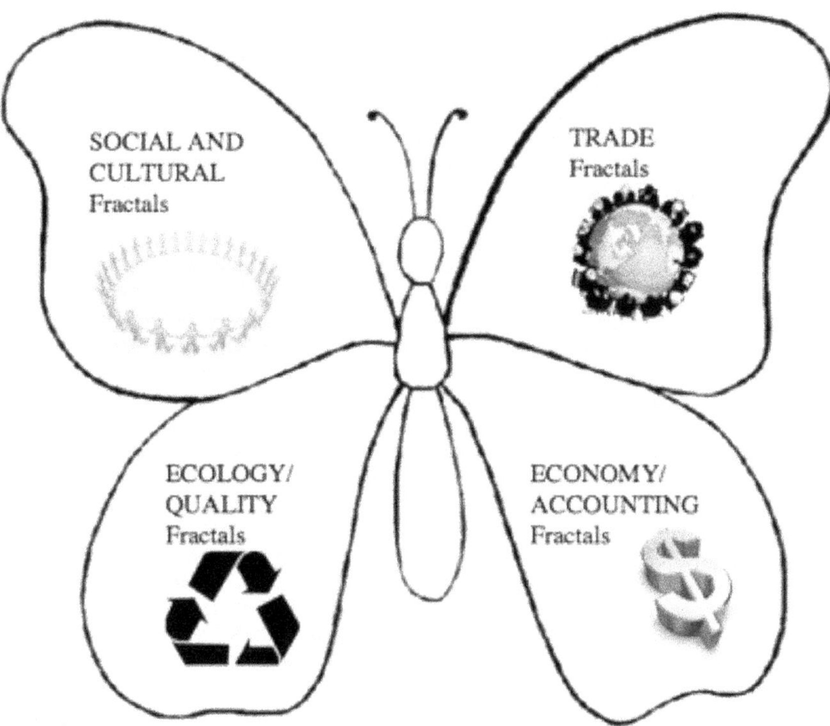

Figure c.1 Wings of Tetranormalizing
Source: By David Boje (2015 in press). Used by permission.

Vrobel is at The Institute for Fractal Research (Kassel, Germany). She addresses the "interfacial cut assumed between the observer and the rest of the world" (p. 229) and stresses our primary experiences of time (succession, simultaneity, duration, and extended Now) affect our sense of "fractal spacetime" (p. 229). For Vrobel (2011) "Fractal time not only nests past events into the present but also includes the notion of anticipation, which adds the idea of the future being embedded into the Now" (p. 238). They base the idea on Bergsonian "duration" of past nows into the present now, and on Husserl's pretension: An anticipation of a future event. They, however favor the social over materiality, stating that the material and semantic (social) are "anthpocentrical and thus derivatives of our subjective experience of time" (p. 238).

Vorbel's work applies to the popularity of grander narrative forms in organization studies. She assumes "our inbuilt desire for complexity reduction" leads us to embed materiality in our abstracting, focusing on a few aspects, while disregarding others (p. 230). For Vrobel (2011) "3rd-order cybernetics then contextualized the observer-participant ontologies of the

2nd-order domain." (p. 230). In other words the subjectivity of the observer is a result of an embedding process in contextualized observer-ontologies that "takes account of both the system-context interface and the observer-involvement interface" (p. 230).

In the Newtonian reductionist approach, there is a linear "container-like time and space" that does not allow the kinds of observer frames that Einstein's relativity or that quantum mechanics theories address. Prigogine's complexity theory is said to assign different internal times to nested systems (Vorbel, 2010, p. 230). The result is emergence becomes a differentiation between levels of description (LODs) by degrees and modes of involvement. Vrobel subscribes to "embodied cognition" (p. 230), the observer's internal different ion and how the observer is embedded in a context of system interfaces and involvements.

What is called for is a new way of knowing, grounded in lived, embodied experience of sociomateriality as it unfolds. This does not amount to knowledge and blind acceptance of a dominant narrative as presented in books (including this one) or the media. While tetranormalizing offers a partial response, there remains much work to do. Areas for further study include ontological systems mapping in more contexts and testing of the simple rules derived in this way, application of the FARM in multiple contexts to adequately assess its efficacy and determine if it can be modified for use in what our colleague, Roland Livingston terms "fast cycle organization development." The four *A*s of Fractal Change Management model can also be applied as a methodology in myriad settings, in hopes of bridging what we perceive as an almost Cartesian split between the realities of the living story web and the imposition of dominant narratives, be they constructive or harmful in nature. There also remains much to do in the realm of working with embodied practices as a means of supporting sustainable change in organizations. Equine therapy, sandplay, and yoga are but a few of the myriad possible techniques, each of which offers us the opportunity to improve our relationships with sociomaterial experiences such that the patterns we propagate are generative and humane ones.

Having explored fractal organizing processes and provided tools for improved understanding and management in a dynamic, multifractal environment, we now challenge the reader to apply these concepts at multiple scales. What kind of fractals will you co-create with the people and things you meet today?

Glossary

Complexity: the study of complex adaptive systems, wherein permeable system boundaries allow for an exchange of information and/or energy with the external environment and the aggregate behaviors of individual elements result in emergent phenomena

Complex adaptive systems: groups of individual agents exhibiting edge of chaos behaviors, with permeable systems boundaries, an exchange of information, energy, and/or resources with the external environment

Fractal: "recurrence of self-similar and/or instability processes across scales: individual, unit, inter-unit, organization, inter-organization, regional, international, global" (Boje, 2015, in press)

Fractal Organizing Process: a sociomaterial pattern of growth or dissipation in a human system that is characterized by scalable self-similarity that is observable in terms of social and/or material factors. These patterns may be manifested through intentional strategic design intended to promote resilience or, more commonly, as a matter of organic self-organizing behaviors.

Fracticality: the exhibition of fractal-like structures

Fractal Action Research Method: an action research method that incorporates fractal change management principles and makes use of ontological storytelling inquiry methods

Fractal Change Management Theory: an approach to change management that is grounded in the understanding and cocreative intra-action with fractal organizing processes

Relational Introspection: a threefold awareness of self, others, and ecosystem

Systemicity: "the dynamic, unfinished, unfinalized, and unmerged, and the interactivity of complexity properties with storytelling and narrative processes" (Boje 2008, p. 264)

Tetranormalizing: Normalizing fractal processes in the areas of trade, social-cultural (SC), ecology-quality (EQ), trade (T), and economy-accounting (EA) as an antidote to overregulation.

References

Abend, Lisa. 2009, June 15. "Sustainable Aquaculture: Net Profits." *Time*. Retrieved from http://content.time.com/time/magazine/article/0,9171,1902751,00.html

Ahmed, N.S., and Yasin, N.M. 2010, March. "Inspiring a fractal approach in distributed healthcare information systems: A review." *International Journal of Physical Sciences* 5(11):1626–1640.

Antonacopoulou, Elena, and Ricardo Chia. 2007. "The social complexity of organizational learning: The dynamics of learning and organizing." *Management Learning* 38(3):277–295. doi: 10.1177/1350507607079029.

Arendt, Hannah. *The human condition*. University of Chicago Press, 2013.

Ashby, W. Ross. 1958. "Requisite variety and its implications for the control of complex systems." *Cybernetica* 1(2):83–99.

Bakhtin, Michel. 1993. *Toward a philosophy of the act. Translated by Vadim Liapunov.* Edited by Michael Holquist, University of Texas Press Slavic Series No. 10. Austin: University of Texas Press.

Bakhtin, M.M. 1981. In M. Holquist (eds.) and C. Emerson and M. Holquist (trans.) *The dialogic imagination: Four essays by M.M. Bakhtin*. Austin: University of Texas Press.

Barad, Karen. 2003. "Posthumanist performativity: Toward an understanding of how matter comes to matter." *Signs* 28(3):801–831. Retrieved from http://uspace.shef.ac.uk/servlet/JiveServlet/previewBody/66890-102-1-128601/signsbarad.pdf

Barad, Karen. 2007. *Meeting the Universe Halfway: Quantum Physics and the Entanglement of Matter and Meaning*. Durham, NC: Duke University Press.

Barber, Dan. 2010. "How I fell in Love with Fish." *Ted Talk*. Retrieved from https://www.youtube.com/watch?v=4EUAMe2ixCI

Barthes, Roland. 1974. "S/Z. 1970." Trans. Richard Miller. New York: Hill and Wang, 115.

Baskin, Ken. 1995. "DNA for corporations: Organizations learn to adapt or die." *The Futurist* 29(1):68–68.

Baskin, Ken. 2003. "Complexity and the dilemma of the two worlds: The dynamics of navigating in fantasyland." *Emergence* 5(1):36–53.

Baskin, Ken. 2005. "Complexity, stories and knowing." *Emergence: Complexity & Organization* 7(2):32–40.

Baskin, Ken. 2007a. "Ever the twain shall meet." *Chinese Management Studies* 1(1):57–68. doi: 10.1108/17506140710735463.

Baskin, Ken. 2007b. "A review of complexity in world politics: Concepts and methods of a new paradigm." *Emergence: Complexity & Organization* 9(3):112–113.

Baskin, Ken. 2008. "Storied spaces: The human equivalent of complex adaptive systems." *Emergence: Complexity & Organization* 10(2):1–12.

Baskin, Ken. 2011. "How Chinese thought can lead the transformation in management practice." *Chinese Management Studies* 5(4):354–367.

Baskin, Ken, and David Boje. 2005. "Guest editors' introduction." *Emergence: Complexity & Organization* 7(3/4):1.
Baskin, K., and Bondarenko, D. 2014. *The axial ages of world history.* Litchfield Park, AZ: Emergent Publications.
Benjamin, W. 1936. "The storyteller: reflections on the works of Nikolai Leskov" [Essay]. In Hannah Arendt (ed.), *Walter Benjamin Illuminations,* pp. 83–109. First published in 1936 (Orien Und Okzident); 1968 is the English translation. New York: Harcourt Brace Jovanovitch.
Bennett, Jane. 2010. *Vibrant Matter: A Political Ecology of Things.* Durham, NC: Duke University Press.
Bevan, David, and Matthew Gitsham. 2009. "Context, complexity and connectedness: Dimensions of globalization revealed." *Corporate Governance* 9(4): 435–447.
Bhagavad Gita, The. 2007. Translated by Eknath Easwaran. Tomales, CA: Nilgiri Press. Original edition, 1985. Reprint, 2007.
Bodunkova, A.G., and Chernaya, I.P. 2012. "Fractal organization as innovative model for entrepreneurial university development." *World Applied Sciences Journal,* 18, 74–82.
Boje, D. 1991. The storytelling organization: A study of story performance. *Administrative Science Quarterly* 36(1):106–126.
Boje, D. 1995. "Stories of the storytelling organization: A postmodern analysis of Disney as 'Tamara-land.'" *Academy of Management Journal* 38(4):997–1035.
Boje, D. 2001. *Narrative Methods for Organizational & Communication Research.* London, UK: Sage.
Boje, David. 2008. *Storytelling Organizations.* Los Angeles: Sage.
Boje, David. 2010a. "Complexity theory and the dance of storytelling in organizations." In David Boje and Ken Baskin (eds.), *Dance to the Music of Story* (pp. 39–59). Litchfield Park, AZ: Emergent Publications.
Boje, David. 2010b. "MGMT 811: R&W Action Research Theory: IAS1" (Summer 2010), Lyon, France.
Boje, D. 2011a, 15 June, 2011. Quantum physics implications of storytelling for socioeconomic research methods: Experiences in small business consulting research form New Mexico State University. Paper presented at the International Meeting of Research Methods Division of the Academy of Management, Lyon, France.
Boje, David. 2011b. "Introduction to agential narratives that shape the future of organizations." In *Storytelling and the Future of Organizations: An Antenarrative Handbook,* edited by D. Boje, 1–15. New York, NY: Routledge.
Boje, David. 2011c. "Quantum storytelling conference." Quantum storytelling conference, Las Cruces, NM. www.quantumstorytelling.org
Boje, D. 2011d. *The cycle and spiral-antenarrative: A quantum-ontology manifesto.* Working Papers. New Mexico State University. Las Cruces, NM. Retrieved from http://business.nmsu.edu/~dboje/655/anteriority_and_antenarrative_spiral.html
Boje, David. 2011c. *Ontological Storytelling Inquiry Methodology—For Dummies.* Las Cruces, NM.
Boje, David. 2011e. *The Quantum Physics of Storytelling.* [Author's Draft ed.].
Boje, David. 2011f. "Quantum storytelling conference." Quantum storytelling conference, Las Cruces, NM.
Boje, David M. 2014a. "Meet our faculty: Dr. David M. Boje, Management." In Wenkai Zhou (ed.), *NM State Business Outlook.* Las Cruces, NM.
Boje, D.M. 2014b. Fractal Story and Fractal Ethnography of Entrepreneurial Sustainability: Daniel Q. Boje's Trash Compactor Patents and Enterprise. Proceedings Paper for 4th Annual Quantum Storytelling Conference, December 17–19 2014, held at 'Inn of the Arts,' Las Cruces, New Mexico.

Boje, David M. 2014c "Quantum Systemicity Theory." Accessed 17 August. http://business.nmsu.edu/~dboje/655/quantum_systems_theory.htm

Boje, D. 2014d. What is Living Story Web? Retrieved 15 May 2015, 2015, from http://peaceaware.com/Boje/What%20is%20Living%20Story.htm

Boje, D. 2014e. *Six Dumb Cultural Habits of Storytelling about War, Veterans, Schooling, and Sustainability*. Paper presented at the 13th IACCM Annual Conference BETWEEN CULTURES AND PARADIGMS: Intercultural Competence & Managerial Intelligence and 6th CEMS/IACCM Doctoral Workshop, Warwick, UK. http://peaceaware.com/Warwick/

Boje, D.M., ed. in press, 2015 expected. *Change Solutions to the Chaos of Standards and Norms Overwhelming Organizations: Four Wings of Tetranormalizing*. London: Routledge.

Boje, David, and K. Arkoubi. 2005. "Third cybernetic revolution: Beyond open to dialogic system theories." *Tamara: Journal of Critical Postmodern Organization Science* 4(1/2):138.

Boje, David, and Ken Baskin, eds. 2010a. *Dance to the Music of Story*. Litchfield Park, AZ: Emergent Publications.

Boje, David, and Ken Baskin. 2010b. "Editorial introduction." In *Dance to the music of story*, edited by David Boje and Ken Baskin, pp. 1–20. Litchfield Park, AZ: Emergent Publications.

Boje, David, and Ken Baskin. 2010c. "Our organizations were never disenchanted: Enchantment by design." [Prepublication version]. *Journal of Organizational Change Management.*

Boje, David, and Ken Baskin. 2010d. "When storytelling dances with complexity—the search for Morin's keys." In David Boje and Ken Baskin (eds.), *Dance to the Music of Story: Understanding Human Behavior through the Integration of Storytelling and Complexity Thinking* (pp. 21–37). Litchfield Park, AZ.

Boje, David, Ivy DuRant, Krisha Coppedge, Ted Chambers, and Marilu Marcillo-Gomez. 2012. "Social materiality: A new direction in change management and action research." In David M. Boje, Bernard Burnes and John Hassard (eds.), *The Routledge Companion to Organizational Change* (pp. 580–597). New York, NY: Routeledge.

Boje, David, and Tonya L. Henderson, eds. 2014. *Being Quantum: Ontological Storytelling in the Age of Antenarrative*. Newcastle upon Tyne, United Kingdom: Cambridge Scholars Publishing.

Boje, D. M., Jørgensen, K. M., and Strand, A. M. C. 2013. Towards a postcolonialist Storytelling Theory of management and organization. *Journal of Management Philosophy* 12(1):43–65.

Boje, David, and Tonya Wakefield. 2011. "Storytelling in systemicity and emergence: A third order cybernetic." In David Boje, Bernard Burnes, and John Hassard (eds.), *The Routledge Companion to Organizational Change*. New York: Routledge.

Bonifer, M. 2008. *Gamechangers: Improvisation for Business in the Networked World*. Gamechangers. Los Angeles: McKava Press.

Booher, David E., and Judith E. Innes. 2002. "Network power in collaborative planning." *Journal of Planning Education and Research* 21(3):221–236. doi: 10.1177/0739456x0202100301.

Bourdieu, P. 1977. *Outline of a Theory of Practice*. New York: Cambridge University Press.

Brown, A.D., Humphreys, M., and Gurney, P.M. 2005. "Narrative, identity and change: A case study of Laskarina holidays." *Journal of Organizational Change Management* 18(4):312–326.

Browne Trading Company: Veta La Palma Seafood. 2015. Retrieved 8 March, 2015, from http://www.brownetrading.com/products/fresh-fish/veta-la-palma-seafood/

Bruner, J. 1986. *Actual Minds, Possible Worlds.* Harvard University Press, Cambridge, MA.

Burnes, Bernard. 2012. "Kurt Lewin and the Origins of OD." In Bernard Burnes and David M. Boje (eds.), *The Routledge Companion to Organizational Change* (pp. 15–30). Abingdon, Oxon, UK: Routledge.

Butler, J. 1993. *Bodies that Matter.* New York: Routledge.

Bygrave, W.D. 1993. "Theory building in the entrepreneurship paradigm." *Journal of Business Venturing* 8(3):255–280.

Bygrave, W.D. 2007. "The entrepreneurship paradigm (I) revisited." In H. Neergaard and J.P. Ulhøi (eds.), *Handbook of Qualitative Research Methods in Entrepreneurship* (pp. 17–48). Northampton, MA: Edward Elgar.

Bygrave, W.D., and Hofer, C.W. 1991. "Theorizing about entrepreneurship." *Entrepreneurship theory and Practice* 16(2):13–22.

Campbell, J. 1987. *The Hero's Journey.* [VHS]. Public Media Video.

Carayannis, E.G., and D.F. Campbell. 2009. "'Mode 3' and 'Quadruple Helix': Toward a 21st century fractal innovation ecosystem." *International Journal of Technology Management* 46(3):201–234.

Carayannis, E.G., and D.F. Campbell. 2012. *Mode 3 knowledge production in quadruple helix innovation systems.* New York: Springer.

Carrera, Jagnath. 2011. *Inside the Yoga Sutras.* Buckingham, VA: Integral Yoga Publications.

Chia, R., and Chia, R. K. G. 1996. *Organizational Analysis as Deconstructive Practice* (Vol. 77). New York: Walter de Gruyter.

Chiva-Gomez, R. 2004. "Repercussions of complex adaptive systems on product design management." *Technovation* 24(9):707–711.

Clarkson, G. 2004. Objective identification of patent thickets: A network analytic approach. *Harvard Business School Doctoral Thesis.*

Clarkson, G., and DeKorte, D. 2006. "The problem of patent thickets in convergent technologies." *Annals of the New York Academy of Sciences* 1093(1):180–200.

Comunian, Roberta. 2011. "Rethinking the creative city." *Urban Studies* 48(6): 1157–1179. doi: 10.1177/0042098010370626.

Cooperrider, David L. 1986. "Appreciative inquiry: Toward a methodology for understanding and enhancing organizational innovation." Ph.D., Department of Organizational Behavior, Case Western Reserve (8611485).

Cooperrider, David L., and Diana Whitney. 2005. *Appreciative Inquiry: A Positive Revolution in Change.* San Francisco, CA: Berrett-Koehler Publishers.

Coppedge, Krisha. 2014. "The preponderance of evidentuality enlightenment in home ownership." In Boje David M and Tonya L. Henderson (eds.), *Being Quantum: Ontological Storytelling in the Age of Antenarrative* (pp. 191–216). Newcastle Upon Tyne, UK: Cambridge Scholars.

Covey, Steven R. 1989. *Seven Habits of Highly Effective People*: Simon & Schuster.

Delany, S. R. 2011. *Silent Interviews: On Language, Race, Sex, Science Fiction, and Some Comics—A Collection of Written Interviews.* Hanover, NH: Wesleyan University Press.

Deleuze, Gilles. 1994. *Difference and Repetition.* Translated by Paul Patton. English translation ed., European Perspectives. New York, NY: Columbia University Press. Original edition, 1968.

Deleuze, G., and Guattari, F. 1987. *A Thousand Plateaus: Capitalism and Schizophrenia.* Translated by B. Massumi. Minneapolis, MN: University of Minnesota Press.

Dourish, P. 2014. Reeconfiguring Sociomateriality: An Ethnographic Investigation of Robotic Deep Space Science. *Stanford Seminars* [Guest Lecture]. Standford, CA: Stanford University.

Down, S. 2006. *Narratives of Enterprise: Crafting Entrepreneurial Self-Identity in a Small Firm.* Northampton, MA: Edward Elgar Publishing.

Duarte, G. A. 2014. *Fractal Narrative: About the Relationship Between Geometries and Technology and Its Impact on Narrative Spaces* (Vol. 12). Deutsche Nationalbibliotekhe

Eberly, Marion, Erica Holley, Michael Johnson, and Terence Mitchell. 2011. "Beyond internal and external: A dyadic theory of relational attributions." *Academy of Management Review* 36(4):731–753.

Eglash, Ron. 2005. *African Fractals: Modern Computing and Indigenous Design* (Reprint, 3rd). New Brunswick, NJ: Rutgers University Press. Original edition, 1999.

Emery, Merrelyn, and Ronald E. Purser. 1996. *The Search Conference* (1st ed.). San Francisco, CA: Jossey-Bass, Inc.

Eoyang, Glenda. 2009. *Coping with Chaos.* Edited by Human Systems Dynamics Institute. Circle Pines, MN: Lagumo.

Etzkowitz, H., and L. Leydesdorff. 2000. "The dynamics of innovation: From National Systems and 'Mode 2' to a Triple Helix of university–industry–govern ment relations." *Research Policy* 29(2):109–123.

Fainstein, Susan S. 2005. "Cities and diversity." *Urban Affairs Review* 41(1):3–19. doi: 10.1177/1078087405278968.

Fischer, D. H. 1996. *The Great Wave: Price Revolutions and the Rhythm of History.* New York: Oxford University Press.

Florida, Richard. 2008. *Who's Your City.* New York, NY: Basic Books.

Foucault, M. 1977. *Discipline and Punish: The Birth of the Prision* (A. Sheridan, Trans.). New York: Random House.

Fractal Analytics: Overview. 2015. Retrieved 1 February, 2015, from http://www.fractalanalytics.com/products-and-solutions/overview

Fractal Analytics Buys Mobile-Based Context-Aware Big Data Startup Mobius Innovations. 2015, 15 January. Retrieved 15 May, 2015, from http://www.fractalanalytics.com/news/fractal-analytics-buys-mobile-based-context-aware-big-data-startup-mobius-innovations

Frazier, Mark. 2012. "What are narrative fractals?" *Quora,* Last Modified 21 August 2012 (original post). Retrieved 6 January 2015, from http://www.quora.com/What-are-narrative-fractals

Fryer, P., and J. Ruis. 2004. What are Fractal Systems? A brief description of "Complex Adaptive and Emergent Systems" (CAES). http://www.fractal.org/

Gabriel, R. P., and R. Goldman. 2006, October. "Conscientious software." In *Acm Sigplan Notices* 41(10):433–450.

Gérard, Genette. 1982. "Palimpsestes." *La littérature au second degré.* Paris: Seuil.

Gershenson, Carlos, and Francis Heylighen. 2003. "When can we call a system self-organizing?" Advances in Artificial Life: 7th European Conference on Artificial Life, ECAL 2003, Dortmund, Germany, 19 February, 2004.

Gibson, W. 1995. *Neuromancer.* 1984. New York: Ace.

Giddens, A. 1979. *Central Problems in Social Theory: Action, Structure, and Contradiction in Social Science.* Berkley, Los Angeles: University of California Press.

Gladstone, Joe S. 2014. "Transplanar wisdom: The quantum spirit of Native American storytelling" In David M. Boje and Tonya L. Henderson (eds.), *Being Quantum: Ontological Storytelling in the Age of Antenarrative* (pp. 217–231). Newcastle upon Tyne, NE6 2XX, UK Cambridge Scholars Publishing.

Gulick, D., and Scott, J. 2010. *The Beauty of Fractals: Six Different Views.* Washington DC: Mathematical Association of America.

Gómez-Pompa, A., and A. Kaus. 1999. "From pre-Hispanic to future conservation alternatives: Lessons from Mexico." *Proceedings of the National Academy of Sciences* 96(11):5982–5986. doi: 10.1073/pnas.96.11.5982.

Grant, Robert M. 2010. *Contemporary Strategy Analysis* (7th ed). West Sussex, UK: John Wiley & Sons.

Haley, Usha C. V., and David M. Boje. 2015. "Storytelling the internationalization of the multinational enterprise." *Journal of International Business Studies* 45 (9): 1115–1132.

Haslett, B. B., and Lipman, S. 1997. *Micro inequities: Up close and personal.* In N.V. Benokraitis (ed.), *Subtle Sexism: Current Practice and Prospects for Change* (pp. 34–53). Thousand Oaks, CA: Sage.

Hawking, Stephen, and Leonard Mlodinow. 2005. *A Briefer History of Time.* Westminster, MD: Random House. [audio-book].

Hazy, James K. 2006. "Measuring leadership effectiveness in complex socio-technical systems." *Emergence: Complexity & Organization* 8 (3):58–77.

Heidegger, Martin. 1962. *Being and Time.* Translated by Ralph Mahnheim (7th ed.). New York: Harper & Rowe Publishers. Original edition, 1926.

Heidegger, M. 1971. *Poetry, Language, Thought,* translated by A. Hofstadter. New York: Harper and Row.

Henderson, Tonya L. 2014a. *Fractal Patterns in Storytelling: A Deeper Understanding of Organizational Complexity.* Academy of Management, Philadelphia, PA.

Henderson, Tonya L. 2014b. Management on the Mat, 12 January.

Henderson, Tonya L. 2014c. "Spotting Patterns in Work and Life: Awareness and Reinvention." FEBE (For Entrepreneurs by Entrepreneurs) Superwoman Leadership Conference, Colorado Springs, CO, 14 June 2014.

Henderson, Tonya L. 2014d. "Are your patterns on purpose?" 21 October. http://www.glysolutions.com/—!Are-your-patterns-on-purpose-The-Four-As-of-Fractal-Management/c1q8z/A5C4A23C-3564-4C7E-B6BC-A91359694E9E.

Henderson, Tonya L., and Daphne Deporres. 2014. "Patterns of Perception Among Yoga Practitioners." International Conferene of Management Cases, Greater Noida, India.

History: 1964–2014: Our 50th Anniversary. 2014. Retrieved 15 May, 2015, from http://business.nmsu.edu/about/history/

Hongzhao, D., L. Dongxu, Z. Yanwei, and C. Ying. 2005. "A novel approach of networked manufacturing collaboration: Fractal web-based extended enterprise." *The International Journal of Advanced Manufacturing Technology* 26(11–12):1436–1442. doi: 10.1007/s00170-004-2125-4.

Houston, Renee. 1999. "Self-organizing systems theory: Historical challenges to new sciences." *Management Communication Quarterly* 13(1):119–134. doi: 10.1177/0893318999131006.

Hoverstadt, Patrick. 2011. *The Fractal Organization: Creating Sustainable Organizations with the Viable System Model.* Hoboken, NJ: John Wiley & Sons.

Interview. 2009. Alexandria, VA: American Society for Training & Development.

Ison, Ray. 2008. "Systems thinking and practice for action research." In Peter Reason and Hilary Bradbury (eds.), *The SAGE Handbook of Action Research: Participative Inquiry and Practice* (pp. 138–158). London: Sage. Original edition, 2008.

Jantsch, Erich. 1973. "Forecasting and systems approach: A frame of reference" *Management Science* 19(12):1355–1367.

Johnson, Neil. 2007. *Simply Complexity: A Clear Guide to Complexity Theory.* Oxford, England: Oneworld Publications.

Joint initiatives for youth and families: An analysis of the collaborative network. 2011. In PARTNER: Program to analyze, record, and track networks to enhance relationships. Denver, Colorado: University of Colorado Denver.

Joyce, Arthur A. 2009. "Theorizing urbanism in ancient Mesoamerica." *Ancient Mesoamerica* 20: 189–196. doi:10.1017/S0956536109990125.

Joyce, A.A., and Winter, M. 1996. "Ideology, power and urban society in pre-Hispanic Oaxaca." *Current Anthropology, 37*(1).

Kauffman, Stuart. 1995. *At Home in the Universe.* New York: Oxford University Press.

Kincheloe, Joe L. 2007. "Postformalism and critical ontology—Part 1: Difference, indigenous knowledge, and cognition." In Joe L. Kincheloe and Raymond A. Horn (eds.), *The Praeger Handbook of Education and Psychology* (Vol. 1, pp. 884–899). Santa Barbara, CA: Greenwood Publishing Group.

Kirikova, M. 2009. "Towards multifractal approach in IS development." In C. Barry et al. (eds.), *Information Systems Development* (pp. 295–306). New York: Springer.

Kondrat′ev, Nikolaĭ Dmitrievich. 1984. *The long wave cycle.* New York: Richardson & Snyder.

Kotak, D., Bardi, S., Groover, W., and Zohrevand, K. 2000. *Comparison of Hierarchical and Holonic Shop Floor Control Using Virtual Manufacturing Environment.* Paper presented at the IEEE International Conference on Systems, Man, and Cybernetics.

Krizanc, J., and Boje, D. 2006. Tamara Journal Interview with John Krizanc: TAMARA. *Journal of Critical Postmodern Organization Science* 5: 70–77.

Kuehnle, H. I. 2002. Guidelines for future manufacturing–necessity of a change of organizational structures in industry and ways to the "fractal company" [Электронный ресурс]. *WEB Journal, 12.*

Lakoff, G. 1990. The Invariance Hypothesis: Is abstract reason based on image-schemas? *Cognitive Linguistics* (includes *Cognitive Linguistic Bibliography*) 1(1): 39–74.

Lakoff, G., and Núñez, R. E. 2000. Where Mathematics Comes from: How the Embodied Mind Brings Mathematics into Being. New York: Basic books.

Latent semantic analysis. 2015, 25 April. Retrieved 15 May, 2015, from http://en.wikipedia.org/wiki/Latent_semantic_analysis

Latour, B. 1999. *Pandora's Hope: Essays on the Reality of Science Studies.* Cambridge, MA: Harvard University Press.

Latour, B. 2004. "How to talk about the body? The normative dimension of science studies." *Body & Society* 10(2–3):205–229.

Latour, Bruno. 2005. *Reassembling the Social: An Introduction to Actor-Network Theory, Clarendon Lectures in Management Studies.* Oxford: Oxford University Press. Original edition, 2005. Reprint, 2007 paperback.

Lee, Deokjae, K.-I. Goh, B. Kahng, and D. Kim. 2010. "Complete trails of coauthorship network evolution." *The American Physical Society* E82 (026112):1–9.

Lefebvre, Henri. 2004. *RhythmAnalysis: Space, Time and Everyday Life.* Translated by Stuart Elden and Gerald Moore with an Introduction by Stuart Elden. London/New York: Continuum Press. Originally in French 1992.

Leibovitch, Larry S. 1998. *Fractals and Chaos for the Life Sciences.* New York: Oxford University Press.

Lesmoir-Gordon, N., Rood, W., and Edney, R. 2009. *Fractals: A graphic guide.* London, UK: Icon Books.

Letiche, Hugo, and David Boje. 2001. "Phenomenal complexity: Theory and the politics of organization." *Emergence* 3(4):5–31.

Lewin, Kurt. 1951. *Field Theory in Social Science.* Dorwin Cartwright (ed.). New York, NY: Harper & Brothers.

Lewin, Roger. 1999. *Complexity: Life at the Edge of Chaos* (2nd ed.). Chicago, IL: University of Chicago Press. Original edition, 1992.

Leximancer (version 2.2) Manual. 2005. Brisbane, Australia: Leximancer. https://www.leximancer.com/wiki/images/7/77/Leximancer_V2_Manual.pdf

Luhman, John T., and David M. Boje. 2001. "What is complexity science? A possible answer from narrative research." *Emergence* 3(1):158–168.

MacLeod, Gordon. 2011. "Urban politics reconsidered." *Urban Studies* 48(12): 2629–2660. doi: 10.1177/0042098011415715.

Mandelbrot, Benoit. 1983. *The Fractal Geometry of Nature.* New York, NY: W.H. Freeman and Company. Original edition, 1977. Reprint, 1983.

Mandelbrot, Benoit, and Richard L. Hudson. 2004. *The (Mis)behavior of Markets: A Fractal View of Risk, Ruin, and Reward*. New York, NY: Basic Books: A Member of the Perseus Books Group.

Mandrell, Patti. 2014. Introduction to Equine-Assisted Psychotherapy: A Comprehensive Overview. Second Edition. ISBY 978-0-9916291-0-7 printed in US, www.refugesservices.

Mataric, Maja J. 1995. "Designing and understanding adaptive group behavior." *Adaptive Behavior* 4(1):51–80. doi: 10.1177/105971239500400104.

Maturana, H.R., and Varela, F.J. 1987. *The tree of knowledge: The biological roots of human understanding*. New Science Library/Shambhala Publications.

Mazmanian, M., Cohn, M., and Dourish, P. 2014. Dynamic reconfiguration in planetary exploration: a sociomaterial ethnography. *Mis Quarterly* 38(3):831–848.

McCulloh, Gerri Elise. 2014. "Summoning Kairos: Atavistic processes in quantum adaptive rhetoric." In Gavid M. Boje and Tonya L. Henderson (eds.), *Being Quantum: Ontological Storytelling in the Age of Antenarrative* (pp. 51–89). Newcastle upon Tyne, NE6 2XX, UK: Cambridge Scholars Publishing.

McDonough, W., and Braungart, M. 2002. *Cradle to Cradle: Remaking the Way We Make Things*. San Francisco: North Point Press.

Meisner, G. 2012, 13 May. Phi 1.618: The Golden Number. Retrieved 3 Mar 2015, from http://www.goldennumber.net/golden-ratio-history/

Meredith, H., and Walker, R. n.d. Wikia Fractal Story. *Information Design*. Retrieved 8 March, 2015, from http://www.gold-collective.com/wikia-fractal-story/

Merleau-Ponty, M. 1962. *Phenomenology of Perception [Phénoménologie de la Perception]*. New York: Routledge & Kegan Paul.

Minahen, C.D. 1992. *Vortex/t: The Poetics of Turbulence*. University Park: Pennsylvania State University Press.

Mitchell, Melanie. 2009. *Complexity: A Guided Tour*. Oxford, New York: Oxford University Press.

NMSU College of Business. 2014. from http://business.nmsu.edu/

Nonaka, I. 1991. The knowledge-creating company. *Harvard Business Review*, 69(6):96–104.

Noon, Jeff. 1993. *Vurt*. UK: Ringpull Press.

Noon, Jeff. 1996a. *Automated Alice*. NY: Crown Publishers.

Noon, Jeff. 1996b *Pollen*. NY: Crown Publishers.

Nottale, L. 1996. "Scale relativity and fractal space-time: applications to quantum physics, cosmology and chaotic systems." *Chaos, Solitons & Fractals*, 7(6):877–938.

Nottale, L. 2011. *Scale Relativity and Fractal Space-Time: A new approach to Unifying Relativity and Quantum Mechanics*. London: Imperial College Press.

Oh, Seungjin, Kwangyeol Ryu, Ilkyeong Moon, Hyunbo Cho, and Moonyoung Jung. 2010. "Collaborative fractal-based supply chain management based on a trust model for the automotive industry." *Flexible Services and Manufacturing Journal* 22:183–213. doi: 10.1007/s10696-011-9082-7.

Palumbo, D. 1998. "The monomyth as fractal pattern in Frank Herbert's Dune novels." *Science Fiction Studies*, 25(3):433–458.

Palumbo, D. 2002. *Chaos Theory, Asimov's Foundations and Robots, and Herbert's Dune: The Fractal Aesthetic of Epic Science Fiction* (No. 100). Westport, CT: Greenwood Press.

Palumbo, D.E. 2004. "The monomyth in Alfred Bester's The Stars My Destination." *The Journal of Popular Culture* 38(2):333–368.

Payne, Ruby K. 2001. *Bridges Out of Poverty*. Highlands, TX: aha! Process, Inc.

Plate, Markus, Christian Schiede, and von Arist Schlippe. 2010. "Portfolio entrepreneurship in the context of family owned businesses." In T. Nordqvist, and T. Zellweger, *Transgenerational Entrepreneurship: Exploring Growth and*

Performance in Family Firms Across Generations (pp. 96–122). Cheltenham, UK: Edward Elgar Publishing.

Polkinghorne, D.E. 2004. Narrative therapy and postmodernism. In L. E Angus and J. McLeod (eds.), *The Handbook of Narrative and Psychotherapy: Practice, Theory and Research* (pp. 53–68). Thoudand Oaks, CA: Sage.

Polkinghorne, D.E. 2007. "Validity issues in narrative research." *Qualitative Inquiry* 13(4):471–486.

Pondy, L.R., and Boje, D. 2005. "Beyond open system models of organization." *Emergence: Complexity & Organization* 7(3/4):119–137.

Potter, James n.d. "Obscenity." *Farlex*. Retrieved from http://legal-ictionary.thefreedictionary.com/obscenity.

Prigogine, I. 1996. *The End of Certainty*. New York: The Free Press, A Division of Simon & Schuster.

Prigogine, I., & Stengers, I. 1984. *Order out of Chaos*. Toronto: Bantom Books.

Pugesek, Bruce H. 2014. "Fractal cycle turning points: A theory of human social progression." *Ecological Complexity* 20: 157–175.

Quade, Kristine. 2011. "Simple rules leaders use to guide their organizations during times of rapid change." Ed.D. Doctoral Dissertation, Graduate School of Education and Psychology, Pepperdine University.

Quade, Kristine, and Royce Holladay. 2010. *Dynamical Leadership: Building Adaptive Capacity for Uncertain Times*. Apache Junction, AZ: Gold Canyon Press.

Ramanathan, J. 2005. "Fractal architecture for the adaptive complex enterprise." *Communications of the ACM* 48(5):51–57.

Rapoport, Anatol, William J. Horvath, and Jeffrey Goldstein. 2009. "Thoughts on organization theory." *Emergence: Complexity & Organization* 11(1):94–103.

Robinson, J.A., and Hawpe, L. 1986. "Narrative thinking as a heuristic process." In T. E. Sarbin, (ed.). *Narrative Psychology: The Storied nature of Human Conduct* (pp. 111–125). New York: Preager.

Rosile, Grace, Ann Boje, and Nez Carma. in review. *Ensemble Leadership Theory of Pre-Hispanic Southwest Mesoamerica*. New Mexico State University.

Ruis, J. J. C. M. 2014, 1 August. Fractal Consultancy. http://www.fractal.org/Fractal-Research-and-Products/Fractal-design-cycle.pdf

Ryu, K., and Jung, M. 2003. Agent-based fractal architecture and modeling for developing distributed manufacturing systems. *International Journal of Production Research* 41(17):4233–4255.

Sandkuhl, K., and M. Kirikova. 2011. "Analysing enterprise models from a fractal organisation perspective-potentials and limitations." In *The Practice of Enterprise Modeling* (pp. 193–207). Springer Berlin Heidelberg.

Savall, Henri, Veronique Zardet, and Marc Bonnet. 2008. *Realizing the Potential of Enterprises through Socio-economic Management*. English Edition. Geneva, Lyon: International Labour Office Bureau for Employers' Activities.

Schindehutte, M., and M. H. Morris. 2009. "Advancing strategic entrepreneurship research: The role of complexity science in shifting the paradigm." *Entrepreneurship Theory and Practice* 33(1):241–276. http://www.pogc.ir/Portals/0/maghalat/890724–1.pdf

Schroeder, Manfred. 1991. *Fractals, Chaos, and Power Laws: Minutes from an Infinite Paradise*. Mineola, NY: Dover Publications.

Seashore, Charles, Mary Nash Shawver, Greg Thompson, and Marty Mattare. 2004. "Doing good by knowing who you are: The instrumental self as an agent of change." *OD Practitioner* 36(3):42–46.

Seashore, E., Seashore, C., & Livingston, R. 2010. *Workshop on Intentional Use of Self*. Workshop materials. Colorado Technical University, Colorado Springs, Colorado.

Sennett, R. 1998. *The Spaces of Democracy*. University of Michigan, College of Architecture & Urban Planning.

Sewell Jr, W.H. 1992. A theory of structure: Duality, agency, and transformation. *American Journal of Sociology* 98(1):1–29.

Sheldrake, Rupert. 1988. *The Presence of the Past: Morphic Resonance and the Habits of Nature*. New York, NY: Vintage Books.

Shirky, Clay. 2008. *Here Comes Everybody: The Power of Organizing without Organizations*. New York, NY: The Penguin Press.

Shrestha, Manoj K., and Richard C. Feiock. 2009. "Governing U.S. Metropolitan Areas: Self-organizing and multiplex service networks." *American Politics Research* 37(5):801–823. doi: 10.1177/1532673x09337466.

Sihn, W. 2002, June. Fractal businesses in an E-buisness world. In the 8th Internaitonal Conference on Concurrent Enterprising. Rome, Italy, pp. 17–19. http://www.manubuild.net/projects/08/CE002/reforms/Business%20to%20Business/05_Sihn.pdf

Smith, R., and Anderson, A.R. 2004. "The devil is in the e-tale: form and structure in the entrepreneurial narrative. Narrative and discursive approaches in entrepreneurship." In D. Hjorth and C. Steyaert (eds.), *Narrative and Discursive Approaches in Entrepreneurship: A Second Movements in Entrepreneurship Book* (pp. 125–143). Cheltenham, UK: Edward Elgar.

Stacey, Ralph D. 1996. *Complexity and Creativity in Organizations* (1st ed.). San Francisco, CA: Berrett-Koehler Publishers.

Stewart, Ian. 2010. "The nature of fractal geometry." In Nigel Lesmoir-Gordon (ed.), *The Colours of Infinity*, pp. 2–23. London: Springer-Verlag London Limited.

Strazdina, Renate and Marite Kirikova. 2011. "Change Management for Fractal Enterprises." In Jaroslav Pokorny, Vaclav Repa, Karel Richta, Wita Wojtkowski, Henry Linger, Chris Barry and Michael Lang (eds.), *Information Systems Development* (pp. 735–745). New York: Springer.

Strand, Anete Mikkala Camille. 2011. Presentation on "material storytelling" to 20th anniversary meeting of S'CMoi, meeting in Philadelphia, April.

Strand, Anete Mikkala Camille. 2012. "The between: on dis/continuous intra-active becoming of/through an apparatus of material storytelling." Doctoral Program in Human Centered Communication and Informatics (HCCI), Aalborg University.

Strauss, R.E., & Hummel, T. 1995. *The new industrial engineering revisited-information technology, business process re-engineering, and lean management in the self-organizing "fractal company."* Paper presented at the Engineering Management Conference, 1995. Global Engineering Management: Emerging Trends in the Asia Pacific., Proceedings of 1995 IEEE Annual International, 28–30 June.

Svyantek, Daniel J. and Richard P. Deshon. 1993. "Organizational attractors: A chaos theory explanation of why cultural change efforts often fail." *Public Administration Quarterly* 17(3):339–354.

TA Associates Announces Investment in Fractal Analytics. TA Associates: TA News. Retrieved 13 May, 2015, from http://www.ta.com/News/Fractal-Press-Release.aspx

Talbot, Michael. 1993. *Mysticism and the New Physics* (2nd ed.). London, England: Arkana, Penguin Books. Original edition, 1981.

Taleb, Nassim Nicholas. 2007. *The Black Swan: The Impact of the Highly Improbable*. Recorded Books, LLC. Audiobook.

Tang, Y. Y. 2012. *Document Analysis and Recognition with Wavelet And Fractal Theories*. Singapore, New Jersey, London: World Scientific Publishing Company.

Tetreault, Donald, and Tonya L. Henderson Wakefield. 2012. "Various." Columbia, SC.

Tharumarajah, A. 2003. From fractals and bionics to holonics. In S.M. Dean (ed.), *Agent-Based Manufacturing* (pp. 11–30). Berlin: Springer Heidelberg.

Tharumarajah, A., Wells, A.J., and Nemes, L. 1998, October. Comparison of emerging manufacturing concepts. In *Systems, Man, and Cybernetics, 1998. 1998 IEEE International Conference on* (Vol. 1, pp. 325–331). IEEE.

Thompson, Lea. n.d. Dirty Dining? "Dateline" hidden cameras investigate cleanlines of America's top 10 fast food chain. In Consumer Alert on Dateline. http://www.nbcnews.com/id/3473728/ns/dateline_nbc-consumer_alert/t/dirty-dining/

Tisby-Cousar, W. 2014. Can onological storytelling perpetuate a breakthrough for leaders to re-enter their organizations with greater impact? In B. David M and T.L. Henderson (eds.), *Being Quantum: Ontological Storytelling in the Age of Antenarrative* (pp. 430–449). Newcastle Upon Tyne, UK: Cambridge Scholars Publishing.

Tsoukas, Haridimos, and Kevin J. Dooley. 2011. "Introduction to the special issue: Towards the eological style: Embracing complexity in organizational research." *Organization Studies* 32(6):729–735. doi: 10.1177/0170840611410805.

Tuckman, Bruce. 1965. "Bruce Tuckman's 1965 Forming Storming Norming Performing team-development model." [Web Page] Retrieved 14 January, 2010, from http://www.businessballs.com/tuckmanformingstormingnormingperforming.htm.

Van de Ven, Andrew H., and Marshall Scott Poole. 2005. "Alternative approaches for studying organizational change." *Organization Studies* (01708406) 26(9): 1377–1404. doi: 10.1177/0170840605056907.

von Bertalanffy, Ludwig. 1969. *General Systems Theory: Foundations, Development, Applications* [Revised ed.]. New York, NY: George Braziller.

Vrobel, S. 2011. *Fractal Time: Why a Watched Kettle Never Boils*. New Jersey, London: World Scientific Publishing Company.

Waddington, C.H. 1961. *The Nature of Life*. Kessinger Legacy Reprints [Lecture Series]. New York, NY: Athenium.

Wahl, Bernt Rainer, Peter Van Roy, Michael Larsen, Eric (Doc) Kampman, and Laura Kelly Gonzalez. n.d. "Chapter 4—Calculating Fractals Dimension." Dynamic Software vis Multimedia University. Accessed 31 Jan. 2015, http://www.wahl.org/fe/HTML_version/link/FE4W/c4.htm.

Wakefield, T. H. 2011. Client Report for the Women's Resource Agency of Colorado Springs. Process consulting practicum report. Colorado Technical University. Colorado Springs, CO.

Wakefield, Tonya L. Henderson. 2012. "An ontology of storytelling systemicity: Management, fractals and the Waldo Canyon fire." Doctorate of Management Doctoral dissertation, Management, Colorado Technical University.

Wakefield, Tonya L. Henderson, and D. Boje. 2012. Gly's Purse: Materiality as Viewed through a Threefold Diffractive Lens. Paper presented at the 2nd Annual Quantum Storytelling Conference. http://peaceaware.com/quantum/pdfs/Wakefield_Boje%20Materiality%20Final%2017%20Nov%202012%20corrected.pdf

Wakefield, Tonya L. Henderson, Alfonso Robertson, and Kenneth Wall. 2012. "Nonprofit board service: a qualitative investigation using appreciative inquiry." Action research report International Conference on the Management Cases, Greater Noida (NCR), India, 29–30 November.

Wakefield, Tonya L. Henderson, David Boje, and Michael Lane. 2013. "Fractals and Food." Standing Conference for Management and Organization Inquiry (SCMOI), Alexandria, VA.

Wakefield, Tonya L. Henderson, Alfonso Robertson, and Kenneth Wall. 2012. "Nonprofit board service: A qualitative investigation using appreciative inquiry."

Action research report International Conference on the Management Cases, Greater Noida (NCR), India, 29–30 November.
"Waldo Canyon Fire After Action Report Suggests Better Training in the Future." 2012. *Huffington Post,* 27 October. Retrieved from http://www.huffingtonpost.com/2012/10/23/waldo-canyon_n_2007447.html
Waldrop, M. Mitchell. 1992. *Complexity: The Emerging Science at the Order of Chaos*. New York: Simon & Schuster.
Warnecke, H.J. 1993. *The Fractal Company—Production in the Network*. New York: Springer-Verlag.
Weick, K. 1995. *Sensemaking in Organizations*. Thousand Oaks, CA: Sage.
Wenaus, A. 2011. "Fractal narrative, paraspace, and strange loops: The paradox of escape in Jeff Noon's Vurt." *Science Fiction Studies* 38(1):155–174.
Wheatley, Margaret J. 2006. *Leadership and the New Science: Discovering Order in a Chaotic World* (1st ed.). San Francisco, CA: Brett-Koehler Publishers.
White, M., and Epston, D. 1990. *Narrative Means to Therapeutic Ends*. W. W. Norton & Company.
Williams, Bob. 2000. "Coping with chaos: Seven simple tools." *Management Learning* 31(3):391.
Worley, Christopher G., David E. Hitchin, and Walter L. Ross. 1996. In Edgar Schein and Richard Beckhard, *Integrated Strategic Change: How OD builds competitive advantage*. Addison-Wesley Series on Organizational Development. Reading, Massachusetts: Addison-Wesley Publishing Company.
Zimmerman, Brenda J., and David K. Hurst. 1993. "Breaking the boundaries: The fractal organization." *Journal of Management Inquiry* 2(4):334–355. doi: 10.1177/105649269324006.

About the Authors

Tonya L. Henderson is a management consultant, author, and speaker at Gly Solutions, LLC. She is an adjunct professor, a yoga teacher, and a veteran of the US navy and the aerospace industry. She recently coedited the book *Being Quantum: Ontological Storytelling in the Age of Antenarrative* with David Boje.

David M. Boje holds the Wells Fargo Professorship, Distinguished University Professor, and Bill Daniels Ethics Fellow in Management Department at New Mexico State University. Professor Boje also has an honorary doctorate from Aalborg University, with a special affiliation to the Material Storytelling Lab founded by Anete Strand. He is informally known as the "godfather" to the lab. Emerging in New Mexico is the Embodied Restorying Processes (ERP) Lab, which is affiliated with the worldwide Material Storytelling Lab community. The New Mexico Embodied Restorying Processes (ERP) Lab does work with veterans including the homeless veterans. ERP contributes to Material Storytelling by combining Little Wow Moments rediscovered from the past, and making new "bets" of fore-seeing new "moments of vision" of potential futures, and selecting a future to bring into actuality.

Index

action research *see* fractal action research model
actor 15, 77; *see also* agent
adaptation 1, 18
adaptive action 75
adaptive capacity 22
ad-hocracy xvi
affordances 8
agency, agent 6, 13–14, 24, 69, 72, 114
agent-based fractal modeling 144
agential cut 7, 31, 57, 117, 176
agential realism 8–9, 12; *see* agential cut
alignment 5, 6, 10, 116, 154, 160, 164
answerability 32, 76, 116, 183
antenarrative xvi, 5, 6, 10, 25, 73, 80–2, 91, 94–5, 97, 100, 149; cyclical 96, 98–9; in storytelling 84–6; rhizomatic antenarrative 87, 99; spiral antenarrative 87, 97, 99; types of antenarrative 58–9, 76; in the Fractal Action Research Method 151, 152–4; Five A's of Fractal Management 160; antenarrative reflection 172–3
apparatus 11, 31, 39, 69, 174
appreciative inquiry 175
archetypes 25
Archimedes-fractal-spiral 16; *see also* Fibonacci spiral
Aristotle 7–8, 13, 76, 92
asbestos xv
Ashby, W. Ross xvii, 17
Ashby's law (of requisite variety) 17, 175
assemblage 2, 7, 12, 31, 69, 89, 170
asymmetry 73
attractor, attractor states 24–5, 39, 74, 94
attunement xiii, 10, 28, 55, 84, 76, 109, 111–12; attunement to moods 6, 52–3, 162–4; in Embodied Restorying Processes (ERP) 95; in the five A's of fractal management 160
authentic self; *see* self
autonomy 17
awareness 10, 109–12, 160, 162

Bakhtin, Mikhail 32, 76, 80, 94, 116, 177
Barad, Karen 3, 9; agential realism 7, 31, 57, 69–70; boundaries 170, 176; co-creation 29; intra-activity 11, 12, 40, 160; posthumanism 9, 13
baseline, rebaseline 153, 156
basin of attraction 24
Beer, Stafford 17, 28
Bennett, Jane 13
being 6, 80, 84, 108, 160, 175
beliefs 21; *see also* values
becoming 14
Bergson, Henri, 31
Bernoulli, Jacob 52
Besicovitch, Abram 52
bias 168
big data 124, 135–7
big story 124–5
bionic 35
Bohr, Neils 31, 59
Bonifer, Mike 66–9, 124
boundaries 3, 6, 7, 18, 20, 176, 178
branching fractal 47–50, 85, 129–32, 140
butterfly effects 20, 77, 155

Cartesian (split) 7, 12
cause 7–8; *see also* Aristotle
change 1, 156, 160
chaos 19, 20
choice 154–7, 162, 165, 167
closed systems 7
Coase's law 18
coast of Britain 52
co-creation xix, 7, 14, 18, 30, 77, 88, 160, 163
coding 179–80
collaboration 114
collective *see* assemblage
commodities 37
communication 20, 115–16
complex adaptive systems (CAS) xviii, 11–12, 14, 84, 155, 187; fractals and complex adaptive systems 6; approaches to working with complex adaptive systems 16, 20, 22; storytelling and complex adaptive systems 27
complexity xiv, xvi, 14, 17, 18, 27, 45, 65, 77, 121, 180, 183, 186, 187; complexity in human systems xvii–xix, 27, 30, 39, 74, 86, 88; in sociomateriality 5–6; smooth and striated spaces 25; complexity theory 11–12, in the symmetry model of sociomateriality 12; in the ensemble model 13; Ashby's law 17; viable systems model 18; General Systems Theory 19; Human Systems Dynamics Institute 19–20; complexity approach to leadership 22–5, 66; in storytelling 94; phenomenal complexity theory 94–5; *see also* complex adaptive systems
computational thinking 139
conflict 175–7
context 14, 124, 175
control 24
core principles 157
coupling 30
courage 171
creativity 23
cycles 76

Deleuze, Gilles; multifractal models i, striated and smooth spaces 25–6, 59; 80, 87–8, 92; spirals 97; rhizomes 99, 139; difference and repetition 167
Descartes, René *see* Cartesian
differentiation 20, 29
discernment 28
dissipation 18, 28–9, 73, 79, 163
diversity 20
dominant narrative 125, 153, 186; *see also* grand narrative
double loop learning 18
Dourish, Paul 10, 13
dynamical leadership 22–3, 121–4

EAGALA 142
ecosystem 111–12, 118, 161, 166
efficient cause 7–8
élan vitale 31
embodied-cognition 6
embodied restorying process (ERP) 32–4, 95
emergence xv, 18, 28–9, 73, 79, 92, 186
emergent phenomena 3, 165
ensemble leadership 139
ensemble model 13–15
entanglement 39
entrepreneurial narrative, entrepreneurship 92–3, 132–5, 156, 158, 184
Eoyang, Glenda 19–22, 65, 109, 175
equilibrium 7, 8, 10
equine-assisted psychotherapy 142
E-R-G-O 127
espoused values 149, 178
ethics 65, 76–7, 183
ethnography 8

feedback, feedback loops 20, 88, 111
feminism 13
feng shui 31
Fibonacci cycles 36–8
Fibonacci spiral 16, 51–2, 130–1, 133
field theory 27
fitness 24, 70
five As of fractal change management 160–2
flexible capitalism 87–8
focus groups 157
four Bs of antenarrative 82
fractal: definitions xiii, xix, 6, 22–3, 28, 36, 58, 65–76; in management science 45–62, 55–6; fractal geometry 51–2, 62; fractal text analysis 58
fractal action research methods (FARM) xiii, 149, 151–8, 183
fractal analytics 135

fractal change management (FCM): definition xiii–xiv, 1–3, 5–44, 76; origins 105–19; examples 138–41; five A's of FCM 160–73
fractal factory 93
fractal generator 2, 20–1, 25, 29, 79, 162, 174, 178; *see also* rules
fractal knowing 28
fractal manufacturing processes 35–6
fractal narrative 80, 91
fractal organization structure 93
fractal organizing processes: definition 65–78, 81;connection to antenarrative 80; examples 88–91, 120–50
fractal storytelling, fractal story 6, 59–60, 76, 79–196, 129–33
Frazier, Mark 24
functionalist systems theory 15
future 80, 95, 154, 185

game changers 124–5
general systems theory (GST) 19
Gleick, James 20
globalization 14–15, 17
Gold 128–30
golden ratio 52
grand narrative: definitions 13–14, 33, 73; entrepreneurial grand narrative 92;in embodied restorying processes 33–4; contrasted with antenarrative 80–2, 152; facets of storytelling 85–8; of institutions 96; *see also* narrative
Guattari, Felix 25–6, 59, 99, 139

habituation 76
Haraway, Donna 13
harmony (model of sociomateriality); *see* symmetry
Hausdorff, Felix 52
Hegel, Georg Wilhelm Friedrich 19, 26, 73
Heidegger, Martin 33–4, 39, 58, 80, 82, 95–6
Heisenberg, Werner 31, 59
Hird, Myra J. 13
Holladay, Royce 22–4, 66
hologram xix
holon 35–6
horses 142–3
Hoverstadt, Patrick 17, 27–8
human systems dynamics institute 19, 74
hypertextuality 92

ideology 15
informal power structures 20, 164
innovation 70
intra-activity (model of sociomateriality) 7, 12, 77, 160; *see also* agential realism
interconnectedness 112–13, 118
iteration 73, 137–40

joy 110
Joyce, A.A. 15
just in time 36

Kairos 32, 170–1
Kanban 36
Koch snowflake 25–6, 53–4, 73, 174

Latour, Bruno xvii, 9, 12, 69, 176
leadership 22–3, 65–6, 121–4
leadership landscape model 22
lean production 36
Lefebvre, Henri 34, 95
levels of analysis 29, 57
levels of description 186
Lewin, Kurt 27
linear fractals 24
linear fractal manufacturing 35
Little Wow Moments (LWM) 33, 96, 99–100, 143
living story: defined 25, 28, 85: antenarrative 80–1, 152; and fractal story 87; restorying 97; ontology 97–99; *see also* living story web
living story web 2, 18, 25, 27, 79–82, 88: compared with grand narratives 73, 81; scaling 85; antenarratives 81, 82, 86; storytelling 94; restorying 97; shifting 174; contrasted with dominant narratives 186
logarithmic spiral 52

machine metaphor 26
management 52–7, 65–6, 76, 162
Mandelbrot, Benôit xiii, xix–xxii, 5, 37, 45, 55, 93, 139
Mandelbrot set 73
manufacturing 34–5, 72
marketing 128–9, 135, 136, 165
Marx, Karl 28, 74
material agency 8, 30, 31
material cause 8
materiality 114–15, 126
material storytelling 79, 84, 142, 144
McCulloh, Gerri 32, 170

meshwork 89
metaphor 28
Mexico 14
micro inequity 99–100
micro stories 27
mission 110–11
Mobius 136
mono-fractal 139–40
monologic narrative 92
moods 163
mosaic transformation 18
multifractal 2, 24, 30, 72, 137, 183–4
multilevel analysis 180

narrative 13–14, 33–4, 94, 97–8
narrative fractals 24
neo-evolutionary history stages 14
neo-evolutionism 14–15
networks 3
New Mexico State University 47–50
Nonaka, I. 15–16
Noon, Jeff 87–9
nonjudgment 168
nonprofit 108
norms *see* social norms
normalization 72–73

Oaxaca 14–15
object-ontology 18
ontology: critical ontology 84; process ontology xvi, 16, 18, 25; sociomaterial ontology 5–6, 59; ontology of time 95; living story ontology 97–9
ontological storytelling 79, 80–4, 107–8, 149, 174, 177–82
ontological systems mapping 149, 177–82
open space, open space technology 157
open system 6, 12, 14, 73; *see also* complex adaptive systems
organic-materialist approach 15
organizational development 76, 151
organizational learning 22, 30
organizational structure 18
outliers 5

patent thicket 134
perception 168–9
phenomenon 11
pinwheel approach 161
posthumanism 7, 13, 27, 31
post-modern 27
post-Newtonian xvi–xvii, 27
poststructuralism 14, 15
power law 37
price cycles
price waves 37
process ontology xvi, 2, 5, 16, 18, 25

Quade, Kristine 22–4, 66, 121–4
quantum 10
quantum storytelling theory, quantum storytelling xvi, 27, 31, 39, 80, 124–6, 132

rationalization of conflict 157
re-con-figuring 10–11, 13; *see also* Dourish
reductionism 3, 5, 6
reengineering 35
reflection 157, 170
relational introspection: defined 108–9, 117–18, 187; related to other concepts 117; as a lens for analysis 123, 134, 146, 160–2, 183
requisite variety xvii
resilience 22
restorying 34, 96–7, 142–4
rhizome, rhizomatic 76, 80–1, 78–8, 99, 130, 139, 155
Richardson, Lewis Fry 52
risk 17, 155, 165
Rosile, Grace-Ann 13
rules: alignment with 155; in E-R-G-O 127; as fractal generators 28, 45, 85, 93, 178; in the military 142–6, 175; in organizational structure 70; social rules as fractal generators xx–xxi, 16, 20–1, 22–3, 27, 87, 95, 100, 105, 117, 128, 140, 149, 159, 175, 180

sandplay 33–4, 142
scale-divergence 55
scale space 39
scale transformation 56
scaling: in antenarratives 154; as a feature of fractals xiii, xxi, 2, 16, 45, 51, 129, 139, 151, 160, 187; in ontological storytelling inquiry 179; in organizations 39, 47; 52–61, 75, 165, 183–4; scale transformations 55–9, 162; in storytelling 79, 84–6
scientific method xv, 168
search conference 157
seci 16

self 29, 32, 34, 96, 110, 118, 166
self-as-instrument 164
self-awareness 110–11, 144, 160
self-organizing: adaptation 35, 70; in complexity xvii–xviii, xix; criticality 94; fractals 139, 187; human systems 70; as part of complexity xvii, xix, 1; as a property of fractals 1, 16, 139, 189; structures xviii
self-select *see* self-organize
self-similarity: addiction 91; in analysis 180; behaviors xv, 109, 153, 162, 178–9; as a feature of fractals xv, xix, 5, 6, 26, 28, 37, 47, 51, 54, 55, 59, 70, 76, 129, 187; lack thereof 71, 75; limitations of self-similarity xviii; in living story webs 62; in manufacturing 35–6; in nature xxi, 6; in organizational behavior 2, 164; in organizational structure 55, 73, 86, 93; in scale transformations 55; in spotting organizational rules 16; in storytelling 85, 151
sensemaking 80, 151
separation (model of sociomateriality) 6–7, 12
shadow system 18
shaping (model of sociomateriality), *see* social domination
shifting patterns 21, 22, 128, 162
Sierpinski triangle, Sierpinski gasket 59–61, 73
simple rules *see* rules
social constructivism/social constructivist 6, 8, 13
social domination (model of sociomateriality) 7–8
social norms 14, 23, 73, 85
socioeconomic management (SEAM) 155, 183–4
sociomaterial ontology 5, 39
sociomateriality: antenarratives 91; defined xiii; embodiment ontology 59; entrepreneurship 158; examples 125–6, 132–5; exercises 93; in fractal change management xiii, 184; fractal-sociomateriality 69–71; living story webs 86; models 5–39; spacetimemattering 79; social norms 184; SPUD'S 120, 142–6
sociotechnical systems theory 88
spacetimemattering 6, 39, 79, 158, 170
SPUD'S 142–4
spiral *see* Fibonacci spiral
stakeholder 6, 154, 157
standards 144
story performance 153, 180
storytelling: complexity 12, 25, 70, 88;facets of storytelling 84–7; in FCM 5, 45; types of storytelling 79–80; transformation 94–5; 174–5; *see also* fractal storytelling, material storytelling, ontological storytelling, quantum storytelling, SPUD'S
Strand, Anete 79, 142
strategy, strategic change, strategic planning 17–18, 159–60, 164
structural coupling 17
structural-functionalism 14, 36
supply chain management 17
sustainability 14, 137–40
symmetry (model of sociomateriality) 7, 8, 12
system, systems theory 6, 8, 13–15
systemicity: and antenarrative 59, 82; complexity 12, 88; cycles 37; defined xvi, 3, 6–7, 13–14, 19, 88, 187; perpetuating generative systemicity 116–17

Tamara 94
Taylorism 1–2, 17
tension 23
tetranormalizing 144, 183–4
text analysis 57–8
theme analysis 179–80
they self, they-self *see* self
third order cybernetic systems xvi, 2, 72, 94, 185
tightly coupled systems 20
time, timing: branching fractals 48; fractals in time 69, 90, 140, 174; future 96; Heidegger 82; hermeneutics 84; intervals 16, 37–8, 50, 57; just in time 17, 36; Kairotic time 32, 168, 170–1; linear 95; managerial time horizons 55; patterns across time 22, 34; perspectives 185; spacetime 39; *see also* Kairos, McCulloh, spacetimemattering
tools 8
transformation 85

trash compactor 132–5
trends 55, 74
triple bottom line 184
trust 16
turbulence 107, 152–3, 159, 165

unintended consequences 77

values 2, 21, 116, 175, 178
Velamakanni, Srikanth 135–7
Veta la Palma 137–40
veterans 142, 175
Viable Systems Model (VSM) 17–18
visual storytelling 136
von Bertalanffy, Ludwig 19
vortex 99

Waldo Canyon fire 107–8
Warneke 27–8
Weber, Max xiv
Wikia 128–9
world story 86

yoga 26–7, 28–9, 31, 162, 168

zoom 52, 79, 174

For Product Safety Concerns and Information please contact our EU representative GPSR@taylorandfrancis.com
Taylor & Francis Verlag GmbH, Kaufingerstraße 24, 80331 München, Germany

www.ingramcontent.com/pod-product-compliance
Ingram Content Group UK Ltd.
Pitfield, Milton Keynes, MK11 3LW, UK
UKHW021608240425
457818UK00018B/438

9781138624078